NO LONGER PROPERTY OF
SEATTLE PUBLIC LIBRARY

D1165020

COOKING
IN COLOR

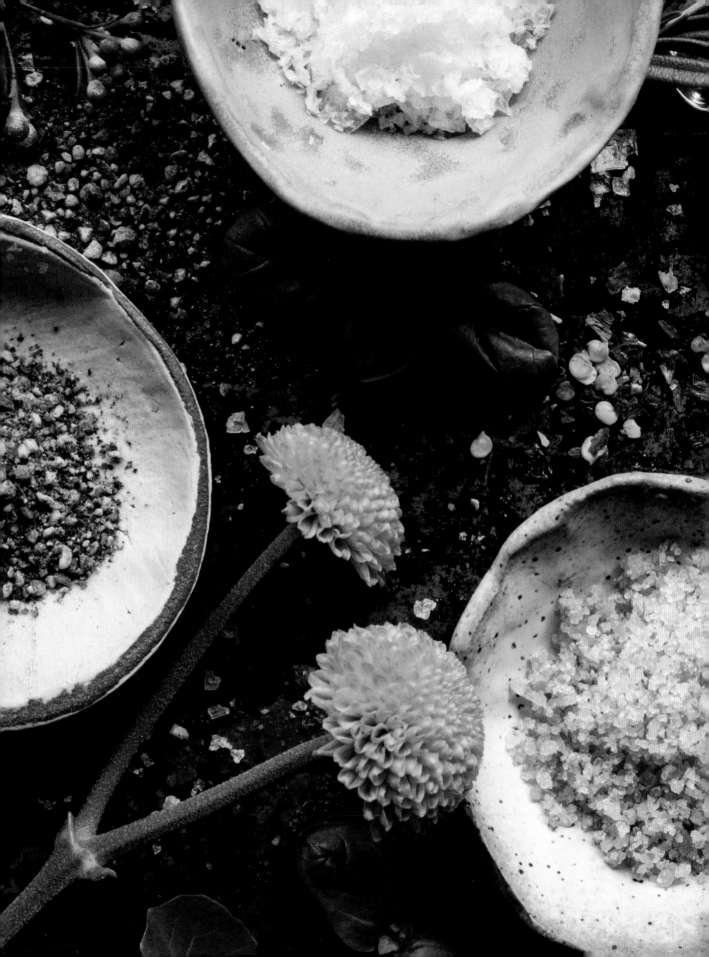

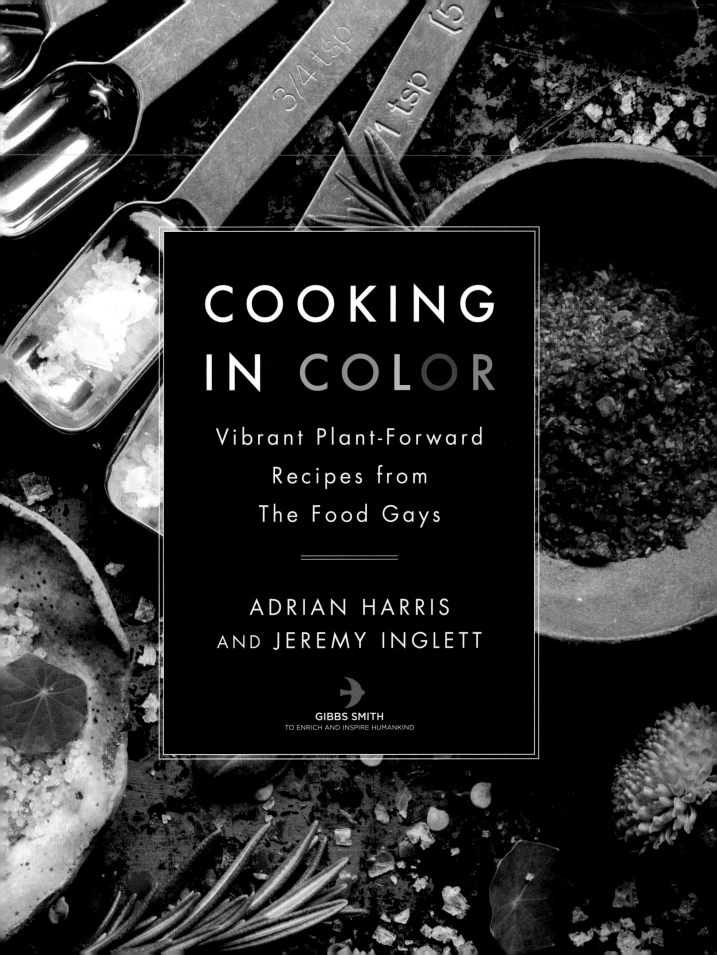

COOKING
IN COLOR

Vibrant Plant-Forward
Recipes from
The Food Gays

ADRIAN HARRIS
AND JEREMY INGLETT

GIBBS SMITH
TO ENRICH AND INSPIRE HUMANKIND

First Edition
22 21 20 19 18   5 4 3 2 1

Text © 2018 Adrian Harris and Jeremy Inglett.
Photographs copyright © 2018 by Adrian Harris and Jeremy Inglett except the
photos on pages viii, 87 and 211, which are copyright © 2018 by Luis Valdizon.

All rights reserved. No part of this book may be reproduced by any means
whatsoever without written permission from the publisher, except brief portions
quoted for purpose of review.

Published by
Gibbs Smith
P.O. Box 667
Layton, Utah 84041
1.800.835.4993 orders
www.gibbs-smith.com

Designed by Greg Tabor
Printed and bound in China
Gibbs Smith books are printed on either recycled, 100% post-consumer waste,
FSC-certified papers or on paper produced from sustainable PEFC-certified
forest/controlled wood source. Learn more at www.pefc.org.

Library of Congress Cataloging-in-Publication Data

Names: Harris, Adrian (Blogger), author. | Inglett, Jeremy, author.
Title: Cooking in color: vibrant plant-forward recipes from the Food Gays /
Adrian Harris & Jeremy Inglett.
Description: First edition. | Layton, Utah : Gibbs Smith, [2018] | Includes index.
Identifiers: LCCN 2018001444 | ISBN 9781423648802
Subjects: LCSH: Food presentation. | Cooking.
Classification: LCC TX740.5 .H36 2018 | DDC 641.3—dc23
LC record available at https://lccn.loc.gov/2018001444

*To all of you
who have supported
and believed in us,
especially our moms,
Jeannie and Kym*

CONTENTS

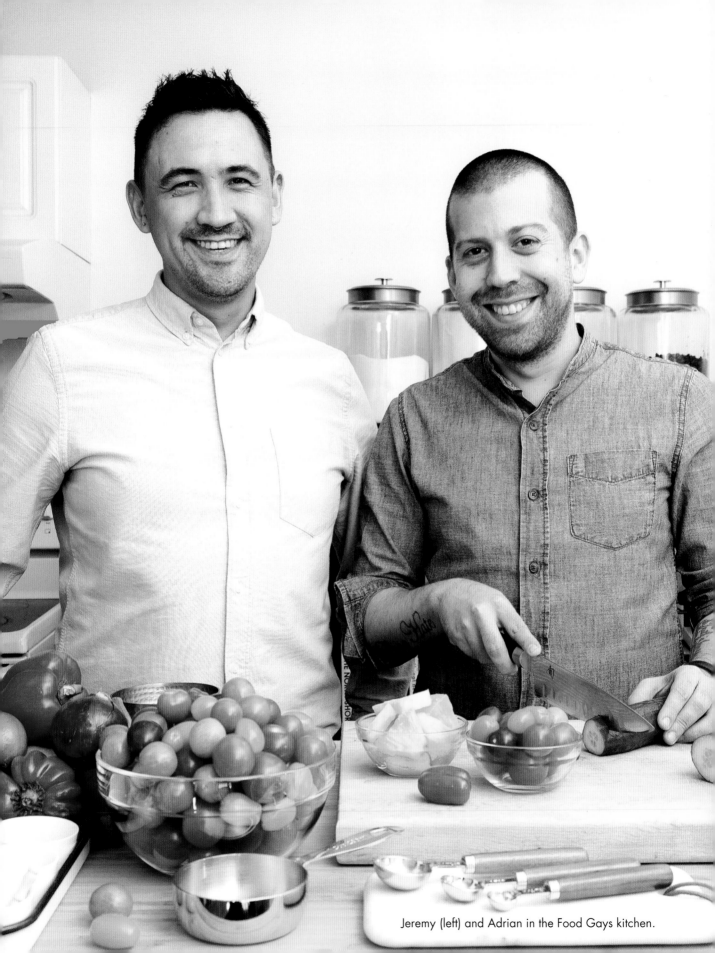

Jeremy (left) and Adrian in the Food Gays kitchen.

INTRODUCTION

Cooking in Color is the culmination of our two loves: deliciously colorful recipes and beautiful presentation. We appreciate the versatility and beauty of fresh produce, and this book reflects our strong point of view that you can add color and originality to just about any dish by way of fresh herbs, crisp seasonal vegetables or crunchy greens.

Like many people today, we find that a diet rich in whole grains, fruits and vegetables, along with the occasional serving of meat and seafood, fits our budget nicely. Sure, we like to indulge from time to time—just wait till you try our Pretzel Bagel Doughnuts (page 77) or our Chocolate Mint Cupcakes with Sour Cream Frosting (page 237)—but on the whole, we strive for balance. If you're looking to shake up your dinner routine, we're your gays . . . er . . . guys.

Many of our recipes are perfect for entertaining or small gatherings, but note that we don't "dinner party" like our parents. As much as we love multicourse, sit-down dinners, we (and our friends) usually prefer more casual fare made up of plates that don't necessarily need to be served piping hot all at once, or in definitive courses. In other words, there are no big expensive roasts to carve, and your kitchen won't be littered with piles of pots and pans at the end of the night.

Once you've prepared food that is naturally colorful, you're most of the way there on presentation. We'll show you some of our secrets behind artful plating, and why we believe a beautifully composed meal just tastes better.

Over time, we have learned there is a harmony to be found in the process of cooking together, one that sparks imagination and mutual communication, and best of all, provides us with a nourishing and vibrant meal that makes us feel good at the same time. We're happier together because of it. In this book, we aim to inspire you to cherish the cooking process and the time spent at the table—not as a chore or as a break to refuel, but as a time to reflect and connect with your friends, with family or just with yourself.

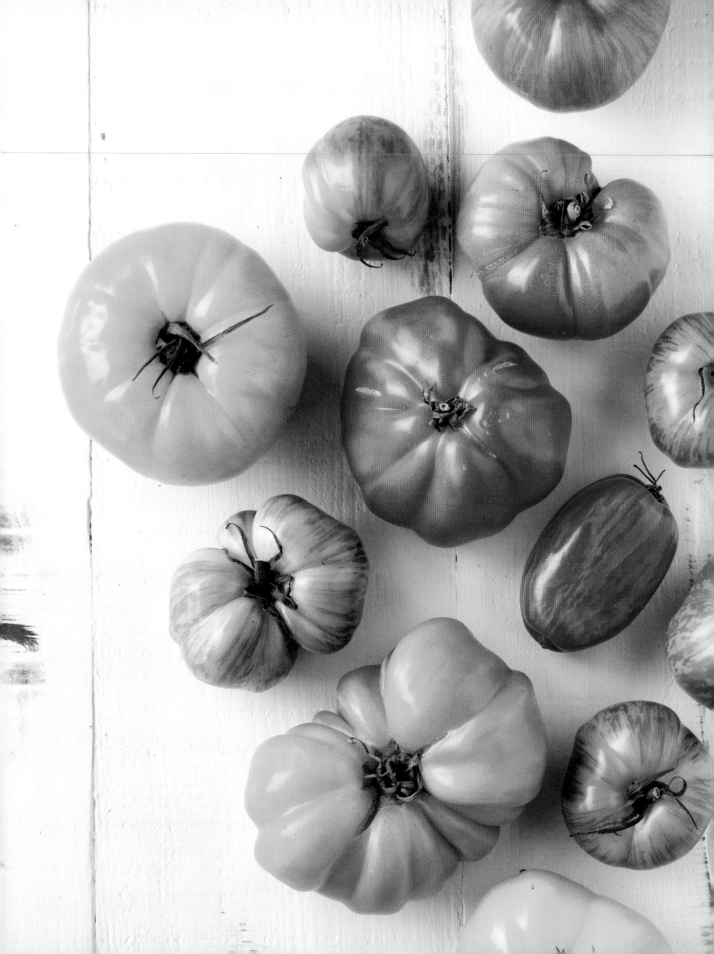

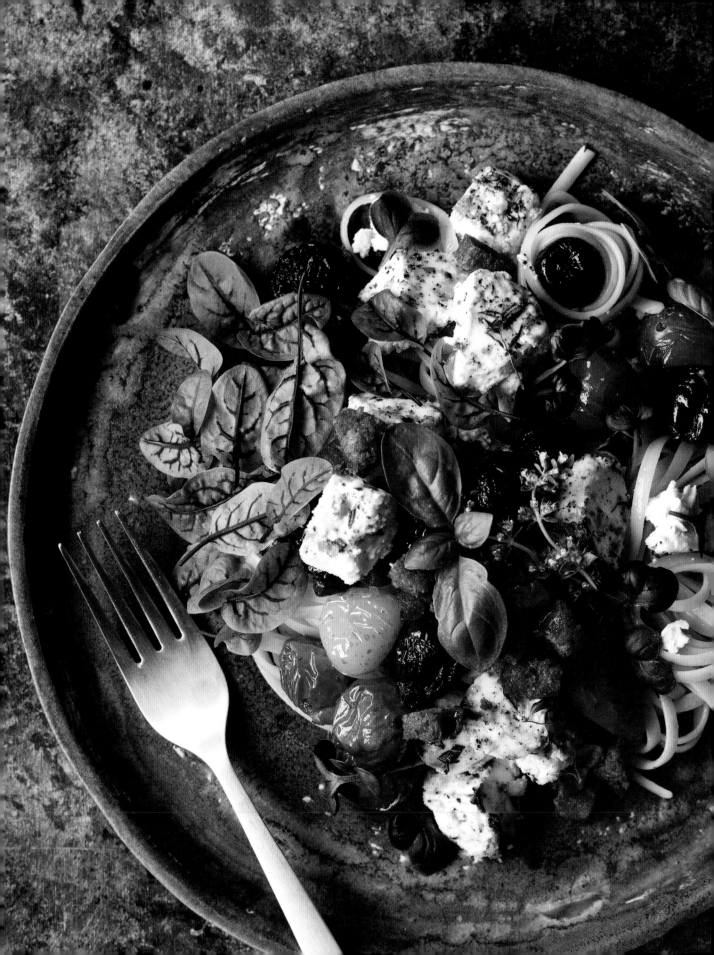

PHOTOGRAPHY AND STYLING

When we were first learning how to take pictures of food, it definitely did not come easily. Some people can pick up a camera and take genius shots with little effort, but that was certainly not us. In the beginning, most of the photos we took were pretty awful. It was to be expected: we were *learning*.

But we persevered and, over time, improved. We each took turns picking up our camera nearly daily, shooting everything from our morning toast and coffee to meals we'd have out and about. It was through this repetitive practice that we really learned what we were doing (and doing wrong). There weren't any shortcuts to take. We simply didn't know what we didn't know, and the only way to learn was by doing.

There are plenty of online resources to help with your photography skills, but the number one thing that will help you improve is actual practice. It might sound trite, but it's action that will have the quickest payoff. Determination is a powerful thing.

Over the years, we've definitely learned what works for us, but those things might not necessarily work for you. Because photography is so personal, we don't believe there's any right or wrong way to approach it, but you may benefit from hearing a bit about what we learned the hard way. What follows are some thoughts and tips about what has worked for us, which we hope will help you as you explore food photography.

LIGHTING

Without a doubt, good lighting is crucial to getting an exceptional shot, and unfortunately there's not much getting around this one. If you've ever tried to photograph something in poor conditions, you know exactly what we mean. Without good lighting, food looks dreadful on camera.

We shoot primarily with natural light, which can be a challenge at times. Understanding how to work with light and shadow takes practice, and as photographers, it's something we're constantly striving to improve. Depending on your taste and aesthetic, lighting can transform the mood of a photo entirely, so don't be afraid to shoot during different times of day, under various conditions. Trial and error is what makes you a better photographer—never be afraid to stumble a few times; you'll soon take off running.

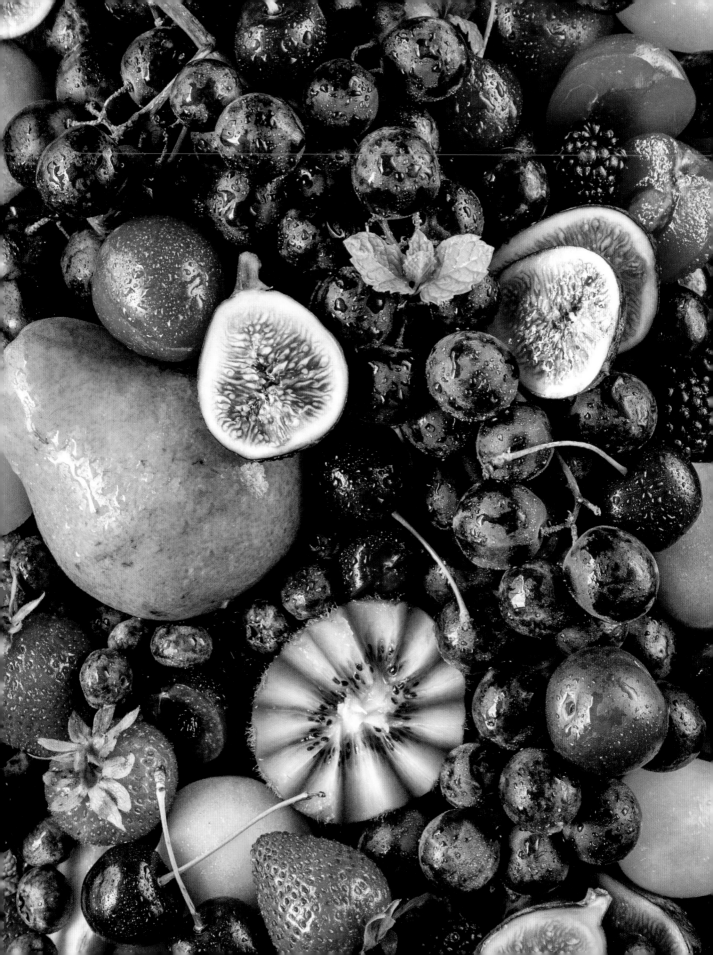

BACKGROUNDS AND SURFACES

One of the biggest trends in food photography over the last couple of years has been the amount of effort and detail that goes into creating food images, including the backgrounds. Scroll through Instagram and you'll see exactly what we mean. For many people, the surface and backdrop are important parts of an image's overall aesthetic, but it's important to remember that the focus should remain on the food, at least at first glance. Ideally, you want your styling to enhance your subject, not draw attention away from it.

If you're just starting out with food styling, make your life simple and consider sticking with a basic setup that will leave you with more energy to focus on what's really important—the food! Your backdrop really doesn't need to be anything fancy to be functional, and sometimes that means thinking outside the box. Hit up thrift shops, rummage through your parents' basement, or check out that neighbor's garage sale. You never know what gems you may find!

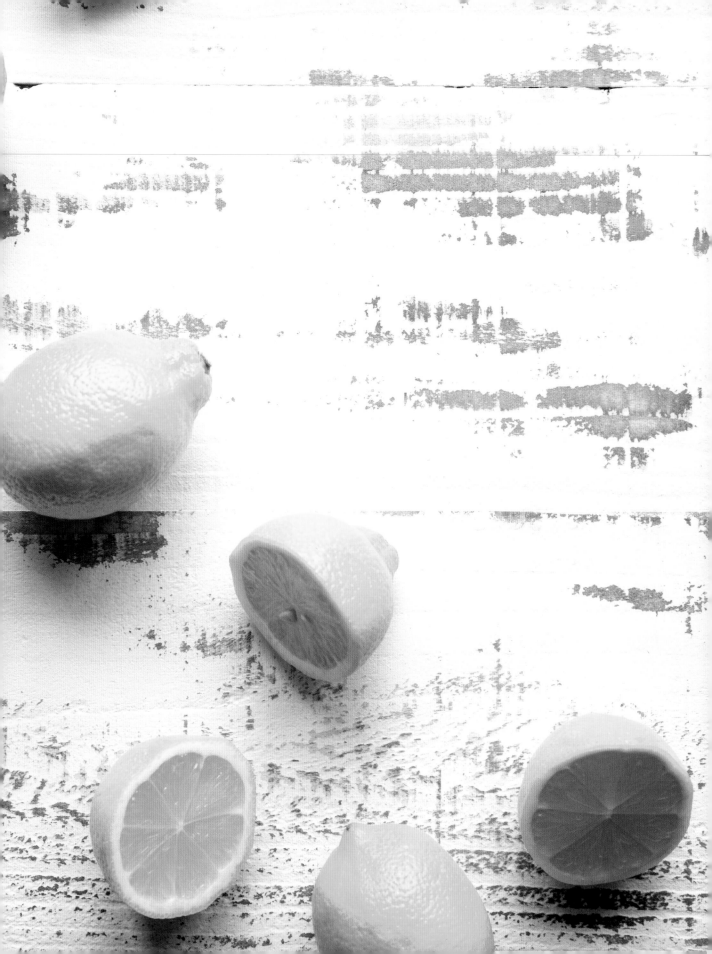

PROPS

When we first began taking photos of food, our prop collection was non-existent. We'd plate our meal and take a quick photo, and that was that. Once we began getting more enthusiastic about food photography, we'd often spend weekends digging through secondhand shops, gleefully searching for cool, low-priced items we could incorporate into our shots. Most of these props have long found their way back to said thrift shop, but some were real gems, and we still use them today. As we expanded and built our hobby into a business, we invested in more specific pieces that served a purpose, both functionally and aesthetically.

Once we took on food photography full time, we could no longer rely on the hit-or-miss selection of a secondhand shop and had to start thinking more about pieces that were going to serve a purpose and bring something extra to our photography to help it stand out.

Over time we've become drawn to a more natural, rustic style that we feel complements the kind of food we make. It's important to explore your personal taste and to find pieces that speak to you. These days we're attracted to minimal food styling, which tends to emphasize texture and touch. Natural objects like metal, clay, porcelain, wood and concrete are commonly used to help set the mood in these types of shots, with special attention to showcasing a slightly more foraged aesthetic. Often times, a handmade plate, bowl or tray is the co-star of the shot, alongside the food itself (the photos of our Cold Soba Noodle Salad with Kimchi and Basil on page 125 and our Roasted Vegetable Gazpacho on page 175 are both great examples). If you're not a food stylist, some of this may be of limited interest, but it's clear that this form of food expression is alive and well.

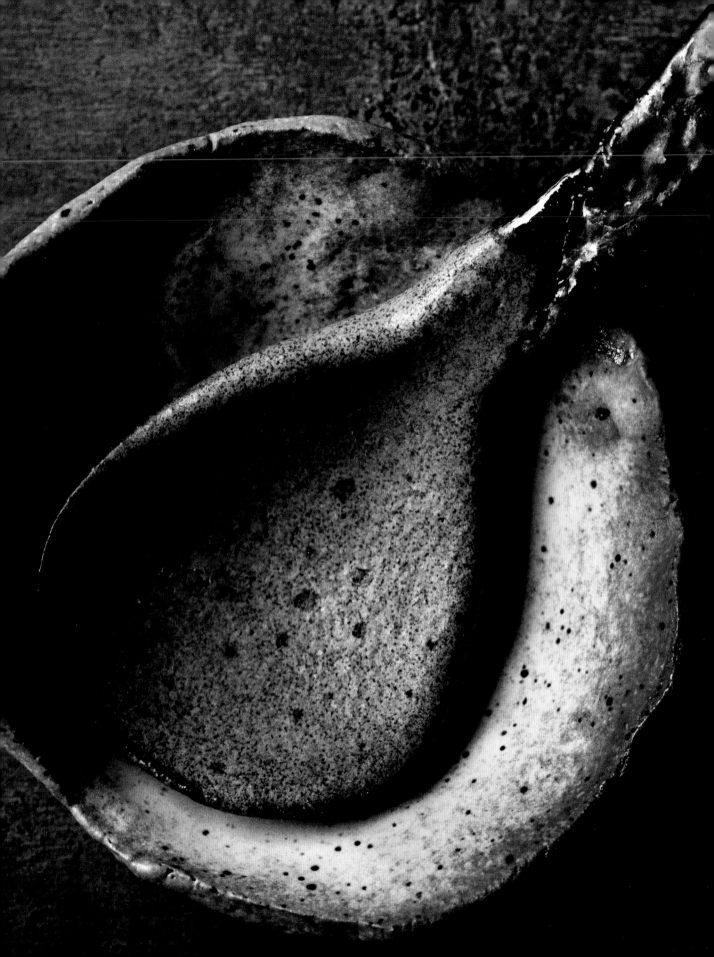

COMPOSITION

For us, composition is one of the most challenging parts of food photography. It's both an art and a science, and it can make or break your shot. If you have any art or design experience, this aspect might be less difficult for you, but for us it is an area for constant improvement. Building an effective, well-composed scene can take a tremendous amount of practice and effort, and some of you may be more artistically inclined than others.

When composing your shot, try focusing on exactly what you'd like to highlight. Is it a beautiful, fresh ingredient that is the star of the show? An oozy, irresistible drip of ice cream running down the cone? Or perhaps it's the elusive steam whirling around a big hearty bowl of ramen—the options are virtually endless, depending on what it is you're looking to capture.

Compare, for instance, the shape and texture of the hollandaise dripping from the spoon in the photo of our West Coast Eggs Benny (page 63) and the gorgeously colored, irresistible ooze of yolk in the shot of our Mac and Cheese Eggs Benny (page 61). These are two "drip" shots, each with different impact. Color, shape and texture are all key players in composition, and knowing how and when to bring these elements into play can make a huge difference between a decent shot and an extraordinary one.

Camera Angles

It's important to play with camera angles and to figure out what works best in different situations. For the most part, when we're planning a shoot, we choose angles based on the way the dish is styled. If it's something with a lot of height, we'd opt for a 0-degree or 20-degree angle, because that will show off the food in a more dramatic fashion (see The Food Gays Burger, page 213, for an example).

If it's a grand spread on a large table with a ton of textures and colors, we might choose a 90-degree angle for a more vivid, bird's-eye view of the scene. Be aware of how different angles change the look and feel of your images, and don't be afraid to play with the setup.

Editing

Editing your images is akin to putting on makeup—a little looks great, but go too far and you risk overdoing it. Making adjustments to exposure, saturation, contrast and tone can help take your photography to the next level. Think of editing not as a problem solver, but rather as an enhancer; if you're starting with a great image, a bit of tweaking will almost surely bring it up a couple of notches. Whatever editing software you decide to go with, just know that it's certainly worth the time and effort to learn some editing basics, even at a beginner level. There are a ton of useful tutorials online to help you get comfortable, so don't feel intimidated to take a crack at teaching yourself.

HARDWARE

Photography can be an extremely expensive hobby, but please don't let that dissuade you if you're just getting started. An entry-level DSLR or point-and-shoot camera is all you really need to pick up some very useful practice. Again, starting small takes a lot of unneeded pressure off the table and allows you to get comfortable and familiar with the basic act of taking pictures without stressing over the thousands of dollars of gear you just bought. These days you can find camera kits including lenses for as little as a few hundred dollars. You'll always want to upgrade, we can guarantee you that, so leave yourself some room to grow. Most of us don't start off with a Bentley as our first car, and photography should be no different.

This is what we are currently loving:
• Canon EOS 5D Mark III
• Canon EF 100mm f/2.8L Macro IS USM Lens
• Canon EF 24-105mm f/4L IS USM Lens

Camera Settings

You'll see that for each food shot, we've noted which manual settings we used (for example, f/10, ISO 1000, 100 sec). We hope you'll find this information useful!

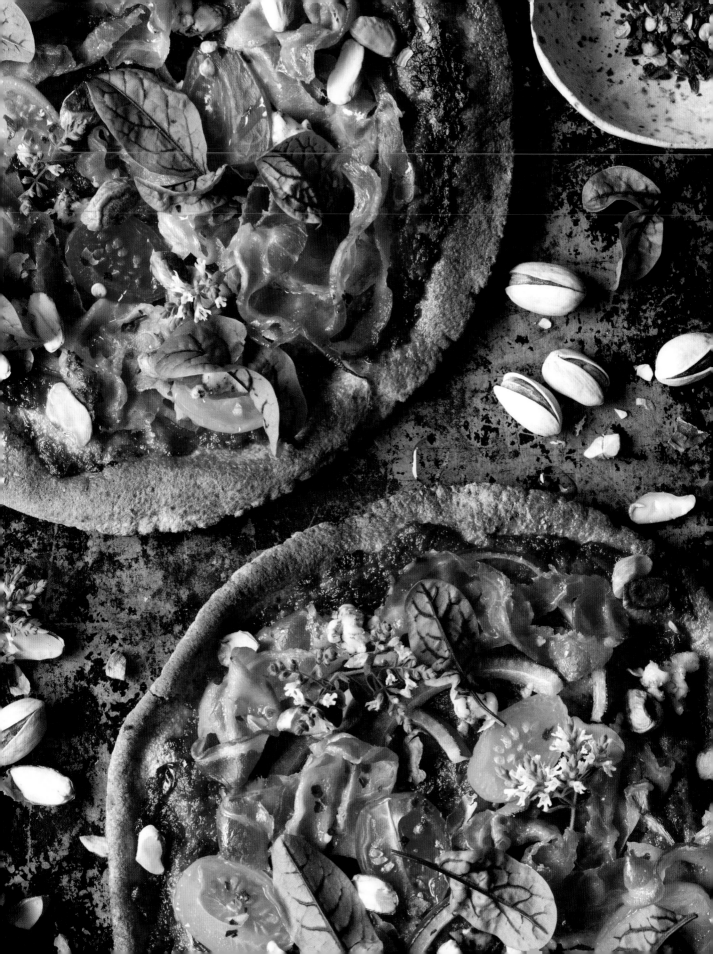

THE FOOD GAYS KITCHEN

We're not going to tell you what you should and shouldn't buy for your pantry. We assume that if you're reading this, you already know that using high-quality ingredients generally yields the best results. Our list on the following pages covers some powerhouse must-haves we always keep on hand and that pop up throughout this book. Don't rush out and buy everything now, though. You will build your pantry naturally as you cook your way through your favorite recipes. It probably goes without saying (but we'll say it anyway!) that when it comes to perishables such as meats, fish, poultry and fresh veggies, it's important to shop as close to cooking time as possible. You don't want to have these things hanging around in your fridge too long.

PANTRY

DRIED HERBS, SPICES AND OTHER SEASONINGS

Ancho chili powder

Basil

Bouillon cubes (regular or reduced-sodium)

Cardamom (whole and ground)

Cayenne powder

Celery salt

Chili flakes

Chinese five-spice powder

Coriander (seeds and ground)

Cumin (seeds and ground)

Curry powder

Flaky sea salt

Garlic powder

Mustard powder

Mustard seeds

Oregano

Paprika (sweet, hot and smoked)

Parsley

Peppercorns (black and white)

Porcini mushrooms

Ras el hanout

Rosemary

Smoked chipotle powder

Thyme

Turmeric (ground)

Vegetable seasoning mix

VINEGARS AND OILS

Balsamic vinegar

Balsamic vinegar crema (reduction)

Extra virgin olive oil

Italian chili oil (olio di peperoncino)

Japanese sesame oil (light or medium)

Neutral cooking oil (such as sunflower or grapeseed)

Red wine vinegar

Rice wine vinegar

White vinegar

RICE, PASTA AND NOODLES

Israeli couscous (medium grain)

Pasta (macaroni, linguine, spaghetti, orzo and soba noodles)

Quinoa (red and white)

Rice (long-grain white, Arborio)

SPECIALTY

Coconut milk (full-fat)

Fish sauce

Gochujang (red chili paste)

Harissa

Hoisin sauce

Passata (raw seeded tomato purée)

Rice paper sheets

Sambal oelek

Soy sauce (regular or reduced-sodium)

Sriracha sauce

Tahini

Tomato paste (canned or tube)

NUTS, SEEDS AND DRIED FRUIT

Almonds (unsalted)

Cashews (unsalted)

Chia seeds

Cranberries (unsweetened)

Dates

Flax seeds

Peanut butter (smooth or crunchy)

Pecans

Pistachios (unsalted)

Raisins

Sesame seeds (white and black;
 raw and toasted)

Sunflower seeds (unsalted)

Walnuts

BAKING

Baking chocolate (semi-sweet)

Baking powder

Baking soda

Brown sugar

Cocoa powder (black or regular
 unsweetened)

Coconut flakes (unsweetened)

Condensed milk

Cornstarch

Flour (all-purpose)

Gelatin powder (unflavored)

Granulated sugar

Honey (liquid)

Icing sugar

Maple syrup (pure)

Rolled oats (large-flake)

Vanilla (pure extract and beans)

FRIDGE

DAIRY

Butter (salted and unsalted)

Buttermilk

Cheddar cheese

Feta cheese

Goat cheese

Greek yogurt

Parmigiano-Reggiano cheese

Ricotta (fresh)

Sour cream

Whipping (35%) cream

Whole milk

FRESH HERBS

Basil

Dill

Mint

Oregano

Parsley (flat-leaf)

Rosemary

Sage

Thyme (lemon, winter)

BREADS AND PASTRY

French bread

Phyllo pastry

Sourdough bread

Tortillas

OTHER ESSENTIALS

Black beans (canned)

Caper berries

Chickpeas (canned)

Dijon mustard

Garlic

Ginger

Horseradish (jarred)

Hot pickled peppers (banana,
    serrano and jalapeño)

Kimchi

Lemons

Limes

Olives (Kalamata, Mediterranean mix)

Onions (white, red and green)

Roasted red peppers (jarred)

Sun-dried tomatoes (jarred, in oil)

BEVERAGES AND SPIRITS

Cointreau

Gin

Ginger beer (nonalcoholic)

Kombucha

Pisco

Tequila

Vodka

Whisky

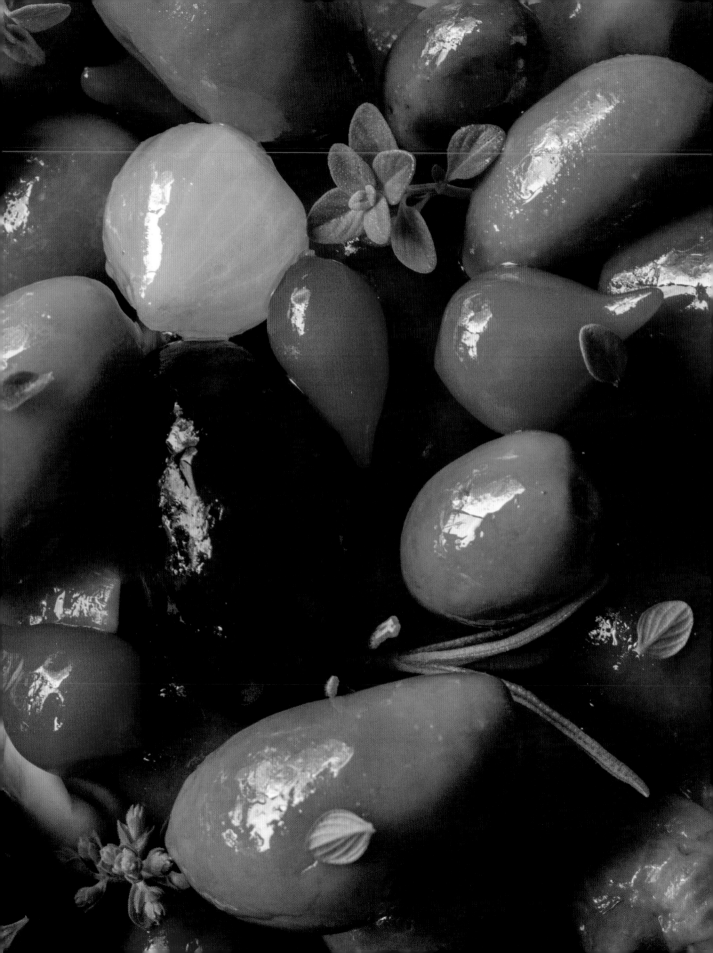

Whether you've just moved into your first apartment and your pantry is in its infancy, or you're like us and clamoring for spare square footage, we're solid believers that a well-stocked condiment selection is the equivalent of a personal arsenal in the kitchen.

Spices, sauces and marinades can mean the difference between bland or blow-you-away, and for us, it's all about keeping a diverse but judiciously chosen selection of flavor-forward ingredients that will work in a multitude of ways.

The last thing anyone needs is to be scouring specialty stores for a jar of something obscure you'll need for only one meal, never to be used again. We promise you that if there is an ingredient for a recipe in this book that you need to go out and buy, it will serve a purpose and be something you can put to work in a variety of dishes.

FLAVORED SALT FIVE WAYS

Each blend makes about ⅓ cup

To add extra flavor to your dishes, try one of these lovely finishing salts. Season steak or roast chicken with Herbed Salt, or add Lemon Petal Salt to a vinaigrette.

⅓ cup flaky sea salt

Lime Coconut Salt

2 tbsp toasted unsweetened
   coconut flakes
1 tbsp finely grated lime zest

Orange Ginger Salt

1 tbsp finely grated orange zest
¼ tsp ground ginger

Chili Salt

½ tbsp chili flakes
½ tsp smoked paprika

Lemon Petal Salt

2 tbsp finely grated lemon zest
1 tbsp dried organic rose petals

Herbed Salt

1 tbsp dried basil
1 tbsp dried parsley
1 tsp dried oregano
1 tsp ground coriander
1 tsp porcini mushroom powder
   (see Tip)

In a small bowl, combine sea salt with chosen flavored ingredients. Using your hands, massage together until well incorporated. Spread evenly on a baking sheet and let air-dry for 2 to 3 hours. Alternatively, bake in a preheated 200°F oven for 15 to 20 minutes; let cool completely before transferring to an airtight jar. Keeps in a cool, dry place for up to 12 months.

Tip: To make porcini mushroom powder, simply place dried porcini mushrooms in a blender or food processor and blend to a fine powder. Add to everything from rice to soup to sauces for an extra boost of flavor. Store in an airtight container in a cool, dry place.

Styling Note:
We built the scene gradually, evoking a feeling of abundance while showing off the beauty of the ingredients.

Settings and Angle:
f/10
ISO 1600
1/200 sec
90 degrees

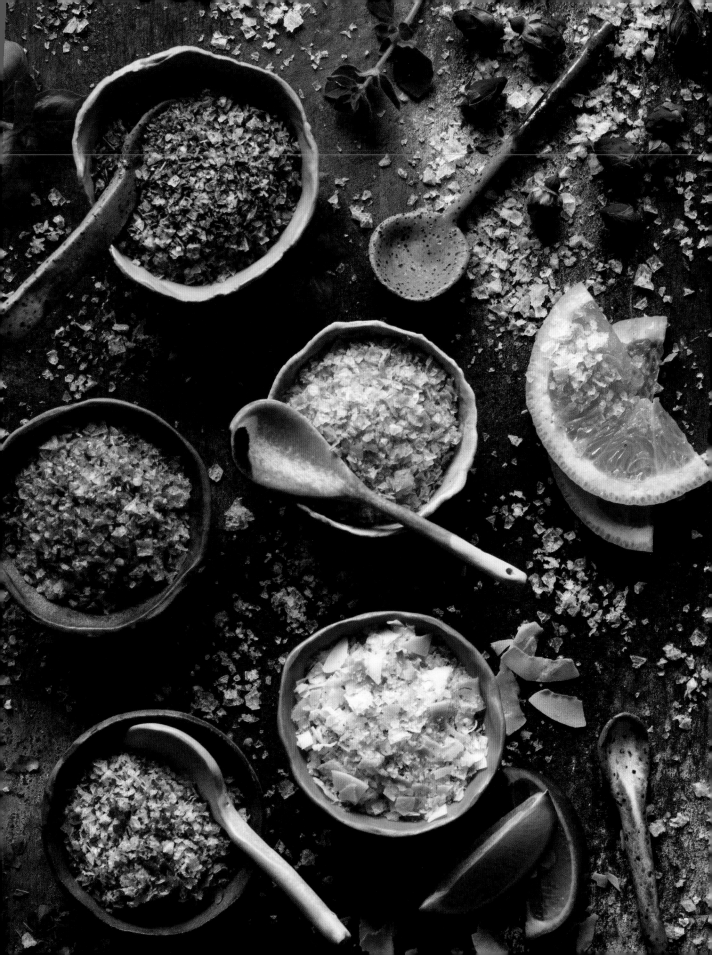

DUKKAH

Makes about 1 cup

Dukkah is a magical Egyptian nut and spice blend that can really elevate a dish with just a little sprinkle. We've used it in a few recipes in this book (see Indian-Spiced Squash, page 180, and Braised Yams with Chimichurri, Eggs and Dukkah, page 192) and encourage you to keep some on hand for when your meal needs a little extra somethin'-somethin'.

¼ cup raw sesame seeds

¼ cup unsalted cashews

¼ cup pecan halves

1 tsp chili flakes

1 tsp coriander seeds

½ tsp freshly ground black pepper

½ tsp smoked paprika

½ tsp flaky sea salt

In a food processor, combine all of the ingredients. Process until everything is well incorporated. (The nuts should be ground to a moderate to fine consistency, but be careful not to over-blend or the mixture will turn into a paste.) Transfer to a mason jar. Keeps in the refrigerator for up to 12 months.

Tip: Customize your own dukkah blend to suit your taste by swapping out different nuts and seeds.

Styling Note:
We've used a lower aperture setting and our 100mm macro lens to highlight the details of the dukkah and create a soft, blurred-out background.

Settings and Angle:
f/4
ISO 640
1/100 sec
45 degrees

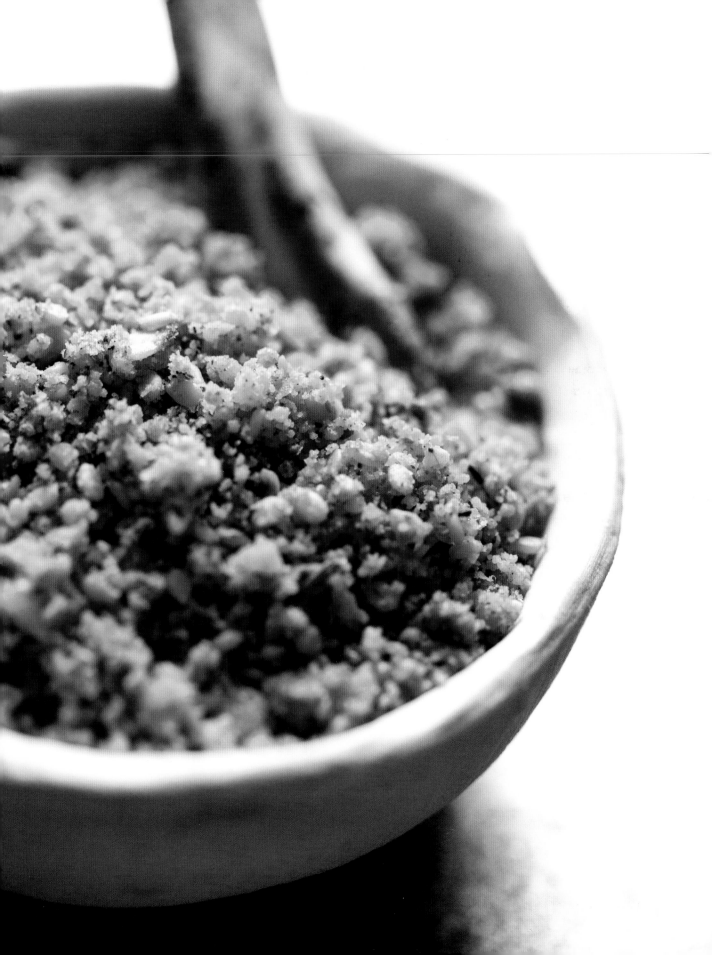

SWEET AND SMOKY SPICE RUB

Makes about 1 cup

A great spice rub is invaluable in the kitchen, and this one works on everything from poultry to seafood, red meat and vegetables. We've even been known to rim our Bloody Caesar cocktails with it!

2 tbsp smoked paprika
1 tbsp brown sugar
½ tbsp granulated sugar
1 tsp salt
1 tsp cayenne pepper
½ tsp cumin seeds
½ tsp dried thyme
½ tsp dried oregano
½ tsp mustard powder
½ tsp celery salt
½ tsp garlic powder
½ tsp freshly ground black
  pepper
2 whole dried juniper berries

In a mortar and pestle or clean spice grinder, combine all of the ingredients and grind to a fine powder.

Transfer mixture to a small mason jar. Keeps in a cool, dark place for up to 6 months.

Styling Note:
For this shot, we wanted a moody scene, enhanced by shadow. The vibrant red spice blend seems almost illuminated by the darkness.

Settings and Angle:
f/9
ISO 6400
1/125 sec
90 degrees

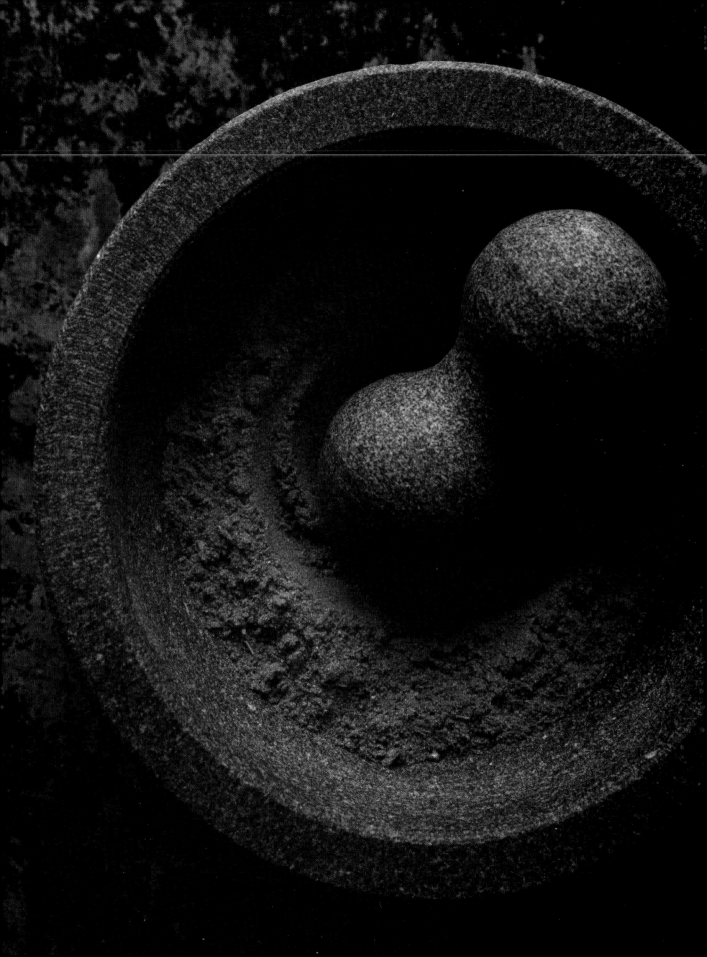

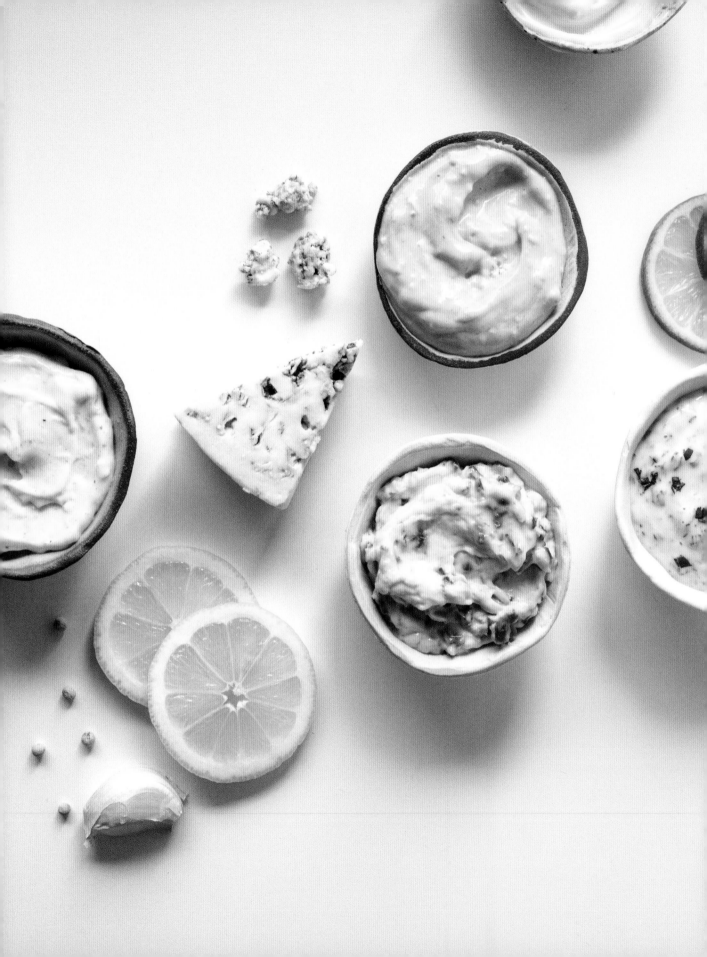

30-SECOND MAYONNAISE FIVE WAYS

We can't remember the last time we purchased mayonnaise. And we're pretty certain that once you make your own, you'll never be buying it again either. It couldn't be easier to whip up — our method is virtually foolproof.

CLASSIC 30-SECOND MAYONNAISE
Makes about 1½ cups

1 large egg
1 cup neutral cooking oil
¼ tsp salt
½ tsp mustard powder or ¼ tsp
  Dijon mustard
1 tbsp fresh lemon juice

In a wide-mouthed mason jar, combine egg, oil, salt, mustard powder and lemon juice.

Whip with an immersion blender for 20 to 30 seconds, until the mixture has thickened and fully emulsified (see Tip). Keeps in the refrigerator for up to 1 week.

Tips: Choose pasteurized, organic, free-range eggs for a silky, ultra-rich, full-bodied mayonnaise that beats anything you'll ever find on store shelves.

To whip the mixture, place your immersion blender directly on the base of the jar, turn it on high and hold it in place until the mixture begins to emulsify. Then move the wand in slow upward motions until everything is completely combined.

(recipes continue on next page)

Styling Note:
Showing off the ingredients that were used to make the flavored mayos gives an otherwise basic photograph a fresh, natural look.

Settings and Angle:
f/10
ISO 500
1/100 sec
90 degrees

(continued from previous page)

SUN-DRIED TOMATO MAYONNAISE
Makes about ¾ cup

½ cup Classic 30-Second
   Mayonnaise (page 31)
¼ cup sun-dried tomatoes in oil,
   drained and finely diced
1½ tsp prepared horseradish
½ tsp freshly ground black pepper

In a small bowl, combine mayonnaise, sun-dried tomatoes, horseradish and pepper. Stir until everything is well incorporated. Cover and keep in the refrigerator for up to 1 week.

Tip: This mayo pairs well with vegetables and seafood.

LEMON GARLIC MAYONNAISE
Makes about ½ cup

½ cup Classic 30-Second
   Mayonnaise (page 31)
2 garlic cloves, minced
Finely grated zest of 1 lemon
1 tsp freshly ground white
   pepper

In a small bowl, combine mayonnaise, garlic, lemon zest and white pepper. Stir until everything is well incorporated. Cover and keep in the refrigerator for up to 1 week.

Tip: This mayo pairs well with seafood, pork and chicken.

BUFFALO BLUE CHEESE MAYONNAISE

Makes about ¾ cup

½ cup Classic 30-Second
Mayonnaise (page 31)
¼ cup crumbled Danish
blue cheese
2 tsp Sriracha sauce

In a small bowl, combine mayonnaise, blue cheese and Sriracha. Stir until everything is well incorporated. Cover and keep in the refrigerator for up to 1 week.

Tip: This mayo pairs well with chicken and beef.

CILANTRO LIME MAYONNAISE

Makes about ½ cup

½ cup Classic 30-Second
Mayonnaise (page 31)
2 tbsp roughly chopped fresh
cilantro leaves
Finely grated zest of 1 lime

In a small bowl, combine mayonnaise, cilantro and lime zest. Stir until everything is well incorporated. Cover and keep in the refrigerator for up to 1 week.

Tip: This mayo pairs well with seafood and chicken.

GRAINY MUSTARD

Makes about 1 cup

This punchy mustard adds a wonderful hit of nose-tingling spice to anything from vinaigrettes to marinades and even sauces. Best of all, it costs just cents to prepare.

2 tbsp whole mustard seeds
¼ to ⅓ cup water
1 tbsp white vinegar
½ tbsp liquid honey
¼ cup mustard powder
½ tsp ground turmeric
¾ tsp salt

Using a pestle and mortar, lightly pound mustard seeds just until they're roughly cracked. Transfer to a medium bowl. Whisk in water, vinegar, honey, mustard powder, turmeric and salt.

Transfer the mustard to a mason jar. You can use it immediately, but the mustard tastes best after it's refrigerated for at least 2 hours. Keeps in the refrigerator for up to 2 months.

Tip: Change up the flavor and intensity of your mustard: try using chardonnay or Champagne vinegar, or bump up the amount of honey for an addictively delicious dip that's a perfect match for fresh veggies or grilled chicken.

Styling Note:
Using a neutral background with a boldly contrasting blue-green serving dish really helped showcase the vibrant yellow of the mustard seeds.

Settings and Angle:
f/10
ISO 1600
1/100 sec
90 degrees

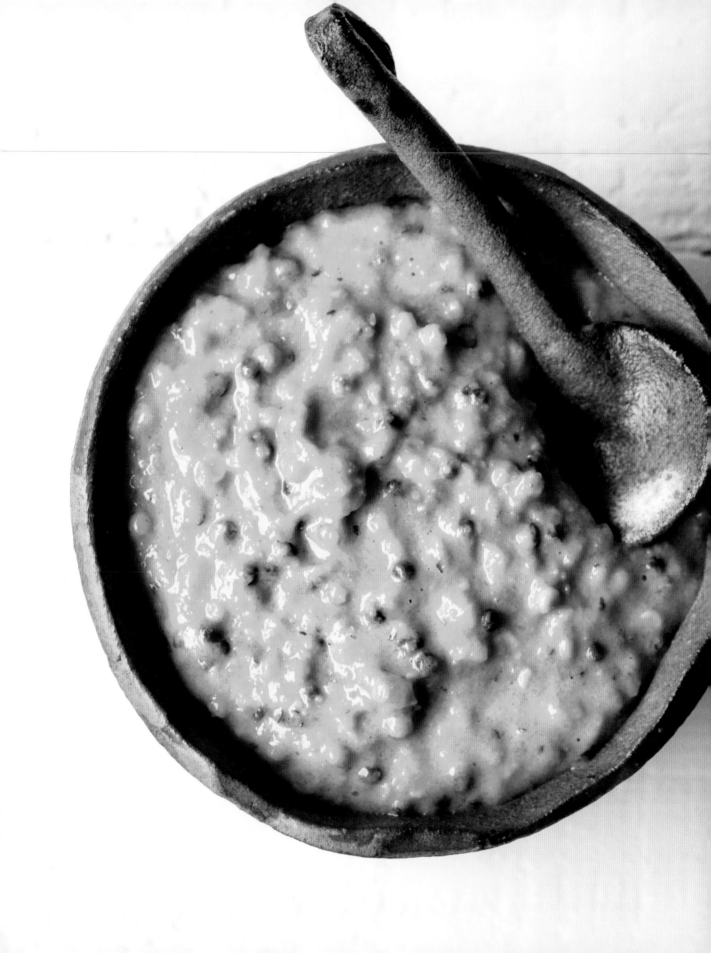

QUICK-PICKLED RED ONIONS

Makes ½ cup

No charcuterie board is complete without accoutrements, and these quick-pickled onions are the ideal add-on. They're also great in a variety of other dishes, from our Buffalo Cauliflower Bánh Mì with Mushroom Pâté (page 93) to Fresh Nachos with Greek Yogurt and Watercress (page 148).

¼ cup red wine vinegar

¼ cup water

1 tsp granulated sugar

½ tsp salt

½ cup thinly sliced red onion

In a mason jar, combine vinegar, water, sugar and salt. Stir (or seal and shake) until sugar and salt are dissolved. Add onion and seal jar tightly. Chill for 6 to 8 hours before eating. Keeps in the refrigerator for up to 5 days.

Tip: Use this brine recipe to quick-pickle other veggies like radishes, carrots and cucumbers.

Styling Note:
The vibrant pink of the onions is elevated against the neutral palette of gray and white.

Settings and Angle:
f/5.6
ISO 2000
1/100 sec
45 degrees

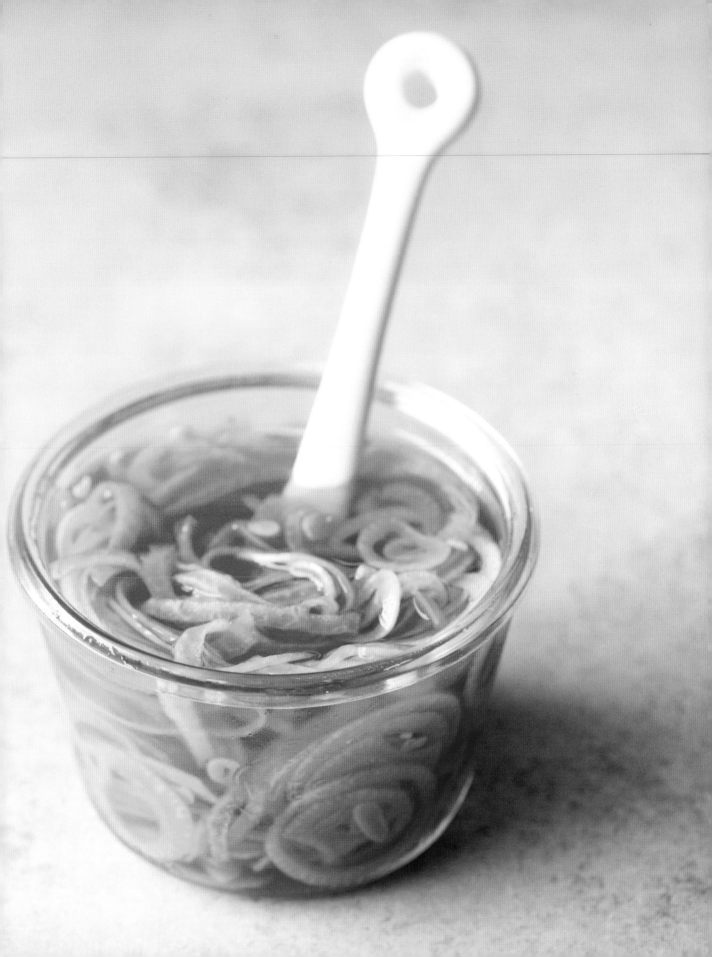

MORNING MEALS

Depending on your lifestyle, the idea of breakfast may seem entirely lavish or absolutely necessary to function. No matter which category you fall into, you'll come around to loving this most important meal of the day, if you haven't already—especially on weekends, when we think it's best enjoyed with extra-comfy PJs and a French-press coffee or two.

Some of these recipes will easily feed a crowd of friends; others are meant just for two or for your solo commute to work. So forget heading out and waiting in some seemingly endless brunch line. Make something remarkable in the comfort of your own kitchen. These morning-inspired recipes have been created to delight and satisfy, and, most importantly, get your day started on the right foot. Sweet or savory, light or stick-to-your-ribs filling, there's a little something for everyone.

GINGER LIME APPLE SMOOTHIE

Serves 2

Hate green drinks? We've probably all had a nasty experience at one time or another that's scarred us. Trust us: the lime juice and serrano pepper combination in this emerald-hued smoothie tastes amazing and packs a kick that'll keep you coming back for more. Try making it the night before and storing it in the fridge so you can enjoy an easy, energizing breakfast that won't slow you down.

1 cup packed spinach leaves
   (including stems)
½ Granny Smith apple, cored
½ tsp minced peeled ginger
1 celery stalk
1 serrano pepper, seeded
½ cup sliced English cucumber
Juice of 1 lime
½ cup coconut water or regular
   water
½ cup ice cubes

In a high-powered blender, combine all of the ingredients (see Tip). Blend until completely smooth. Serve immediately or transfer to an airtight container and refrigerate for up to 24 hours. Shake or stir well before drinking.

Tip: A high-powered blender yields the best results. If you don't have one, you can use a regular blender but the final consistency might not be quite as smooth.

Styling Note:
Blended drinks some-
times pose a challenge, as
they separate easily. We had
to work quickly and swap in
a fresh batch of juice to
get the final
shot.

Settings
and Angle:
f/5
ISO 1000
1/100 sec
0 degrees

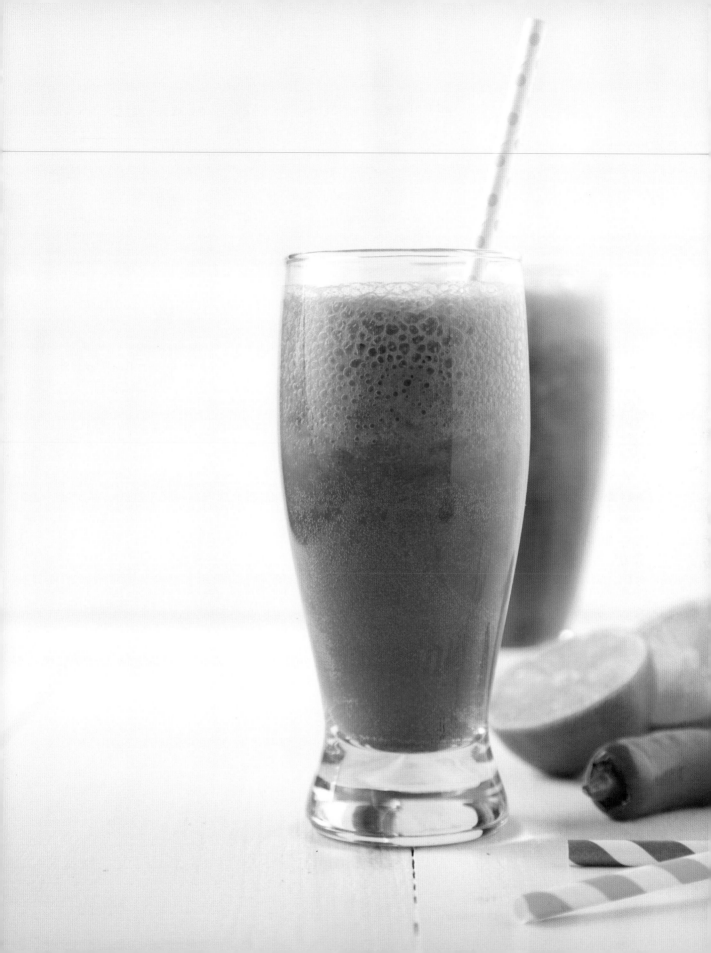

CARROT CAKE OVERNIGHT OATMEAL

Serves 1

Who doesn't want dessert for breakfast? This dreamy morning meal evokes the same feelings as an indulgent slice of cake, but you're really eating nothing but goodness. You can have your cake and eat it too. Yay for adulting!

¼ cup grated carrot

⅓ cup large-flake rolled oats

1 tbsp chia seeds

¼ cup plain Greek yogurt

1 tbsp pure maple syrup

2 tbsp chopped walnuts

2 tbsp raisins

⅓ to ½ cup whole milk or almond milk

Combine all of the ingredients in a medium bowl and stir well. Cover and refrigerate overnight before eating. Enjoy cold or warmed up (see Tip).

Tip: If you'd prefer this dish warm, simply add a splash of milk and heat in a small pan on medium heat, stirring occasionally, for about 2 minutes, until warmed through.

Styling Note:
We love the natural architecture of this bowl. Pairing neutrals together can be an effective, clean way of showing off pops of color (in this case, the bright orange carrot).

Settings and Angle:
f/10
ISO 4000
1/100 sec
90 degrees

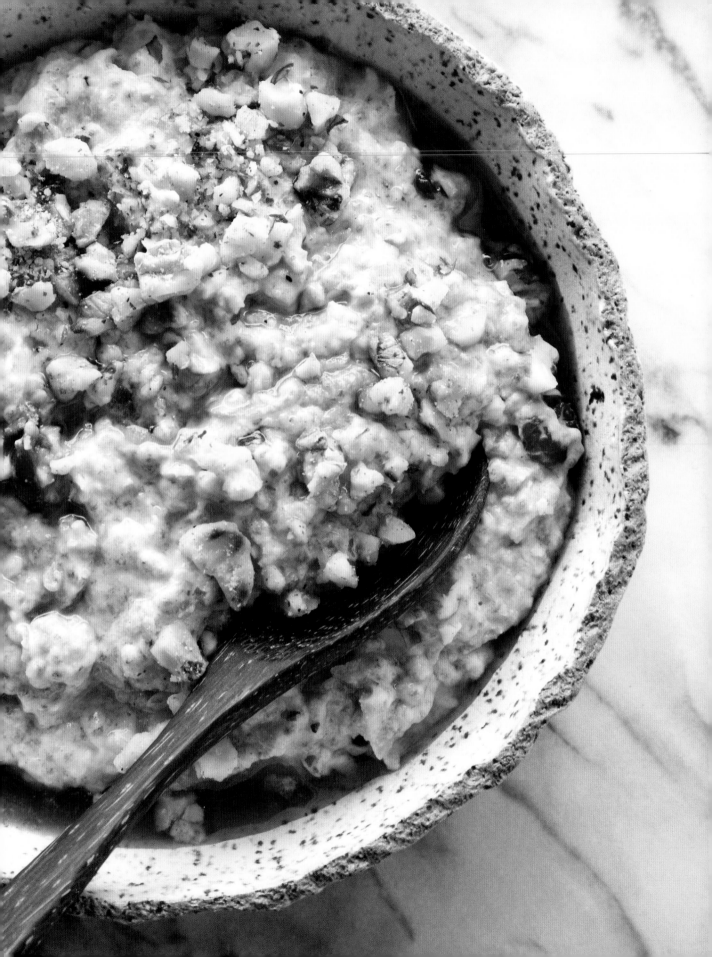

MUSHROOM AND KALE SAVORY OATMEAL

Styling Note:
We wanted this shot
to be minimal and rustic,
with lots of negative space.
We added a dose of color
by combining purple
and green kale.

Serves 1

If you haven't tried savory oatmeal before, you're in for a treat. The rolled oats are prepared like a grain rather than a soft porridge: they're pan-toasted until golden and cooked until al dente. If poaching your eggs seems intimidating, no one will fault you for frying them instead.

2 large eggs

1 tsp white vinegar

1 tbsp butter

⅔ cup large-flake rolled oats

¼ tsp dried thyme

½ cup water

1 garlic clove, smashed

1 tbsp neutral cooking oil

½ cup sliced brown mushrooms

½ cup roughly chopped green
  and purple kale, stems removed

Microgreens, to garnish
  (optional)

Bring a medium saucepan of water to a boil. Fill a medium bowl with cold water (to make a cold-water bath). Crack each egg into a small bowl. Add vinegar to the boiling water and then reduce heat to a simmer. Add cracked eggs, one at a time, to the simmering water. Cook for 3½ minutes. Using a slotted spoon, transfer poached eggs to the cold-water bath for 10 seconds to stop the cooking. Reserve simmering water to rewarm egg before serving.

Add butter to a small saucepan on medium heat. Let the butter melt, stirring frequently, until it begins to brown (it should have a nutty aroma and be a dark golden color). Add rolled oats and stir until lightly toasted, about 5 minutes. Stir in thyme and ½ cup water, and cook, uncovered, until the oats have absorbed all of the liquid, 5 to 10 minutes. Set aside.

Meanwhile, in a small frying pan or skillet on medium-high heat, sauté garlic in oil for 1 minute. Add mushrooms, and cook for 2 minutes, stirring occasionally. Add kale, and cook until wilted, 1 to 2 minutes. Remove the pan from the heat, and discard the garlic. Add the toasted oats to the vegetable mixture and toss to combine. Transfer oat mixture to a bowl, top with poached eggs (rewarm in reserved hot water for 15 seconds before serving) and garnish with microgreens (if using). Enjoy.

Settings
and Angle:
f/9
ISO 6400
1/100 sec
90 degrees

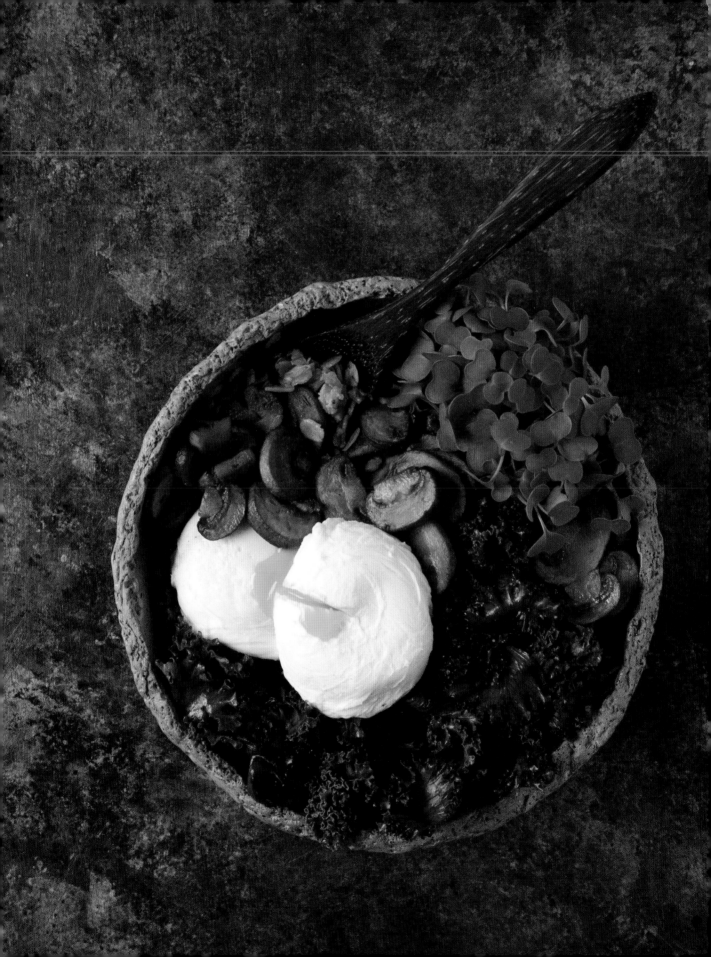

QUINOA FRUIT SALAD

Serves 2

In the summer months when berries are fresh and the sun is shining, this pretty salad is without a doubt one of our favorites to make in bulk and eat throughout the week to stay cool. The addition of red quinoa may seem strange at first, but trust us, it just works, adding great body and texture to an otherwise typical fruit salad.

½ cup red quinoa, rinsed and
   drained
½ cup raspberries
½ cup blueberries
½ cup pitted and quartered
   cherries
Juice of 1 lime
2 tsp liquid honey
Plain Greek yogurt, to serve
   (optional)
Fresh mint, to garnish

Cook quinoa according to the package instructions. Set aside to cool at room temperature for about 20 minutes.

Meanwhile, in a medium bowl, gently smash the raspberries with a fork to help release their juices. Add blueberries, cherries, lime juice and honey. Stir in the cooled quinoa and toss until well combined.

Serve with yogurt (if using) and garnish with mint.

Tip: Feel free to change up the berries depending on your taste, the season and what's available in your area.

Styling Note:
A clean white canvas seemed like a perfect fit for this vivacious red salad. The final shot conjures up a light, airy feeling, which lends itself nicely to the summer-themed ingredients in the recipe.

Settings and Angle:
f/10
ISO 1600
1/80 sec
90 degrees

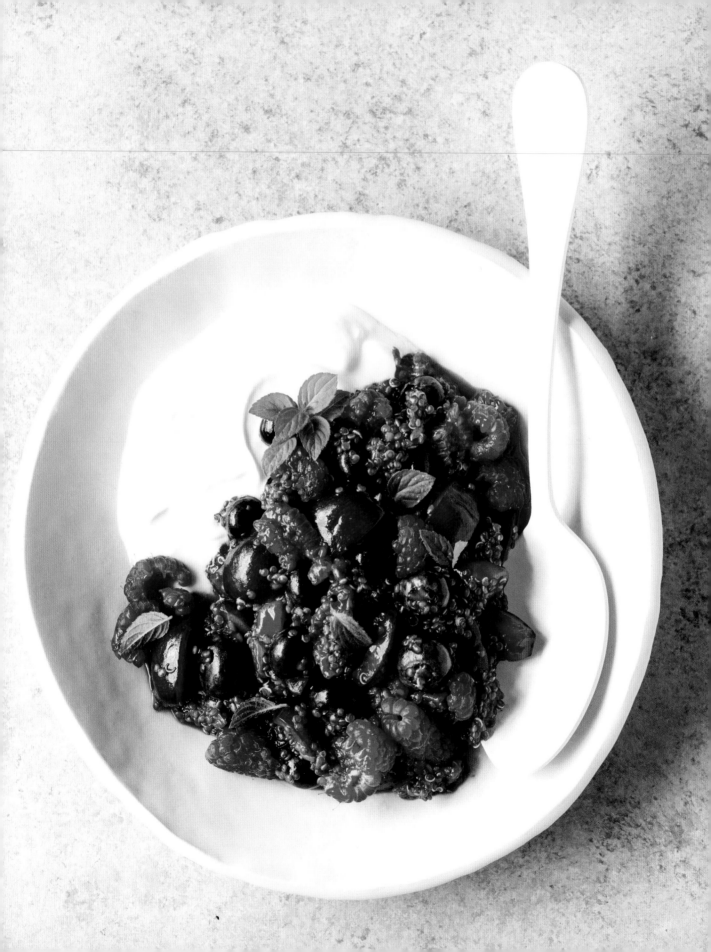

CRANBERRY COCONUT BREAKFAST POWER BARS

Styling Note: Freshly cut bars suggest to the viewer that they're getting the first piece.

Makes 12 bars

We can't tell you how many years we spent buying those so-called "natural" snack bars, blissfully unaware of just how much hidden refined sugars and calories they contained. These babies are full of nothing but good things.

½ cup unsalted almonds, roughly chopped

½ cup large-flake rolled oats

¼ cup large unsweetened coconut flakes + ¼ cup more for topping

2 tbsp flax seeds

2 tbsp unsalted raw sunflower seeds

2 tbsp chia seeds

½ cup unsweetened dried cranberries + 2 tbsp for topping

1 cup pitted dates

¼ cup smooth or crunchy peanut butter

¼ cup liquid honey

Preheat oven to 350°F. Line a 6- x 10-inch baking dish with parchment paper and set aside. Pull out a baking sheet.

On the baking sheet, spread out almonds, rolled oats, ¼ cup coconut flakes, flax seeds, sunflower seeds and chia seeds. Toast in preheated oven for 5 to 7 minutes, until golden. Transfer to a large bowl. Stir in ½ cup cranberries. Set aside.

In a small bowl, soak the dates in very hot water for 1 minute, or until softened, then strain. Transfer softened dates to a food processor and process until smooth. Stir into the oat mixture.

In a small saucepan on medium heat, warm peanut butter and honey, stirring occasionally, for 5 minutes. Add to oat and date mixture. Stir until well combined. Using a spatula, spread the mixture evenly over the bottom of the prepared baking dish. Sprinkle with the remaining 2 tbsp cranberries and ¼ cup coconut. Cover with plastic wrap and refrigerate for 24 hours. Using a sharp knife, cut into squares or bars.

Tips: Swap out the dried fruits, nuts and seeds for any you might have in the cupboard.

Brush your knife with oil for a precise, clean cut.

Settings and Angle: f/10 ISO 2000 1/100 sec 90 degrees

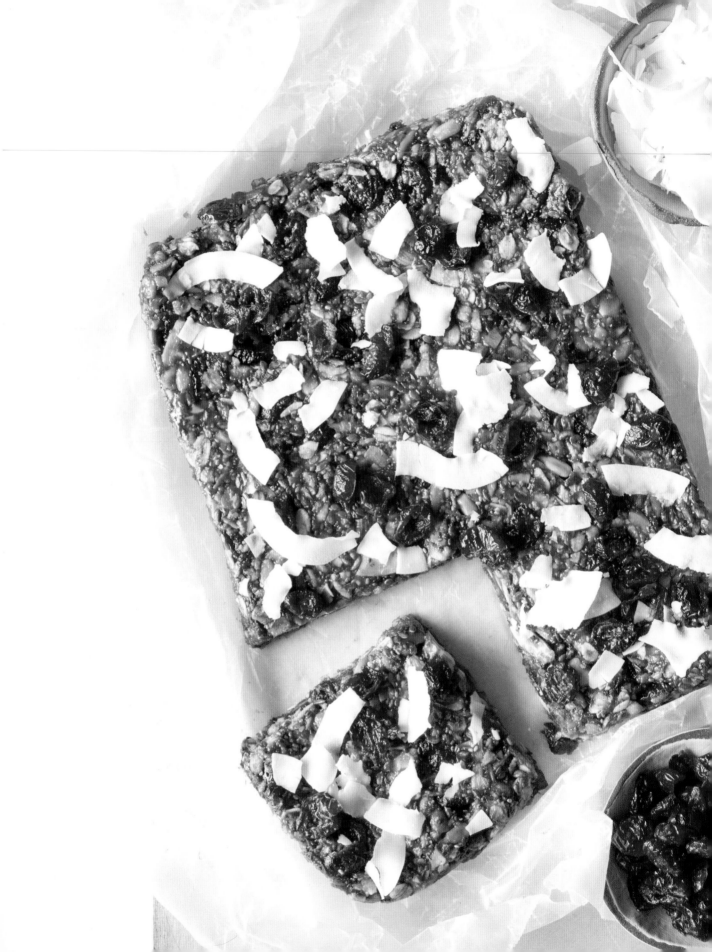

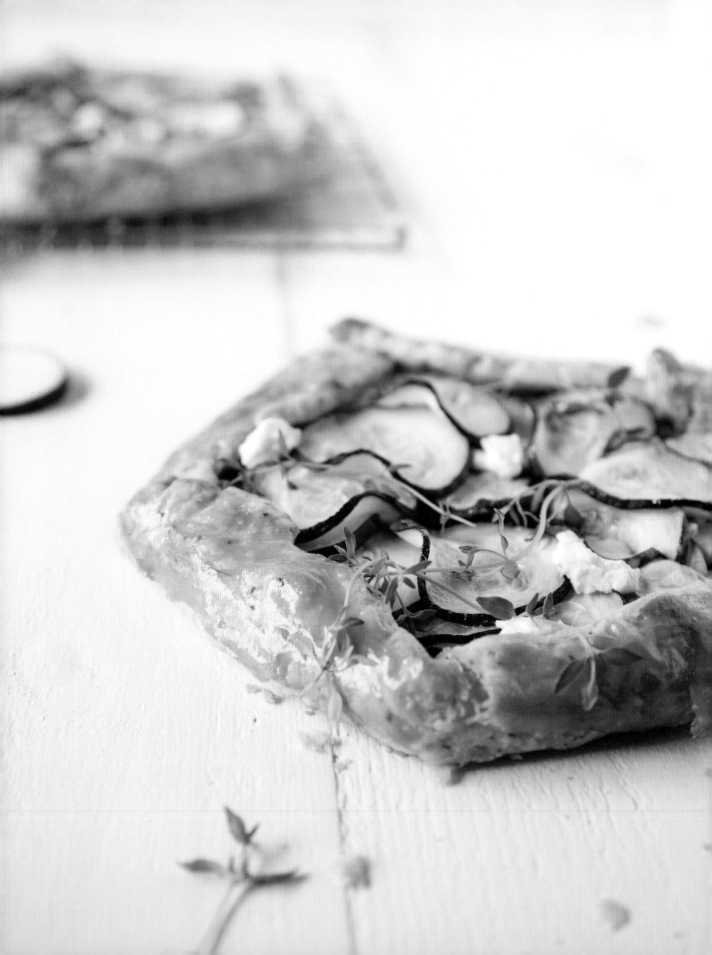

CARAMELIZED ONION, ZUCCHINI AND GOAT CHEESE GALETTES

Makes 2 galettes

These buttery, flaky beauties are most definitely one of our guilty pleasures. I'm always asking Jeremy to come up with irresistible savory baked ideas, and can say with confidence that this one is going to be on your favorites list, too. Don't skip the step of salting the zucchini; otherwise, you'll end up with a soggy galette that no one will want to eat!

Dough:

1 cup butter, cubed

1½ cups all-purpose flour

1 tsp salt

1 tsp dried basil

½ tsp dried oregano

½ tsp dried thyme

¼ cup ice-cold water

1 large egg yolk, beaten, for
  egg wash

Make dough: Using a fork or pastry cutter, break up the butter in a large mixing bowl, leaving some big chunks. Mix in flour, salt, basil, oregano and thyme. Add ice-cold water and mix just until the dough begins to come together. Avoid overworking your dough, or it will become very dense and lack the flaky, delicate qualities you want.

Once your dough comes together, divide it into two even pieces. Flatten each into a disc and cover in plastic wrap. Refrigerate for 30 minutes.

(recipe continues on next page)

Styling Note:
Amp up the color in your final dish by using both yellow and green zucchini.

Settings and Angle:
f/4.5
ISO 250
1/100 sec
10–20 degrees

(continued from previous page)

Filling:

2 cups sliced (¼ inch thick) zucchini

Pinch of salt + more for seasoning

2 tbsp neutral cooking oil

2 cups thinly sliced white onion

½ cup crumbled goat cheese

¾ cup finely grated Parmigiano-Reggiano cheese

Drizzle of olive oil

Freshly ground black pepper, to taste

Sprigs of thyme, to garnish

Make filling: Meanwhile, arrange zucchini rounds in a single layer on a baking sheet lined with a clean cloth or paper towel. Sprinkle lightly with a pinch of salt and let rest for at least 20 to 30 minutes to draw out the moisture.

Heat cooking oil in a large frying pan or skillet on medium heat. Add onion, and cook for 20 to 25 minutes, until caramelized, stirring often to keep from burning. Season with salt to taste. Remove from heat and set aside to cool.

Preheat oven to 400°F. Line a baking sheet with parchment paper.

Assemble galettes: On a lightly floured work surface, roll out each dough disc into a circle about ¼ inch thick (see Tip). To the center of each circle, add half the cooled caramelized onion and crumbled goat cheese. Leave yourself a border of 1 to 1½ inches for folding. Sprinkle each galette with half of the grated Parmigiano-Reggiano. Then arrange your zucchini slices in a neat circular pattern on top of each portion. Drizzle with a small amount of olive oil and add a dash of pepper. Carefully fold the uncovered edge of the dough up towards the center of each galette. Arrange side by side on your prepared baking sheet. Let chill in the refrigerator for 10 minutes.

Gently brush edges of each chilled galette with beaten egg yolk. Bake in preheated oven for 30 to 35 minutes, until golden brown. Rotate the tray halfway through to help ensure an even bake.

Let the galettes cool on a wire rack for 5 to 10 minutes before serving. Garnish with fresh thyme and enjoy.

Tip: For the best bake, work with only one portion of dough at a time, to keep the dough as cold as possible.

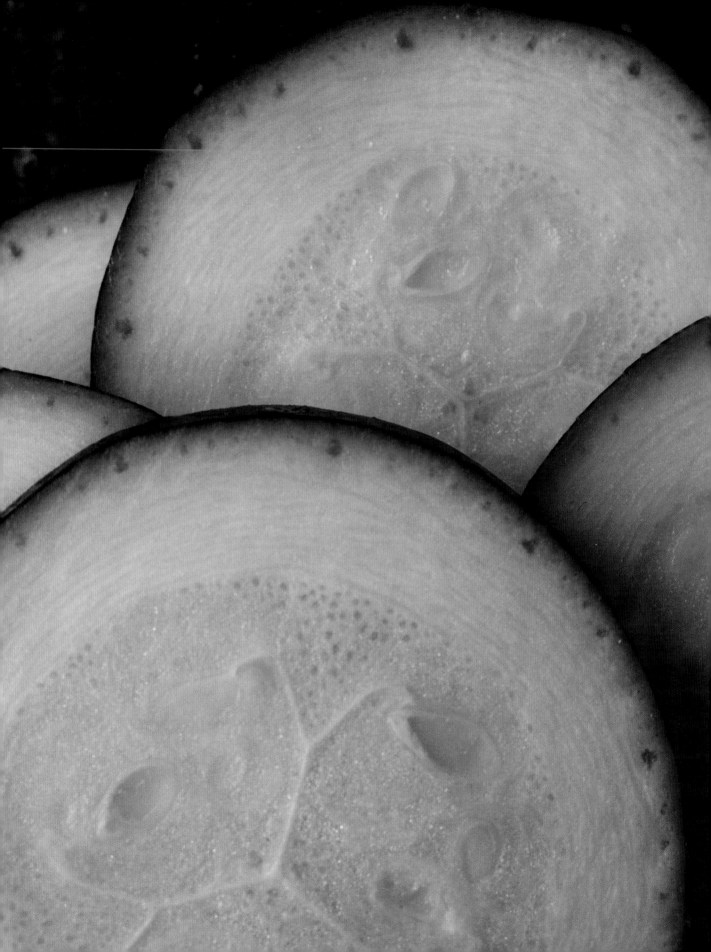

CHORIZO AND SWEET POTATO TOSTADAS

Serves 2

This makes for the ultimate satiating breakfast, if you ask us. You can pile on as much or as little as you want depending on how hungry you are, or what you've got hanging around the kitchen.

1½ tsp neutral cooking oil, divided

½ cup diced white onion

2 garlic cloves, minced

1 cup chopped Spanish chorizo

1½ to 2 cups diced sweet potatoes

1 tsp vegetable seasoning

½ tsp salt

2 to 3 tbsp water

2 small flour tortillas

2 large eggs

1 avocado, pitted, peeled and sliced

¼ cup cherry tomatoes, halved

2 tbsp crumbled feta cheese

Cilantro leaves, to garnish

Sour cream or plain Greek yogurt, to serve (optional)

Preheat oven to 375°F.

Heat 1 tsp oil in a medium frying pan or skillet on medium heat. Add onion, and cook until it begins to soften and become translucent, 2 to 3 minutes. Add garlic and chorizo, and cook for another 2 minutes, stirring occasionally. Add sweet potatoes, vegetable seasoning and salt. Add water, and cook, stirring with a wooden spoon to pick up any brown bits at the bottom of the pan, for 1 to 2 minutes. Cover pan with a lid and simmer for 3 to 4 minutes, until the potatoes are tender.

Meanwhile, place tortillas in the preheated oven, directly on the oven rack, for 2 to 3 minutes to let them crisp up slightly.

Heat the remaining ½ tsp of oil in a small frying pan or skillet on medium-high heat, and fry the eggs to desired doneness.

Top each toasted tortilla with even amounts of the sweet potato and chorizo mixture. Add avocado slices, fried egg, tomatoes, feta and cilantro. Serve with sour cream or Greek yogurt (if using).

Styling Note:
The wood tones in this setup make the colors in the tostada really pop!

Settings and Angle:
f/10
ISO 800
1/100 sec
90 degrees

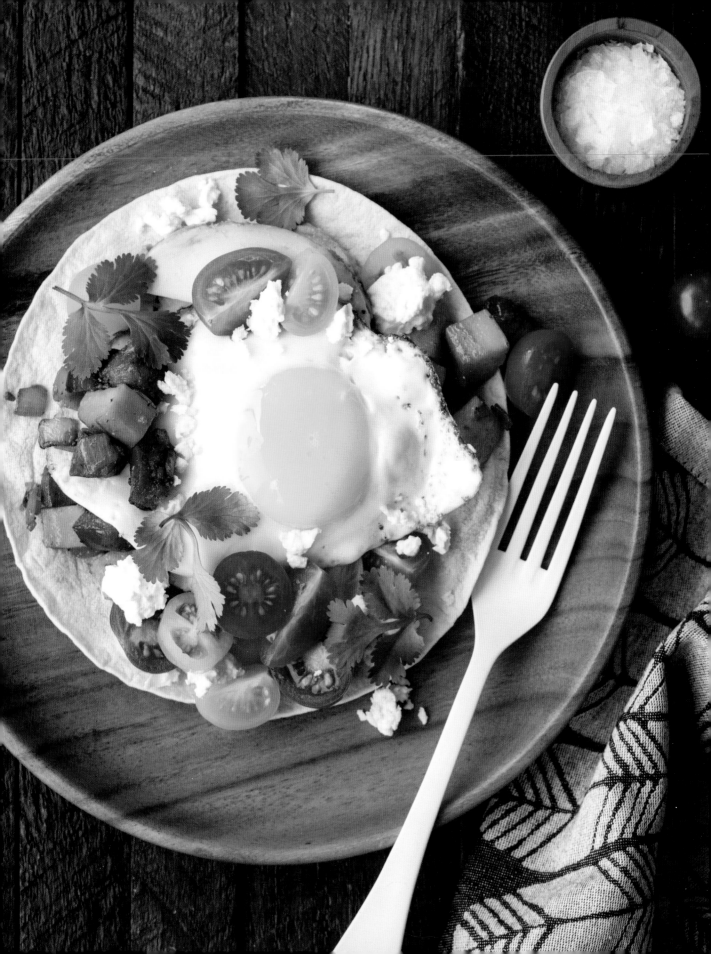

STEAK AND EGG SALAD

Serves 4

We're pretty sure this is one morning meal you'll be keeping in your back pocket, and we wouldn't blame you for taking full credit either. Putting a whole new spin on the classic steak and eggs, this epic brekkie-salad has evolved in various forms in our household. We prefer to use an inexpensive cut of steak for this dish, and tenderize it really well before cooking it to medium-rare.

Dressing:

¼ cup Classic 30-Second
   Mayonnaise (page 31)

¼ cup sour cream

¼ cup crumbled feta cheese

½ cup roughly chopped cilantro
   leaves

1 garlic clove, minced

Juice of ½ lemon

Salad:

4 large eggs

2 tsp neutral cooking oil,
   divided

2 cups cubed red potato, skin on

Salt and pepper, to taste

½ lb steak (sirloin or shoulder
   cuts work well)

1 to 2 tbsp Herbed Salt
   (page 24)

4 cups loosely packed tender
   greens

Make dressing: In a medium bowl, combine mayonnaise, sour cream, feta, cilantro, garlic and lemon juice. Cover and refrigerate.

Make salad: Bring a medium saucepan of water to a boil. Prepare a large bowl of ice water and set aside. Submerge eggs in boiling water, and cook for 7 to 8 minutes (see Tip, page 58). Using a slotted spoon, transfer eggs to the ice water and let cool for 1 to 2 minutes. Carefully peel eggs and set aside.

Heat 1 tsp oil in a large frying pan or skillet on medium heat. Add potatoes and season with salt and pepper. Cook for 5 to 7 minutes, until they're browned and tender. Remove from heat, transfer potatoes to a bowl, cover and set aside; reserve pan.

(recipe continues on page 58)

Styling Note:
We love the family-style appearance of this salad, and think it looks especially impressive when served on an oversized plate or platter.

Settings and Angle:
f/9
ISO 4000
1/100 sec
90 degrees

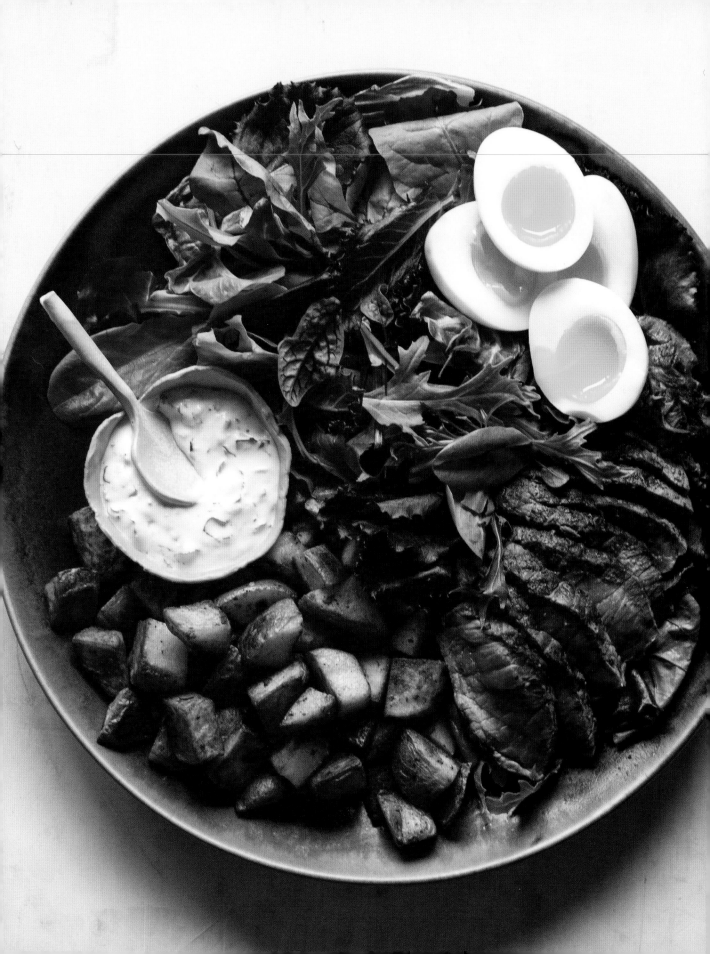

(continued from page 56)

Season steak with herbed salt. If you're using a tougher cut of meat, you may want to tenderize it first. (We do this by simply placing the meat in a plastic bag and whaling down on it with a rolling pin for a while. It's a great way to release some pent-up energy.)

In the reserved pan, heat the remaining 1 tsp oil. Cook steak for a few minutes on each side until desired doneness (it should take 7 to 8 minutes total for medium-rare). Let rest, loosely covered in foil, for 2 to 3 minutes. Cut into ¼-inch slices.

Arrange your greens on a platter. Top with the sliced steak, potatoes and sliced soft-boiled eggs. Gently toss with the dressing. Serve immediately.

Tip: We prefer our eggs soft-boiled for this dish (7 minutes), but if you prefer a less yolky consistency, just boil them for an additional minute.

MAC AND CHEESE EGGS BENNY

Serves 4

This recipe was created as a bit of a happy accident, when on a whim we combined leftover mac and cheese on toast with poached eggs . . . as boys do, duh. Sounds crazy, we know, but it was actually a pretty incredible mashup. Separately, these are all good things. But together? Pure magic, friends!

1 tsp butter

1 tsp all-purpose flour

¾ cup whole milk

1½ cups shredded aged cheddar cheese

½ tsp ground smoked chipotle pepper

½ tsp freshly ground black pepper

¼ to ½ tsp salt, to taste

1 cup dried macaroni

1 tsp white vinegar

4 large eggs

4 slices sourdough bread, toasted

1 to 2 tbsp Classic 30-Second Mayonnaise (page 31)

1 cup red lettuce, sliced

In a medium saucepan on medium heat, melt butter and heat until golden, 1 to 2 minutes. Add flour and whisk together for 2 minutes, or until a smooth paste has formed and the flour has cooked. Slowly drizzle in milk, whisking constantly, and cook until the mixture has thickened (see Tip, page 60). Once the mixture can coat the back of a spoon, add shredded cheese in handfuls, stirring constantly until smooth. Add chipotle and black pepper. Taste, and season with salt, as needed.

Bring a large pot of water to a boil, and cook macaroni according to the package instructions. Drain pasta, reserving 1 tbsp of the starchy water. Add pasta and reserved starchy water to the sauce, and stir everything together. Set aside at room temperature for at least 10 minutes to set or, for best results, cover and chill overnight in the refrigerator.

Heat a dry frying pan on medium-high heat. Add about ½ cup mac and cheese per person, and cook for 5 to 6 minutes, stirring only occasionally, until it begins to get crispy. Remove from heat and set aside. Meanwhile, bring a medium saucepan of water to a boil. Reduce heat to a simmer and add vinegar. Crack eggs into separate small bowls, then carefully, one at a time, add to the simmering water. Cook for 3½ minutes. While eggs are cooking, toast the bread.

(recipe continues on next page)

(continued from previous page)

Spread mayonnaise over each piece of toast. Top with lettuce, a few spoonfuls of the crispy mac and cheese, and finish with a poached egg. Serve immediately.

Tips: When making the cheese sauce, be careful not to add the milk to the pan too fast; otherwise, the mixture will have to sit on the stove for at least 5 to 10 minutes to thicken while you stand there and whisk. Our method of slowly drizzling in the milk while whisking works to quickly thicken up the sauce, saving you time.

Make the mac and cheese the night before to get a head start.

Styling Note:
Did someone say
yolk porn? This dish was
begging for something
ooey-gooey and totally
graphic—and a yolky
egg always
satisfies.

Settings
and Angle:
f/5.6
ISO 640
1/200 sec
10–20 degrees

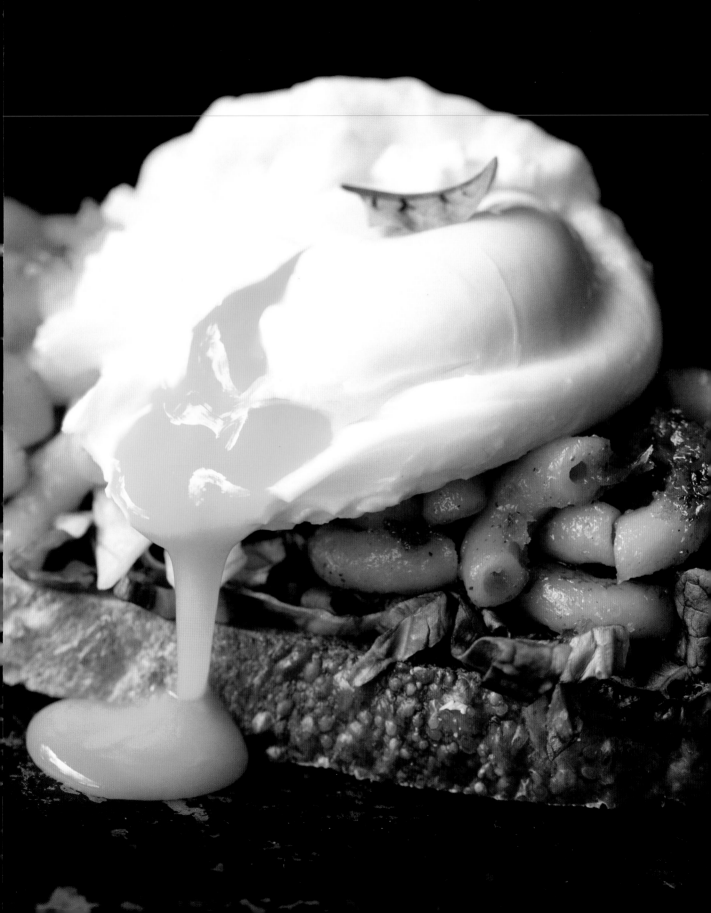

WEST COAST EGGS BENNY

Serves 2

When we say "West Coast," we're talking Canada, and here in British Columbia few things in life bring pleasure quite like smoked salmon. Combined with our irresistible Serrano Pepper and Cheddar Bagels (page 69), a thick schmear of cream cheese and a super easy hollandaise sauce, this is one flavorful bite that is both light yet indulgent.

Eggs Benny:

1 tsp white vinegar

4 large eggs

2 bagels, split (see Tip, page 70)

4 large caper berries, thinly sliced

¼ cup cream cheese

½ cup smoked salmon

thinly sliced red onion

Fresh dill, to serve

Hollandaise Sauce:

¼ to ⅓ cup butter

3 large egg yolks

1 tbsp fresh lemon juice

¼ tsp ground turmeric

Pinch of salt

Poach eggs: Bring a medium saucepan of water to a gentle simmer. Add vinegar. Crack each egg into a small bowl, then carefully, one at a time, add to the water. Cook for 3½ minutes. Using a slotted spoon, carefully transfer poached eggs to a plate. Reserve pan of hot water to reheat eggs before serving, if desired.

Make sauce: Melt butter in a small pan and let cool slightly. In a flat-bottomed cup, combine the egg yolks, lemon juice, turmeric and salt. Using an immersion blender, blend until smooth. While blending, add the cooled melted butter in a slow stream and mix until completely emulsified (the result should be thick and creamy, but still smooth and pourable); set aside. In the empty butter pan, toast the bagels, and then fry the caper berries until golden and slightly crisp.

Spread cream cheese on cut sides of each bagel and divide between serving plates. Top each with onion, smoked salmon, fried caper berries and a poached egg. Finish with a cascade of hollandaise sauce and garnish with dill.

Styling Note:
The irresistible drip of hollandaise from the spoon was the highlight of this shot. It basically screams "Come eat me!"

Settings and Angle:
f/4.5
ISO 800
1/100 sec
10–20 degrees

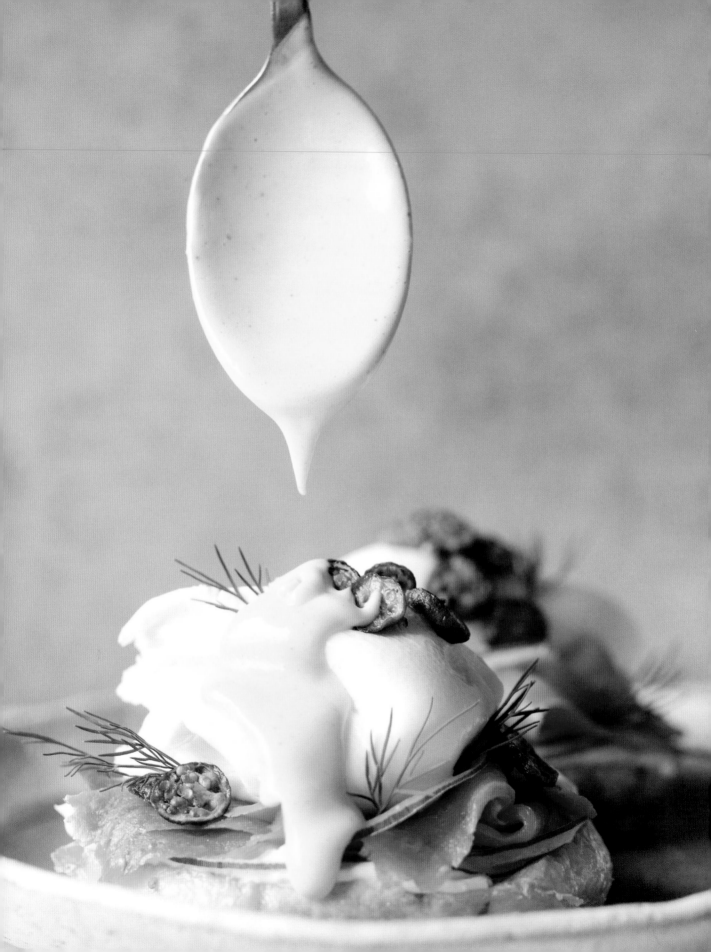

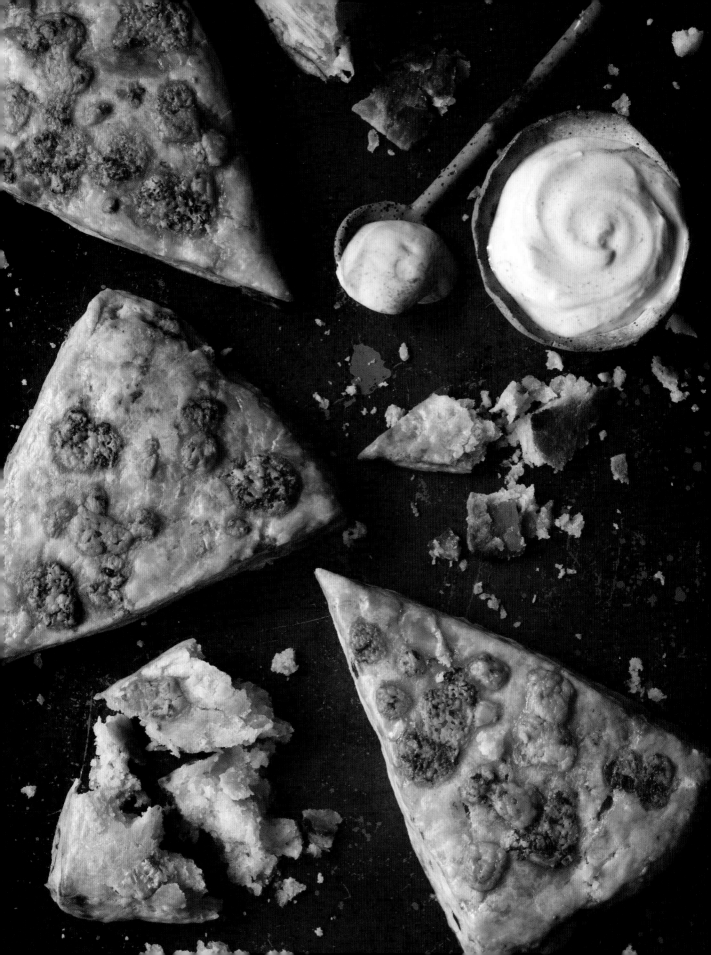

SERRANO PEPPER AND CHEDDAR BAGELS

Makes 1 dozen

Without a doubt, bagels are one of Adrian's biggest vices (if his waistline permitted, he would happily eat one generously piled with cream cheese every day of the week). So needless to say, as good as these babies are, they don't hang around our house too long. Great all on their own, they also make for a killer BLT sandwich, or give them a try in our irresistible West Coast Eggs Benny (page 62).

1⅓ cups warm water

2½ tsp active dry yeast

2 tsp granulated sugar, divided

3½ cups all-purpose flour

1 tsp salt

1½ cups shredded cheddar cheese
  + ½ cup for topping

½ cup roughly chopped serrano
  peppers + ¼ cup for topping

2 tbsp buttermilk

¼ tsp salt

In the bowl of a stand mixer, combine warm water, yeast and 1 tsp sugar. Let stand for about 10 minutes to allow the yeast to activate. Once you see foam, it's time to add the flour, remaining 1 tsp sugar and salt.

Affix the dough hook and mix until a rough dough starts to form. Add 1½ cups cheddar and ½ cup chopped serrano peppers, and mix until the dough is smooth and doesn't stick to the bowl. Cover and set aside at room temperature for 45 minutes, or until the dough doubles in size.

Preheat oven to 425°F. Line a baking sheet with parchment paper.

Punch down the dough, and turn out onto a lightly floured surface. Divide into 12 even balls.

(recipe continues on next page)

Styling Note:
Because a plain bagel isn't the most exciting thing to photograph, we jazzed things up by incorporating a bit more color.

Settings and Angle:
f/8
ISO 2000
1/100 sec
90 degrees

(continued from previous page)

Working with one ball at a time, use your index finger to poke a hole through the center of the ball, then stretch the dough gently with your hands until you can fit three fingers in the hole. Place on prepared baking sheet. Repeat with remaining dough balls. Let rise for 10 minutes.

Bring a large pot of water to a boil. Place bagels in boiling water, three at a time, and cook for 1 minute. Using a slotted spoon, carefully flip them over, and cook the other side for 1 minute. Transfer the bagels back to the baking sheet, then brush with buttermilk. Top with the remaining ½ cup cheddar and ¼ cup chopped serrano peppers. Bake in preheated oven for 30 to 35 minutes, until golden brown. Remove pan from oven and transfer bagels to a wire rack to cool before eating.

Tip: Got too many bagels? Just cut them in half, put them in a resealable bag and pop them in the freezer to toast and enjoy another time.

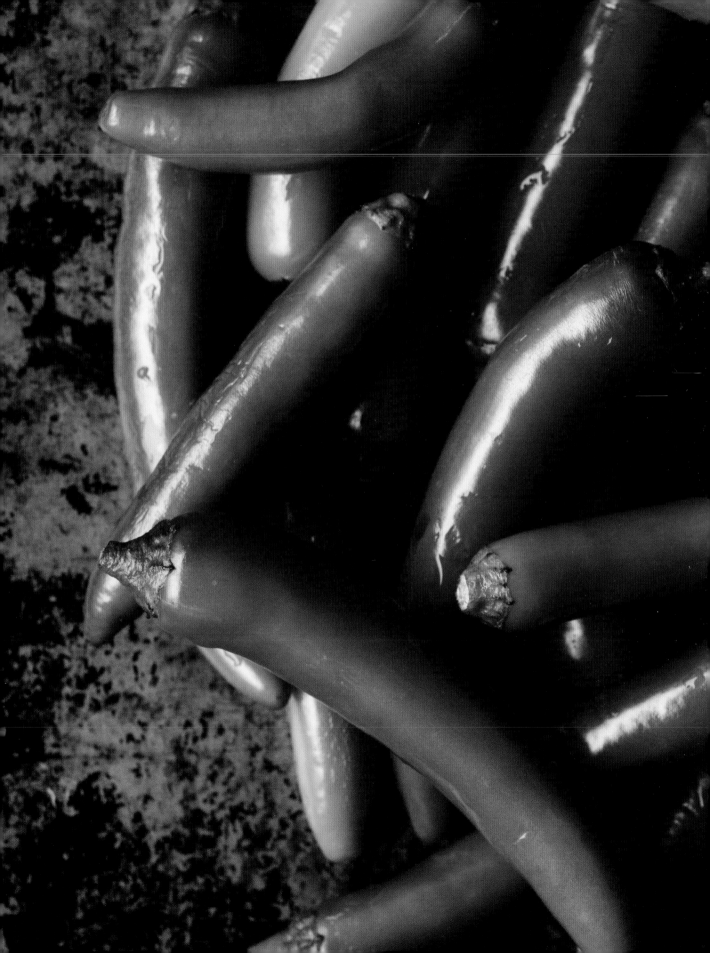

FRENCH TOAST WAFFLES WITH WHIPPED CREAM AND FRUIT

Serves 2

Adults and kids alike will love this dish. We like to use whatever fruit is in season, such as strawberries in the summer or blood oranges in the winter.

1 can (14 oz) coconut milk, chilled

1 cup whole milk

1 large egg

1 cup all-purpose flour

6 tbsp granulated sugar

1 tsp baking powder

1 tsp ground cinnamon

1 to 2 slices French bread, cut into 1-inch cubes

1 peach or any other fresh fruit, sliced, to serve

Sprigs of mint, to garnish

Refrigerate the can of coconut milk overnight. Scoop out the solid cream at the top (reserve the remaining milk for another use) and whip using an electric mixer until desired consistency for topping. Refrigerate until ready to use. Preheat your waffle iron.

In a large bowl, whisk together milk and egg.

In a separate bowl, whisk together flour, sugar, baking powder and cinnamon. Add the egg mixture and stir until well combined. Add cubed bread and let sit for 5 minutes, or until waffle iron has warmed up. Cook waffles according to the manufacturer's instructions.

Serve waffles topped with whipped coconut cream and fresh fruit. Garnish with mint.

Styling Note:
The gorgeous red inside of these white peaches complemented the waffles beautifully. Choose produce that's in season and you're already halfway there.

Settings and Angle:
f/10
ISO 1600
1/100 sec
90 degrees

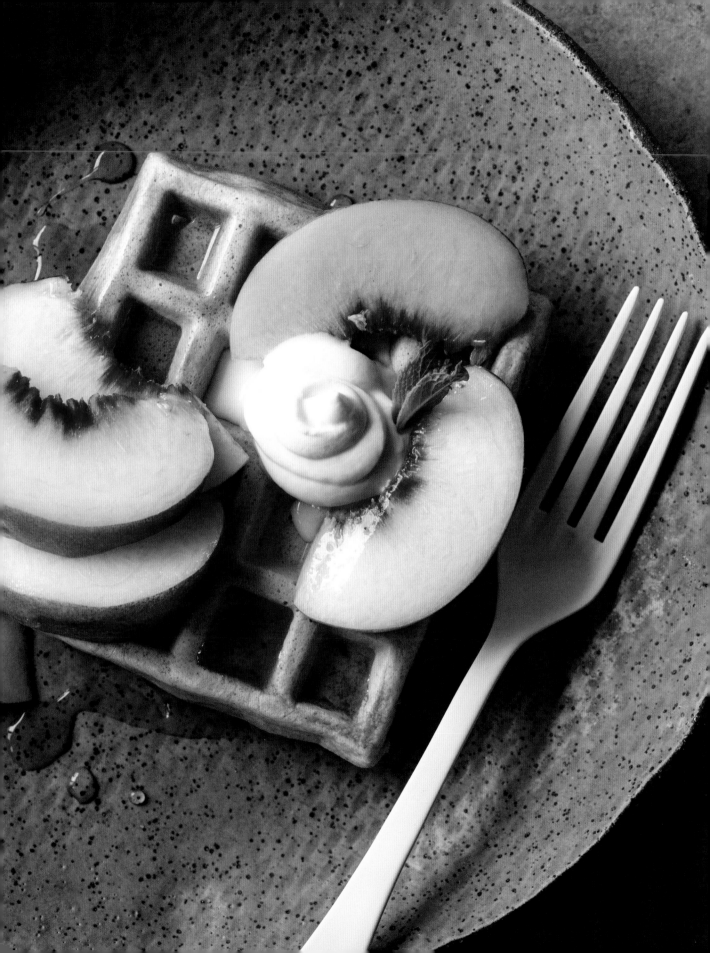

KOREAN-STYLE
BULGOGI BEEF WAFFLES

Serves 4

Packed full of punchy, bold flavors like sesame and ginger, and accompanied by bright, crunchy carrots and purple cabbage, this is one epic brunch masterpiece we're certain you'll be making more than once. Many elements in this recipe can be made the day before your brunch, meaning you'll have even more time to enjoy good food and great friends.

Waffle Batter:

1 cup whole milk

2 tbsp neutral cooking oil

1 large egg

1 cup all-purpose flour

1 tsp baking powder

½ tsp salt

Bulgogi Beef:

10 oz beef tenderloin (see Tip, page 76)

Beef Marinade:

½ cup soy sauce

5 tbsp mirin

2 tbsp sesame oil

Juice of ½ lime

5 tbsp granulated sugar

2 tbsp toasted sesame seeds

2 tbsp finely chopped green onion

2 garlic cloves, minced

Make batter: In a medium bowl, combine milk, oil, egg, flour, baking powder and salt. Mix well, cover and refrigerate overnight (or up to 24 hours; see Tip, page 76).

Make beef: Wrap beef tenderloin tightly in plastic wrap, and freeze for 1 to 2 hours, until firm but not frozen all the way through. Remove plastic wrap and cut beef into very thin slices.

Make marinade: In a medium bowl, combine soy sauce, mirin, sesame oil, lime juice, sugar, sesame seeds, green onion and minced garlic. Stir well and reserve ⅓ cup for the sauce.

(recipe continues on page 76)

Styling Note:
Brown foods, while often delicious, can be especially challenging to photograph. Green and purple play off each other well and brighten up the dark slices of beef.

Settings and Angle:
f/5.6
ISO 1250
1/100 sec
10–20 degrees

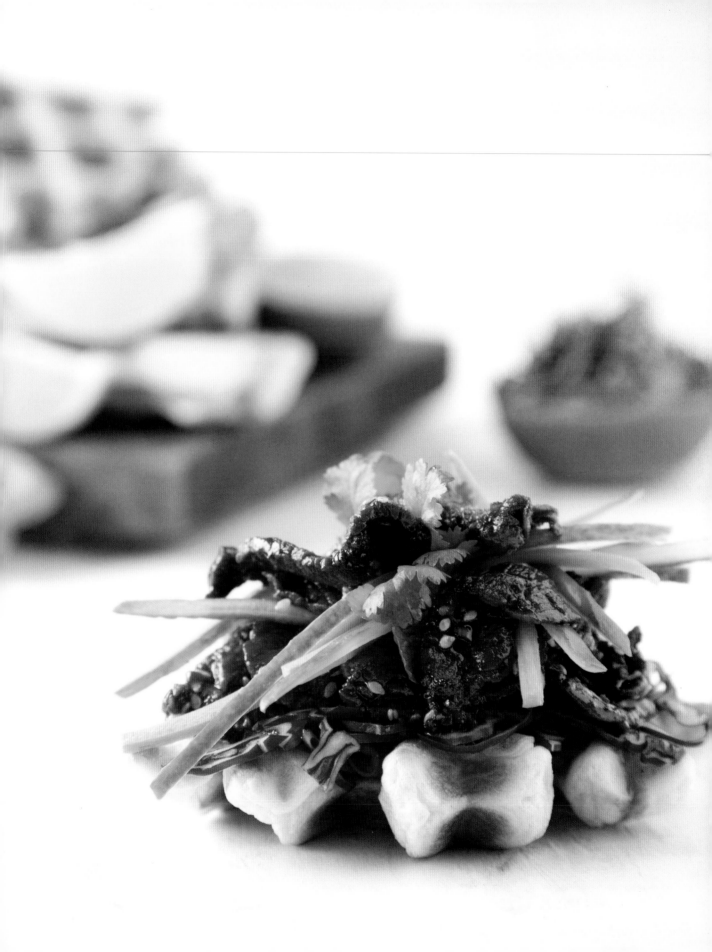

(continued from page 74)

Sauce:

4 tbsp Classic 30-Second Mayonnaise (page 31)

1 tbsp reduced Beef Marinade (page 74)

Juice of ½ lime (about 1 tsp)

For Serving:

½ cup thinly sliced purple cabbage

½ cup chopped carrots (cut into matchsticks)

½ cup chopped English cucumber (cut into matchsticks)

Fresh cilantro, to garnish

In a resealable bag, combine sliced beef and marinade. Refrigerate overnight (or up to 24 hours). Drain beef and discard marinade.

In a medium frying pan or skillet on medium-high heat, cook beef for 1 to 2 minutes, until cooked through.

In a small saucepan on medium-high heat, bring the ⅓ cup of reserved marinade to a boil. Cook until thickened, 3 to 5 minutes. Set aside to cool. (You will need 1 tbsp of the reduced marinade for the sauce.)

Cook waffles: Preheat waffle iron. Cook waffles according to the manufacturer's instructions.

Make sauce: In a small bowl, whisk together mayonnaise, 1 tbsp reserved marinade and lime juice.

Serve waffles with purple cabbage, bulgogi beef and sauce, topped with carrots, cucumber and cilantro.

Tips: Letting the batter sit overnight (or up to 24 hours) results in lighter, fluffier waffles.

Sirloin, tenderloin or skirt steak are all great choices for this dish.

PRETZEL BAGEL DOUGHNUTS

Makes 12 doughnuts

This is by far one of the most popular recipes on our blog, so we knew it had to make an appearance here. These little savory carb-babies combine a pretzel, bagel and doughnut into one, and are stuffed to the brim with herbed cream cheese. Your diet can start tomorrow.

Doughnut Batter:

3½ cups all-purpose flour

2¼ tsp active dry yeast

2 tsp granulated sugar

2 tsp salt + more for seasoning

1⅓ cups warm water

1 tbsp neutral cooking oil

½ onion, diced

2 garlic cloves, minced

1 tbsp butter

Olive oil, to coat dough

Lye Solution:

4 cups room-temperature water

2 tbsp food-grade lye (see Tips for safe handling, page 78)

Make batter: In the bowl of a stand mixer fitted with the dough hook, combine flour, yeast, sugar and 2 tsp salt. Mix on medium speed, and add warm water. Continue to mix until a dough ball forms, about 6 minutes or so.

Meanwhile, heat cooking oil in a small frying pan or skillet on medium heat. Add onion, and cook for 2 to 3 minutes, until translucent. Season with salt to taste. Add garlic and butter, and cook for another 2 to 3 minutes. Set aside and let cool completely.

Once the dough has formed, let the mixer run for another 8 minutes or so, checking for elasticity. When you stretch the dough out between your hands, it should not tear, and it should have a springy quality. Using a sharp knife, cut dough into small pieces. Return dough pieces to the mixer, add cooled onion mixture, and mix together until one large dough ball reforms. Transfer the ball to a lightly oiled medium bowl, and coat dough with a drizzle of olive oil. Cover dough with a clean kitchen towel and let rise in a warm, draft-free place for about 1 hour, or until doubled in size.

Preheat oven to 425°F. Line a baking sheet with parchment paper. Punch dough down to release some of the gas. Turn dough out onto a lightly floured work surface and cut into 12 equal pieces. (We recommend using a kitchen scale to be as accurate as possible.)

(recipe continues on next page)

(continued from previous page)

Topping:

1 tbsp raw sesame seeds

1 tbsp poppy seeds

1 tbsp flax seeds

½ tsp flaky sea salt

Chives, to garnish

Filling:

1 package (9 oz) cream cheese, softened

2 tbsp minced fresh herbs (your choice)

Styling Note: Incorporating hands in the shot provides a sense of movement to the still frame.

Settings and Angle: f/7.1 ISO 1600 1/100 sec 90 degrees

Roll each piece into a ball, then flatten slightly with your hand to form a doughnut-like shape. Cover with a clean kitchen towel and let rise for 5 to 10 minutes.

Make lye solution: Pour water into a nonreactive bowl. Add lye (see Tips below) and stir until lye is completely dissolved. Set aside.

Make topping: In a small bowl, combine all of the topping ingredients except chives. Set aside.

Bake pretzel bagel doughnuts: Wearing rubber gloves and using a slotted wooden spoon, dip each dough round in the lye solution for at least 15 to 20 seconds. Once dipped, transfer to the prepared baking sheet. Sprinkle with the topping, and let stand for 5 minutes.

Bake pretzel bagel doughnuts in preheated oven for 18 minutes, or until a nice dark golden-brown exterior has developed. Transfer to a wire rack and let cool for at least 10 minutes.

Make filling: In a small bowl, mix together cream cheese and fresh herbs until cream cheese is soft and airy. Transfer to a resealable bag, and snip the tip off the corner of one side.

Fill doughnuts: Using the tip of a knife, poke a hole (big enough to insert the tip of the bag) in the top of each of your pretzel bagel doughnuts. Fill generously with herbed cream cheese. Top with another dollop of the filling and sprinkle with chopped chives. Enjoy!

Tips: For us, lye adds the quintessential pretzel flavor (baking soda is no subsitite). You can purchase lye through online retailers.

Be extremely careful when handling lye, as it is caustic. Do not ingest it or get it on your skin. Wearing rubber gloves is essential. Always add lye to water (never pour water onto lye) to avoid a volcano-like reaction.

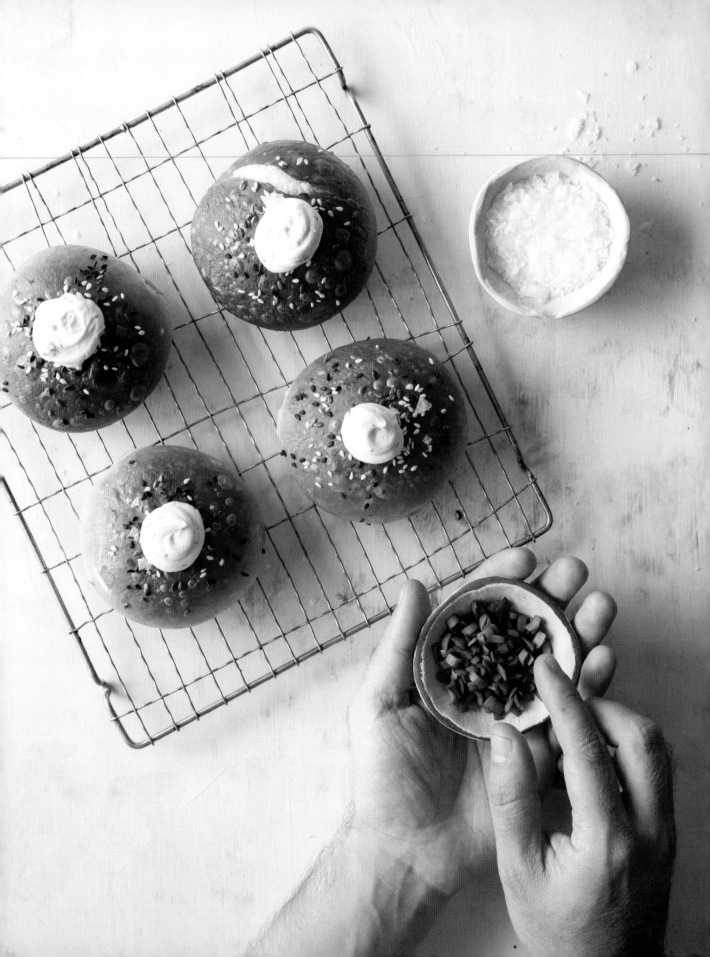

EAT WITH YOUR HANDS

We're all about bright, vibrant meals that are simple enough to prepare but, most of all, are satisfying to eat. Many of the recipes in this chapter are great make-aheads and work overtime by suiting lunch or dinner, depending what you're in the mood for.

Whether you're craving something utterly sinful and rich like our Moroccan Pulled Pork Sandwich Dip with Kohlrabi Slaw (page 103), or light and refreshing like our Rainbow Spring Rolls with Miso Peanut Dip (page 82), we've got you covered. So forget the sad desk lunch and up your game with something exceptional.

RAINBOW SPRING ROLLS WITH MISO PEANUT DIP

Serves 2

Flavorful, fast and oh-so-easy to make! These colorful little spring rolls are a cinch to prep ahead of time. Have your ingredients pre-sliced in the fridge and these can be put together in a flash. The dipping sauce keeps, refrigerated, for up to 1 week.

Dip:

¼ cup smooth peanut butter

½ tbsp soy sauce

½ tbsp hoisin sauce

1 tsp yellow miso paste

1 tsp fish sauce

½ cup water + more if desired

Pinch of sesame seeds, to garnish

Rolls:

6 sheets rice paper

5 leaves red lettuce

1 cup thinly sliced bell peppers (any color)

⅔ cup thinly sliced purple cabbage

⅔ cup thinly sliced carrot

⅔ cup thinly sliced daikon

⅔ cup thinly sliced English cucumber

2 green onions, thinly sliced

¼ cup fresh basil leaves

¼ cup fresh mint leaves

Make dip: In a small saucepan on medium heat, combine peanut butter, soy sauce, hoisin sauce, miso paste, fish sauce and water. As soon as the mixture comes to a simmer, remove from heat and set aside to cool at room temperature. Once cool, store in a small jar with a resealable lid.

Make rolls: Soak rice paper sheets in a large bowl of warm water for a few seconds, just until they become pliable. Lay them side by side on a clean work surface, and layer even amounts of vegetables and herbs on top, starting with the lettuce. (Resist the urge to overfill, or you'll tear your rice paper!)

Working with one sheet at a time, first fold in both sides of the rice paper, then fold up the bottom, and then gently roll it into a cylinder, keeping the rice paper taut. The result should be fairly tidy, but don't feel bad if each one takes a couple tries. Cut the rolls into 1½-inch pieces, and arrange on a serving platter. Serve immediately with a small bowl of dip alongside, sprinkled with sesame seeds.

Styling Note: Use a mandoline to cut vegetables into super-thin matchsticks.

Settings and Angle: f/10 ISO 800 1/100 sec 90 degrees

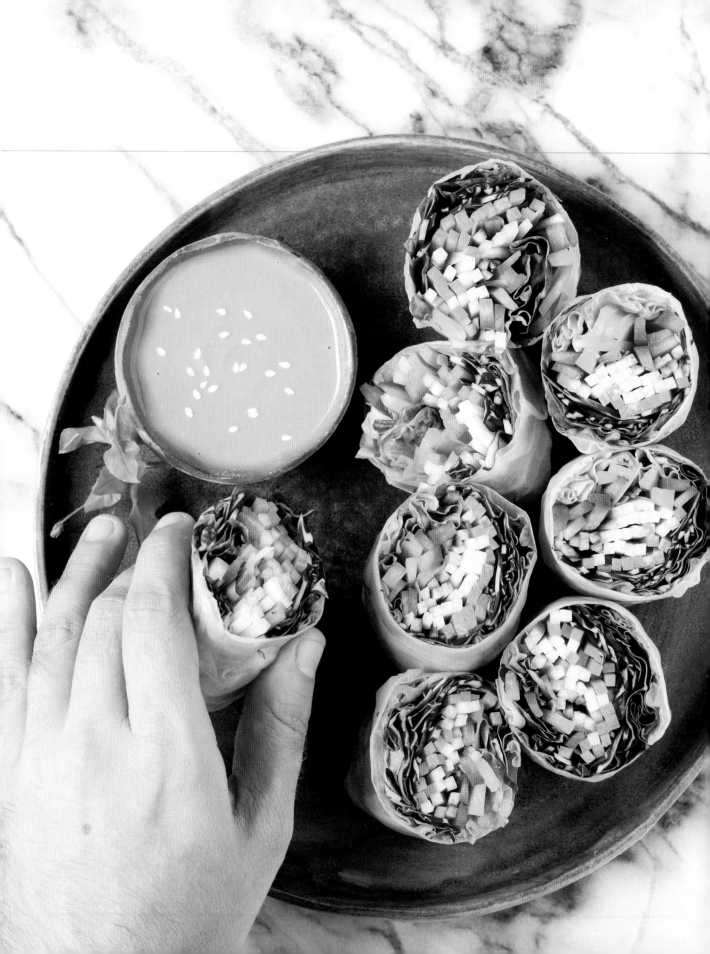

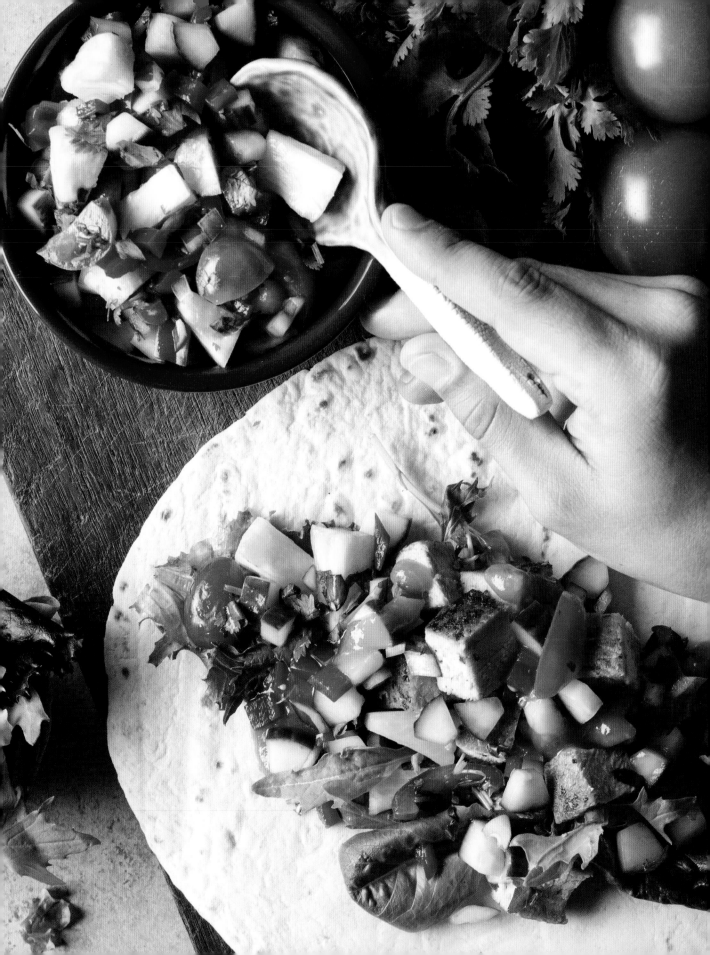

SEARED PORK AND PINEAPPLE SALSA WRAP

Serves 4

Haven't tried pineapple salsa? Now's the time! Pork and pineapple go together like cheese and wine, and this tasty wrap proves once and for all that the two were meant to be.

Salsa:

1½ cups diced fresh pineapple

¼ cup diced red onion

½ cup halved cherry tomatoes

1 cup diced English cucumber

½ cup diced red bell pepper

2 tbsp roughly chopped fresh mint

2 tbsp roughly chopped fresh cilantro leaves

Juice of ½ lime

⅛ tsp salt

Sauce:

1 cup puréed pineapple (see Tip, page 86)

2 tbsp soy sauce

2 tbsp liquid honey

2 tsp minced peeled ginger

2 tsp minced garlic

1 tbsp cornstarch

¼ cup water

½ tbsp neutral cooking oil

1 lb lean pork tenderloin

4 flour tortillas, to serve

2 cups packed mixed greens, to serve

Make salsa: In a medium bowl, combine pineapple, red onion, cherry tomatoes, cucumber, red pepper, mint and cilantro. Add lime juice and salt, stir and taste for seasoning. Cover and refrigerate until ready to serve.

Make sauce: Preheat oven to 350°F. In a small saucepan on medium-high heat, combine puréed pineapple, soy sauce, honey, ginger and garlic and bring to a boil.

In a small bowl, whisk together cornstarch and water until smooth. Once the pineapple mixture begins boiling, reduce the heat to medium-low and whisk in the cornstarch slurry. Simmer until thickened. Remove from heat and set aside.

(recipe continues on next page)

Styling Note:
This is one colorful wrap, full of texture and vibrantly fresh ingredients. We have always thought that action shots with hands add extra character.

Settings and Angle:
f/10
ISO 800
1/100 sec
90 degrees

(continued from previous page)

Heat oil in a large, ovenproof frying pan or skillet on medium-high heat until the oil begins to smoke. Add pork and sear on each side for 3 minutes. Transfer skillet to the preheated oven, and cook pork for an additional 5 to 10 minutes, until pork is cooked through (it should reach an internal temperature of 145°F when tested with a meat thermometer). Remove from the oven and let pork rest for another 5 to 10 minutes before cutting into ½-inch cubes.

Top your tortilla with greens and pineapple salsa, cubed pork and a drizzle of the pineapple sauce. Wrap and serve.

Tip: To make pineapple purée, simply add fresh pineapple chunks to a blender or food processor and blend until smooth.

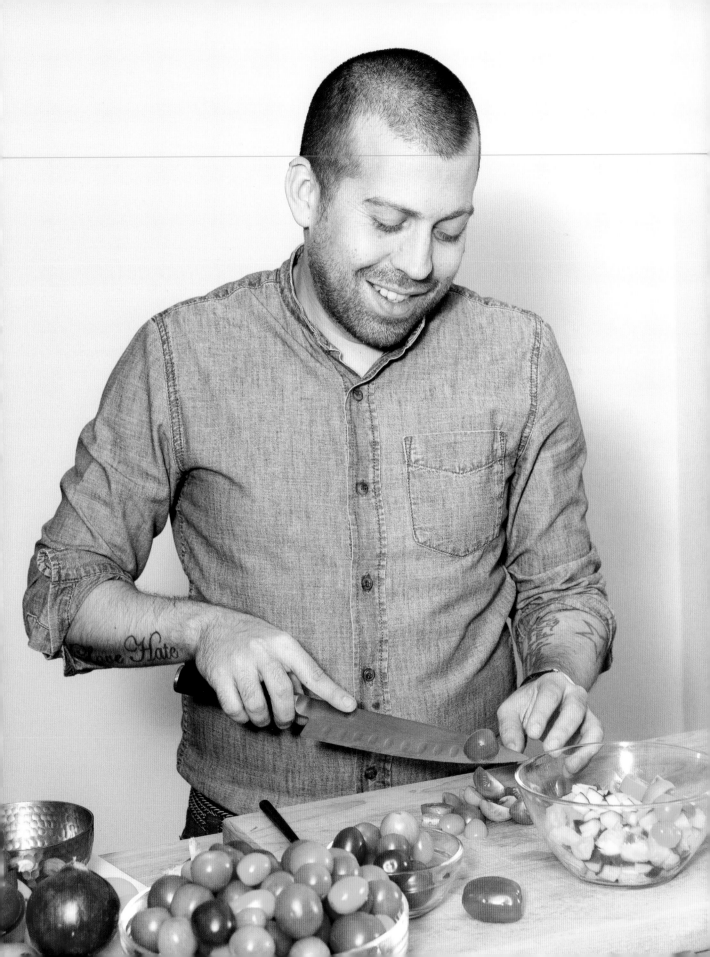

LEMON PEPPER GRILLED CHICKEN WRAP

Serves 4

Incredibly simple to make, this addictive wrap is sure to become a new lunchtime fave. Our lemon pepper marinade requires only a handful of ingredients, and when left overnight it infuses the chicken with a wallop of intense, citrusy flavor.

2 tbsp extra virgin olive oil

Zest and juice of 2 lemons

½ tbsp freshly ground black pepper

½ tsp flaky sea salt

2 boneless skinless chicken breasts

Classic 30-Second Mayonnaise (page 31), to serve

4 flour tortillas, to serve

1 cup packed baby arugula

2 roma tomatoes, sliced

1 avocado, pitted, peeled and sliced

¼ cup crumbled gorgonzola cheese

In a resealable bag, combine olive oil, lemon zest and juice, pepper and salt. Place chicken inside the bag, seal and turn to coat. Refrigerate for 12 to 24 hours. Discard marinade.

In an oiled grill pan on medium-high heat, cook chicken breasts for about 5 minutes per side, or until cooked through (they should reach an internal temperature of 165°F when tested with a meat thermometer). Let rest for 5 minutes before cutting into ¼-inch slices.

Spread some mayonnaise on a tortilla, then top with arugula, tomato, avocado, gorgonzola and sliced chicken. Wrap and serve.

Styling Note:
We photographed this wrap open-faced, to show off the mouth-watering grilled chicken, tomatoes and fresh arugula.

Settings and Angle:
f/4
ISO 500
1/100 sec
10–20 degrees

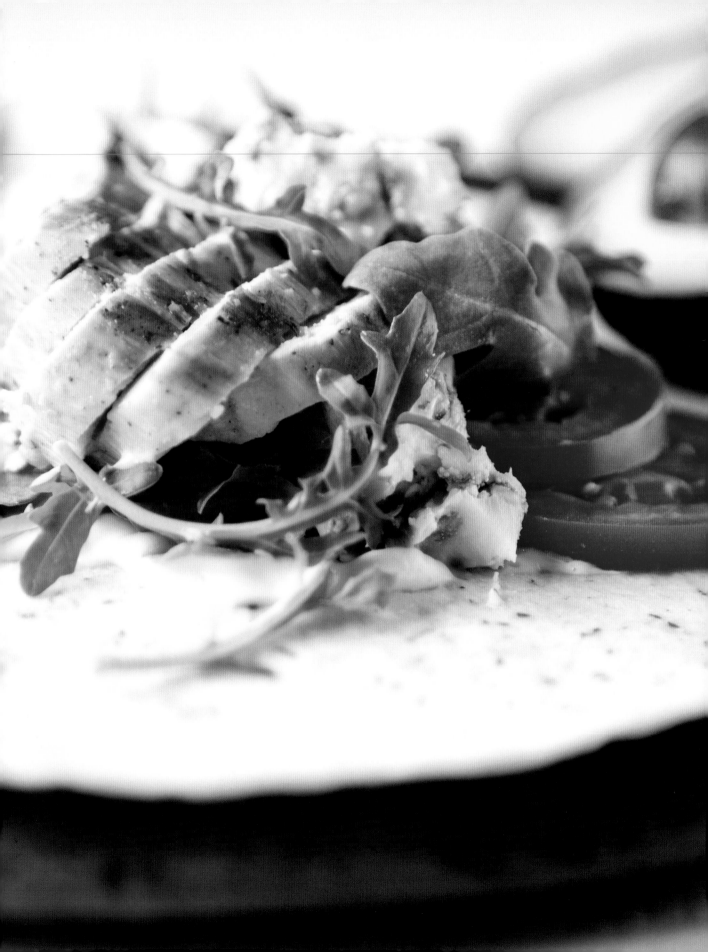

HUMMUS VEGGIE WRAP

Serves 4

While purists may have strong opinions about what is and isn't acceptable in a hummus recipe, we've thrown caution to the wind and taken an alternative approach here. Blending in other veggies like roasted red peppers is a great way to ramp up the nutrition and taste — not to mention a fun way to inject color.

Hummus:

1 can (15 oz) chickpeas, rinsed and drained, reserving 2 tbsp chickpea water

1 cup seeded and diced roasted red pepper

½ cup tahini

Juice of 1 lemon

Salt, to taste

2 garlic cloves

For Serving:

Tortillas

Kale leaves

Alfalfa sprouts

English cucumber, cut into ribbons

Cherry tomatoes, halved

Avocado, pitted, peeled and sliced

Salt and pepper, to taste

Prepare hummus: In a blender or food processor, combine chickpeas and chickpea water, roasted red pepper, tahini, lemon juice, salt and garlic. Blend until completely smooth.

On each tortilla, spread a few tablespoons of the hummus, then top with as little or as much of the kale, sprouts, cucumber, tomato and avocado as you'd like. Season with salt and pepper. Roll it up and chow down!

Styling Note:
The ingredients do most of the work here, offering bold color and texture.

Settings and Angle:
f/9
ISO 3200
1/100 sec
90 degrees

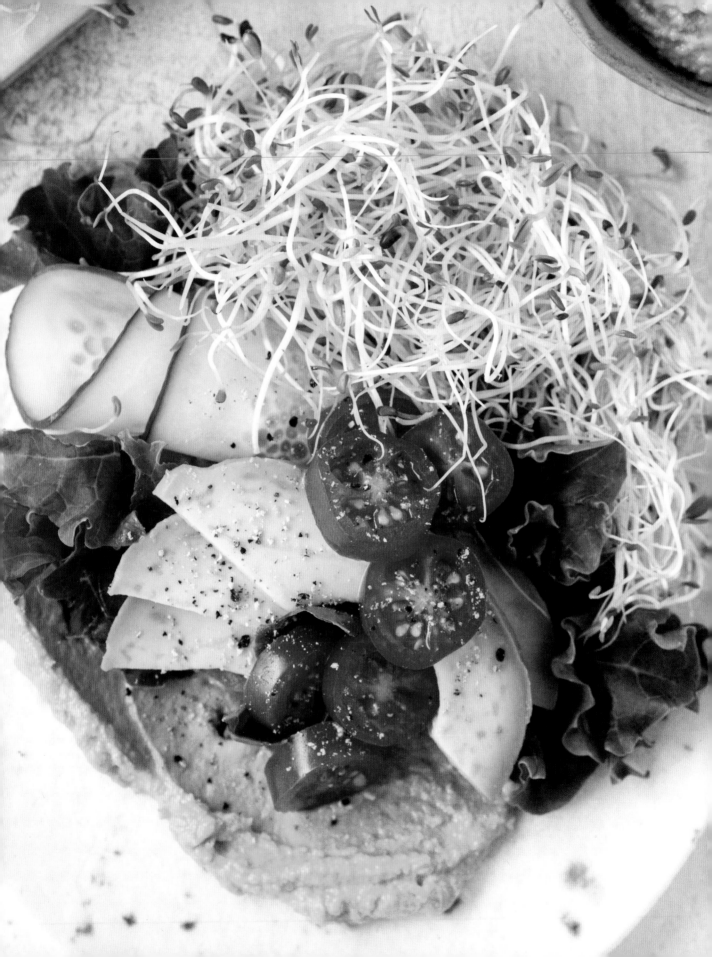

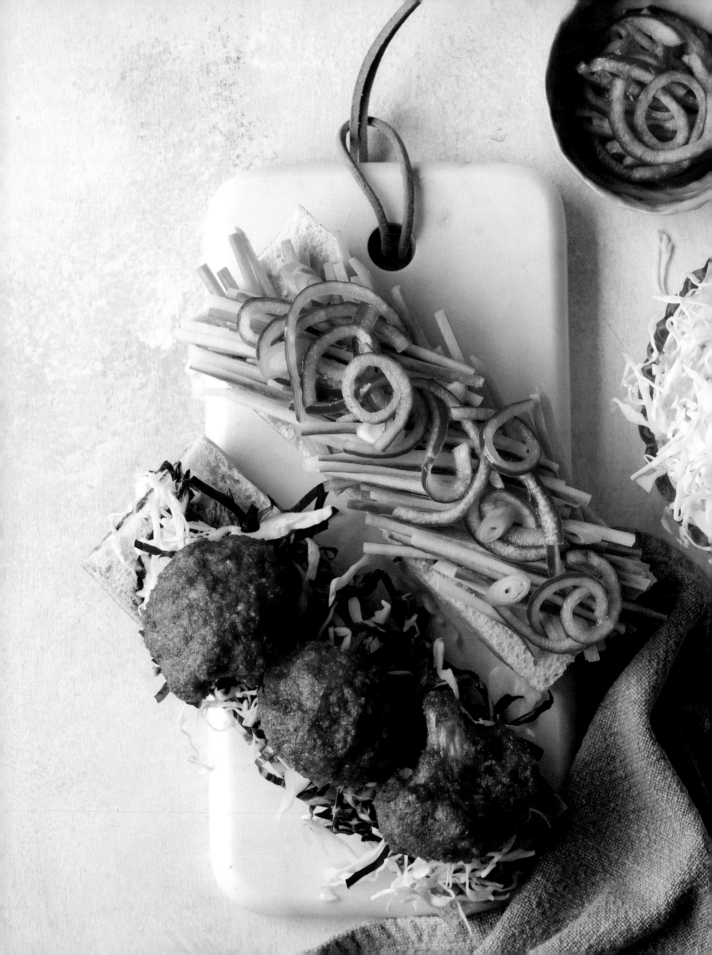

BUFFALO CAULIFLOWER BÁNH MÌ WITH MUSHROOM PÂTÉ

Serves 4

This sandwich has major swagger and is nowhere near your average, boring vegetarian bánh mì. Made with a rich, umami-packed mushroom pâté, then stuffed with crispy, spicy buffalo cauliflower bites and generously topped with quick-pickled onions, this baby is a flavor bomb that demands attention.

Mushroom Pâté:

3 tsp olive oil, divided

1 cup diced onion

2 cups diced brown mushrooms

½ tsp dried thyme

¾ cup unsalted cashews

½ tsp salt

⅛ tsp freshly ground black pepper

Juice of ½ lime

Preheat oven to 375°F. Line a baking sheet with parchment paper and set aside.

Make pâté: Heat 1 tsp olive oil in a large frying pan or skillet on medium heat. Add onion, and cook for 2 to 3 minutes, stirring occasionally, until translucent. Add mushrooms, and cook for 2 to 3 minutes. Stir in thyme, and cook for another 2 minutes. Add cashews and sauté for another 5 minutes. Transfer mixture to a high-speed blender or food processor, and blend until a soft paste forms. Stir in salt, pepper, lime juice and remaining 2 tsp olive oil. Taste for seasoning, and adjust as needed. Transfer to an airtight jar and refrigerate for up to 1 week.

(recipe continues on next page)

Styling Note:
Styling a sandwich open-faced is the easiest way to show off what's going on inside.

Settings and Angle:
f/8
ISO 800
1/80 sec
90 degrees

(continued from previous page)

Buffalo Cauliflower:

1 cup unseasoned breadcrumbs

½ tsp ground smoked chipotle pepper

½ tsp garlic powder

½ tsp salt

½ tsp freshly ground black
  pepper

2 large eggs, beaten, for egg wash

1 head of cauliflower, cut into
  florets

Sauce:

⅓ cup Sriracha sauce

½ tsp sambal oelek

2 tbsp unsalted butter

1 tbsp brown sugar

For Serving:

Baguette, split and toasted

Fresh cilantro leaves

Daikon, cut into matchsticks

English cucumber, cut into
  matchsticks

Grated cabbage

Quick-Pickled Red Onions
  (page 36)

Make cauliflower: In a medium bowl, combine breadcrumbs, chipotle, garlic powder, salt and pepper. Set up a breading station: place seasoned breadcrumbs mixture and beaten eggs in separate shallow dishes. Dunk each cauliflower floret first into the egg wash, then coat with breadcrumbs. Arrange in a single layer on the prepared baking sheet. Bake in preheated oven for 25 to 30 minutes, until golden brown and cooked through (test for doneness by inserting a toothpick or fork; if they're tender, they're done!).

Make sauce: In a small saucepan on medium heat, combine Sriracha, sambal oelek, butter and brown sugar. Cook for 2 to 3 minutes, just until it starts simmering. Remove from heat and set aside.

Remove the cauliflower from the oven and toss with sauce. Bump the oven temperature to 400°F, and bake cauliflower for another 5 minutes.

Spread mushroom pâté on cut sides of the toasted baguette. Fill with a few pieces of spicy buffalo cauliflower, and as much cilantro, daikon, cucumber, cabbage and pickled red onions as you like. Slice sandwich in half, if desired, and serve immediately.

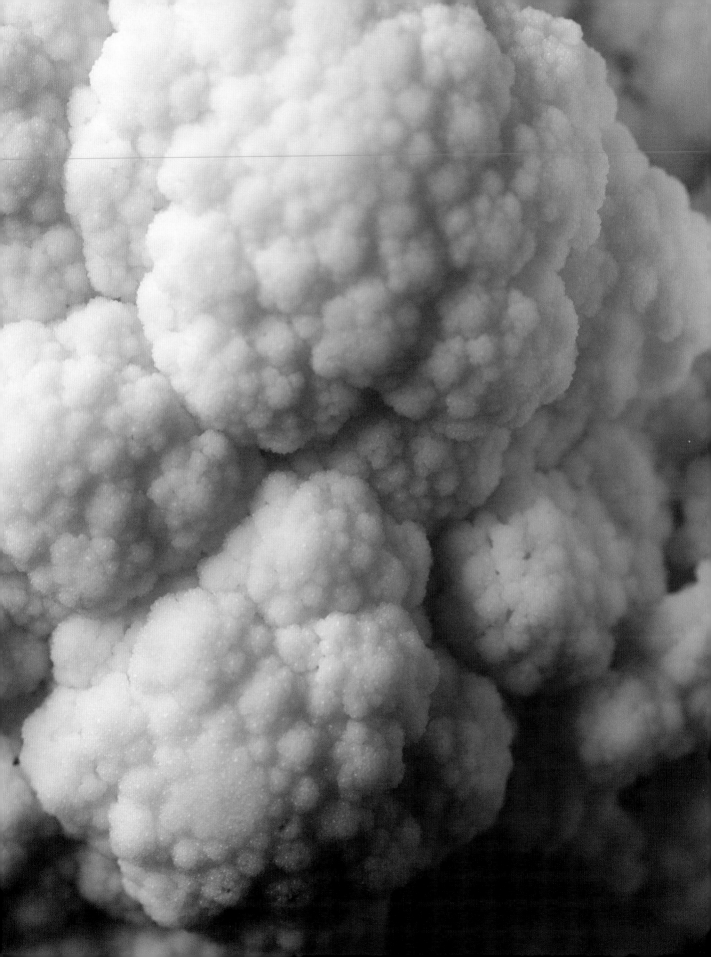

VEGGIENORMOUS SANDWICH

Serves 2

When we say eat the rainbow, we really mean it! This colossal sandwich is made with a ton of delicious and nutritious veggies, so you're sure to feel like a million bucks after eating it. Use whatever you have on hand, and remember: More is more here. Be sure to use a sturdy bread like rye or sourdough or best results.

4 slices of bread

Spread:
¼ cup plain Greek yogurt
2 tbsp tahini
Fresh basil leaves, sliced
Salt and pepper, to taste

Toppings:
¼ cup spinach leaves
¼ cup alfalfa sprouts
¼ cup sliced tomato
1 avocado, pitted, peeled and
  sliced
¼ cup thinly sliced radish
¼ cup thinly sliced English
  cucumber
¼ cup thinly sliced radicchio
¼ cup thinly sliced red onion
Fresh basil leaves, sliced

Lightly toast the bread.

In a small bowl, combine yogurt, tahini, basil, salt and pepper. Spread mixture on one side of each piece of toasted bread. Build your sandwich as desired.

Serve and enjoy.

Styling Note: Because of the sheer size of this sandwich, a 0-degree shot felt like the natural choice for showing off its impressive height.

Settings and Angle:
f/4
ISO 640
1/100 sec
0 degrees

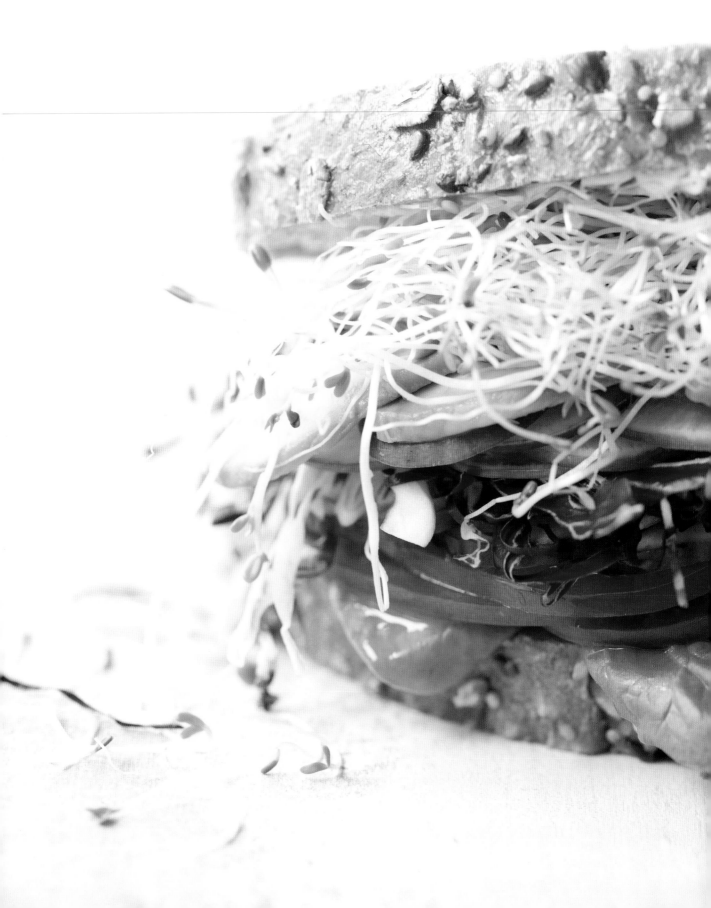

OPEN-FACED BRIE, PEACH AND PROSCIUTTO SANDWICH WITH WALNUTS AND HONEY

Serves 2

Ideal for a snack, light lunch or just because you can! This open-faced sandwich hits all the salty, sweet, creamy and crunchy notes, making it a flawless bite.

2 slices of sourdough bread

3½ oz soft unripened brie cheese, sliced

2 oz Prosciutto di Parma, thinly sliced

1 peach, pitted, peeled and sliced

2 tbsp crushed walnuts

Liquid honey, to serve

Lightly toast bread in a toaster oven or preheated 375°F oven for 2 to 3 minutes. Top with sliced brie and return to the oven until cheese is melted, 1 to 2 minutes (optional).

Divide prosciutto evenly between toasts, along with a few peach slices and a sprinkle of crushed walnuts. Finish with a lovely drizzle of honey. Devour immediately.

Styling Note:
We photographed this recipe at a variety of angles, but ultimately a bird's-eye view was the most dramatic and appetizing.

Settings and Angle:
f/10
ISO 1250
1/100 sec
90 degrees

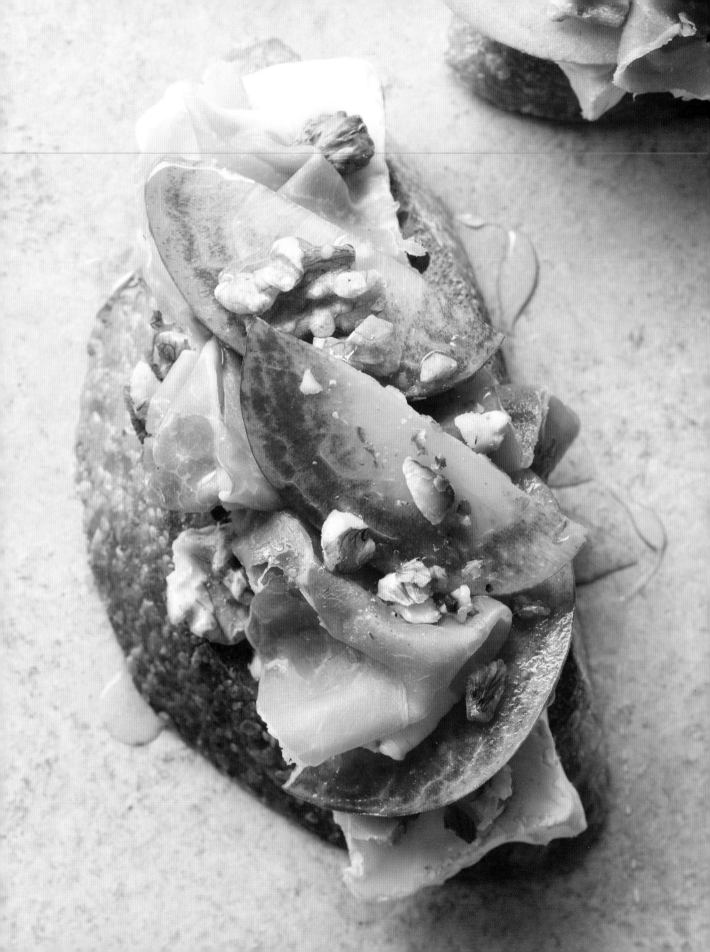

ZUCCHINI "MEATBALL" SUB

Serves 4

We're usually not fans of vegetarian dishes bearing the names of their meat-driven counterparts, but this sandwich is satisfying enough to break all those rules.

"Meatballs":

1 tbsp neutral cooking oil

4 cups grated zucchini

2 tbsp chopped green onion

3 garlic cloves, minced

Salt and pepper, to taste

½ tsp sweet paprika

1 cup unseasoned breadcrumbs

2 tbsp roughly chopped fresh flat-leaf parsley

½ cup finely grated Parmigiano-Reggiano cheese

1 large egg, lightly beaten

Sauce:

1 cup passata

½ tsp brown sugar

½ tsp dried oregano

¼ tsp dried porcini mushroom powder (see Tip, page 24)

For Serving:

4 hoagie rolls, toasted

½ cup fresh basil leaves

Mozzarella cheese, shredded

Preheat oven to 375°F. Line a baking sheet with nonstick foil and set aside.

Make "meatballs": Heat oil in a medium frying pan or skillet on medium heat. Add zucchini, green onion and minced garlic. Season with salt, pepper and paprika. Cook for 5 to 7 minutes, stirring frequently, until vegetables are tender. Transfer to a fine-mesh sieve, and place in the sink to drain for 5 to 10 minutes.

In a large bowl, combine breadcrumbs, parsley, Parmigiano-Reggiano, beaten egg and the drained zucchini mixture. Shape into even-size balls, and place on the prepared baking sheet. Bake in preheated oven for 25 to 30 minutes, until golden brown. Transfer meatballs to a wire rack and let cool for a few minutes while you make the sauce.

Make sauce: In a small saucepan on medium heat, combine the passata, brown sugar, oregano and porcini mushroom powder and bring to a simmer. Add meatballs to sauce and gently toss until well coated.

Serve on toasted rolls, with fresh basil and shredded mozzarella.

Styling Note: As meatball sandwiches tend to be messy, we paired this one with an impossibly white backdrop, just for fun.

Settings and Angle: f/5.6 ISO 1000 1/100 sec 10–20 degrees

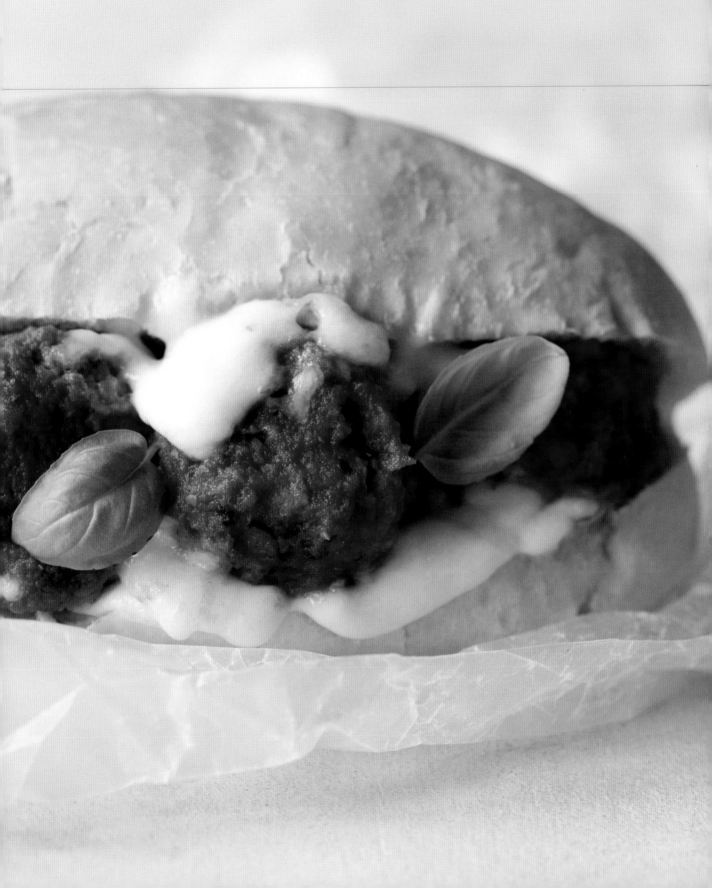

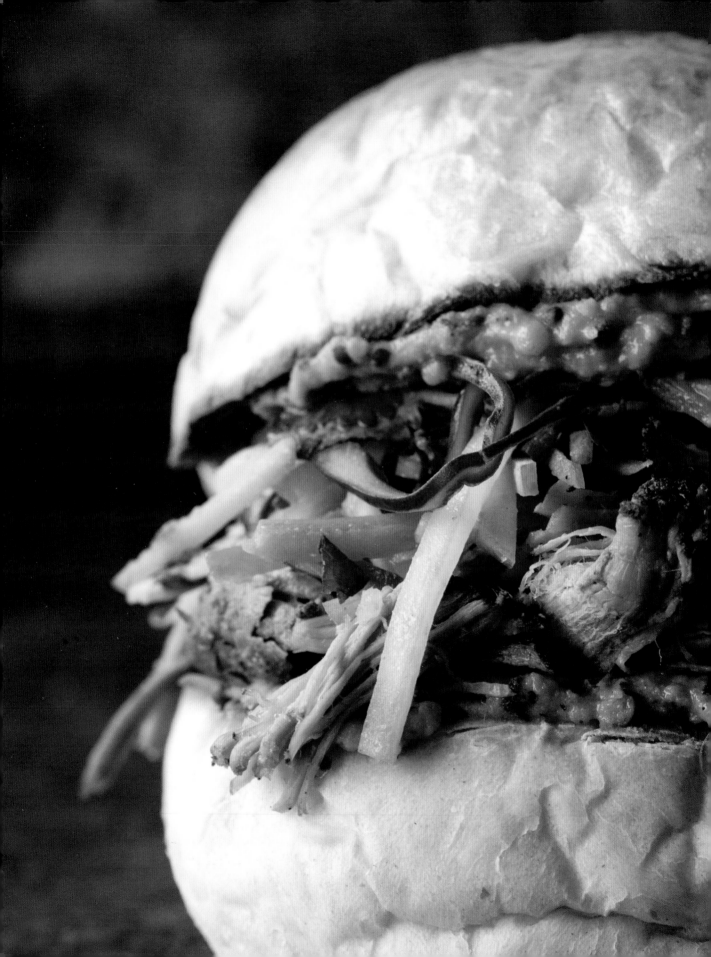

MOROCCAN PULLED PORK SANDWICH DIP WITH KOHLRABI SLAW

Serves 6

There's something about cooking with a crockpot that is so supremely satisfying. It's like you're gaming the system, letting dinner (practically) cook itself while you're off doing other important things. Another bonus: the cooking liquids double as a dipping "jus" for the sandwiches. Paired here with our crisp Confetti Kohlrabi Slaw (page 112), it's a delicious (albeit messy) way to amp up lunchtime!

Styling Note:
When styling a messy sandwich, it's important to remember that there's beauty in imperfection. With moist ingredients, make sure your bun is extra toasted.

1 tbsp neutral cooking oil

2⅔ cups thinly sliced white onions (about 2 medium)

½ tsp salt

2½ to 3 lb boneless lean pork shoulder

2 tbsp ras el hanout (see Tip)

4 cups chicken or vegetable broth

2 cups hot water

Confetti Kohlrabi Slaw (page 112)

6 of your favorite buns

Grainy Mustard (page 34), to serve

Settings and Angle:
f/10
ISO 2500
1/100 sec
0 degrees

Heat oil in a large frying pan on medium-low heat. Add onions and salt, and cook for 20 to 25 minutes, stirring frequently, until onions have caramelized. Transfer to the slow cooker; reserve pan.

Rub the pork shoulder all over with ras el hanout.

Heat reserved pan on medium-high heat. Sear seasoned pork shoulder for 1 to 2 minutes per side, just until it begins to take on some color.

Transfer seared pork to slow cooker. Pour broth and hot water alongside. Cover with a lid, and cook on High for 8 to 10 hours (the meat should be tender and break up easily). Using two forks, shred the pork into small pieces. Reserve cooking liquid ("jus").

Prepare Confetti Kohlrabi Slaw and refrigerate until ready to serve.

Slice and, if desired, toast buns. To serve, top toasted buns generously with grainy mustard, pork and slaw. Serve with reserved cooking "jus" as a dip.

Tip: Ras el hanout is a spice blend from North Africa. It can frequently be found in gourmet spice shops or Middle Eastern specialty markets.

CHAPTER 4

BOWLS
AND SALADS

Bowls and salads are a great way to get creative in the kitchen, allowing you to explore different flavor profiles without too much effort. And they shouldn't just taste good—they should look great, too.

This chapter has a recipe for all occasions and moods. Feeling fancy? Try our Grilled Cantaloupe Salad with Burrata and Asparagus (page 108). Or how about straight-up lazy? Our Teriyaki Chicken Salad Bowl (page 135) will do ya, with minimal effort required.

WATERMELON AND CUCUMBER SALAD WITH HERB VINAIGRETTE

Serves 4 to 6

With a punchy, fragrant herb vinaigrette made from mint, serrano pepper and dill, this sweet-and-savory creation is a departure from the usual watermelon-and-feta combo we see so often.

Salad:

1½ cups cubed (½ inch) seedless watermelon, rind removed

1½ cups cubed (½ inch) English cucumber

½ cup cubed (¼ inch) Gruyère cheese (see Tip)

½ cup quartered radishes

Sprigs of mint and dill, to garnish

Vinaigrette:

3 tbsp neutral cooking oil

1 tbsp red wine vinegar

½ tsp liquid honey

½ serrano pepper, thinly sliced

½ cup fresh dill fronds, roughly chopped

6 mint leaves, roughly chopped

¼ tsp salt

Make salad: In a serving bowl, combine the watermelon, cucumber, Gruyère and radishes. Set aside.

Make vinaigrette: In a blender or food processor, combine oil, red wine vinegar, honey, sliced serrano pepper, most of the dill and mint (saving some for garnish) and salt. Blend until smooth.

Drizzle vinaigrette on salad, and toss until well coated. Garnish with remaining dill and mint. Serve immediately.

Tip: We like using Gruyère in this recipe, but crumbling in a sharp cheddar will also do just fine.

Styling Note:
We used pretty pink radishes to add another layer of brightness to this dish, but regular red radishes would work just fine, too.

Settings and Angle:
f/4.5
ISO 1250
1/160 sec
45 degrees

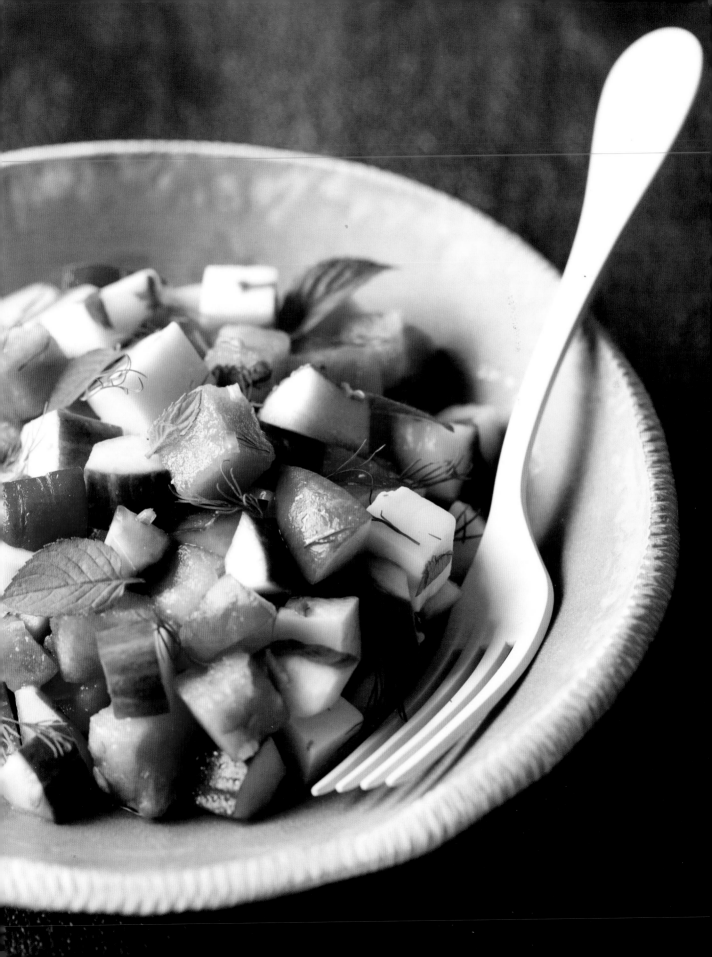

GRILLED CANTALOUPE SALAD WITH BURRATA AND ASPARAGUS

Serves 4

Close your eyes and imagine yourself on a patio somewhere in Italy, soaking up the sun, sipping wine and being fabulous. That's how you'll feel after taking a bite of this salad. Grilling the cantaloupe brings out even more sweetness in the fruit, and offers an impressive char. We pair it with burrata because, well, it's downright amazing, with an unctuous, creamy texture and luscious mouthfeel — but a fresh buffalo mozzarella would work nicely, too.

1 large bunch of asparagus, woody ends trimmed

¼ cup plain skyr or Greek yogurt

1 tbsp fresh lemon juice

5 fresh mint leaves, finely sliced

Pinch of flaky sea salt

4 thick slices of cantaloupe, rind removed

8 oz burrata cheese

Fresh mint and sorrel, to garnish (optional)

Zest of ½ lemon, to finish

Organic edible flowers, to garnish (optional)

Lemon wedge, to serve

Bring a large pot of water to a boil. Cook asparagus for 30 seconds, just until it turns bright green. Using tongs, transfer the asparagus to a bowl of ice water to stop the cooking. Drain asparagus, and then place on paper towel. Set aside.

In a small bowl, whisk together skyr, lemon juice, sliced mint and salt. Set aside. Heat a grill pan on high heat. Grill cantaloupe for 1 minute per side, just until char marks appear and cantaloupe is slightly softened.

Arrange blanched asparagus on a plate. Top with skyr sauce, grilled cantaloupe and burrata. Garnish with mint and sorrel (if using), and sprinkle with lemon zest. Serve family-style, garnished with edible flowers (if using) and a lemon wedge.

Styling Note:
These ingredients look stunning all on their own, so this shot is really about complementing their natural beauty. Red props can be difficult to use, but this plate worked nicely with the other colors.

Settings and Angle:
f/5
ISO 1600
1/100 sec
90 degrees

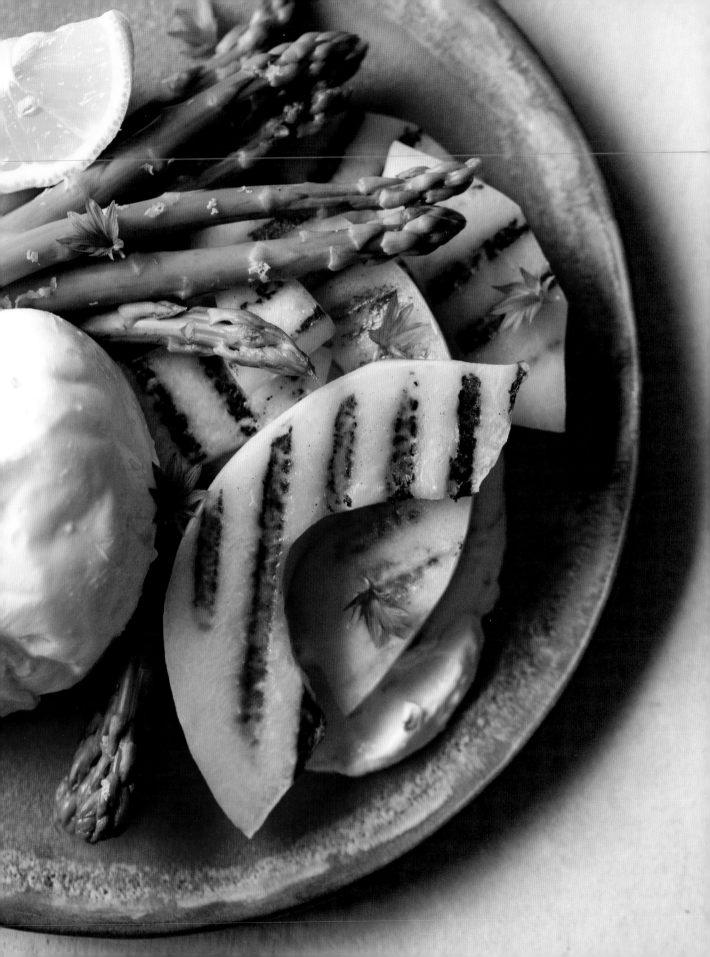

ROMAINE SALAD WITH FRESH TOMATO SALSA AND RICOTTA

Serves 2

This salad is a riff on a recipe we once developed for Food & Wine magazine. The mango vinaigrette is downright addictive and reminds us of a homespun Thousand Island dressing. Our Grainy Mustard (page 34) gives it a real kick, but store-bought mustard will do just fine.

Salsa:

2 cups cherry tomatoes, halved

¼ cup chopped red onion

¼ cup finely chopped fresh cilantro

¼ cup chopped fresh basil leaves

2 garlic cloves, minced

Zest and juice of 1 lime

¼ tsp Sweet and Smoky Spice Rub
(page 28)

Salt, to taste

Vinaigrette:

1 ripe mango, pitted, peeled and cubed

2 tbsp Classic 30-Second Mayonnaise
(page 31)

1 tbsp Grainy Mustard (page 34)

1 tsp red wine vinegar

1 tbsp neutral cooking oil

2 tbsp fresh lemon juice

Salt and pepper, to taste

Salad:

1 head of romaine lettuce, chopped

½ cup ricotta or goat cheese

Make salsa: In a medium bowl, combine tomatoes, red onion, cilantro, basil, garlic, lime zest and juice and spice rub. Stir well, and taste for seasoning. Add salt, if needed.

Make vinaigrette: In a blender or food processor, combine mango, mayonnaise, mustard, red wine vinegar, oil, lemon juice, and salt and pepper. Blend until completely smooth, then set aside.

Place romaine on a serving platter, then drizzle with vinaigrette. Spoon over salsa and dot with cheese. Run to the table and eat it immediately.

Tip: Using three of our pantry superstar items to make this recipe means this dish comes together in a flash.

Styling Note:
This salad can be served deconstructed, as shown, or tossed together. Here, we stacked the lettuce and topped it generously with tomatoes and cheese to give it a home-style feel.

Settings
and Angle:
f/11
ISO 3200
1/200 sec
90 degrees

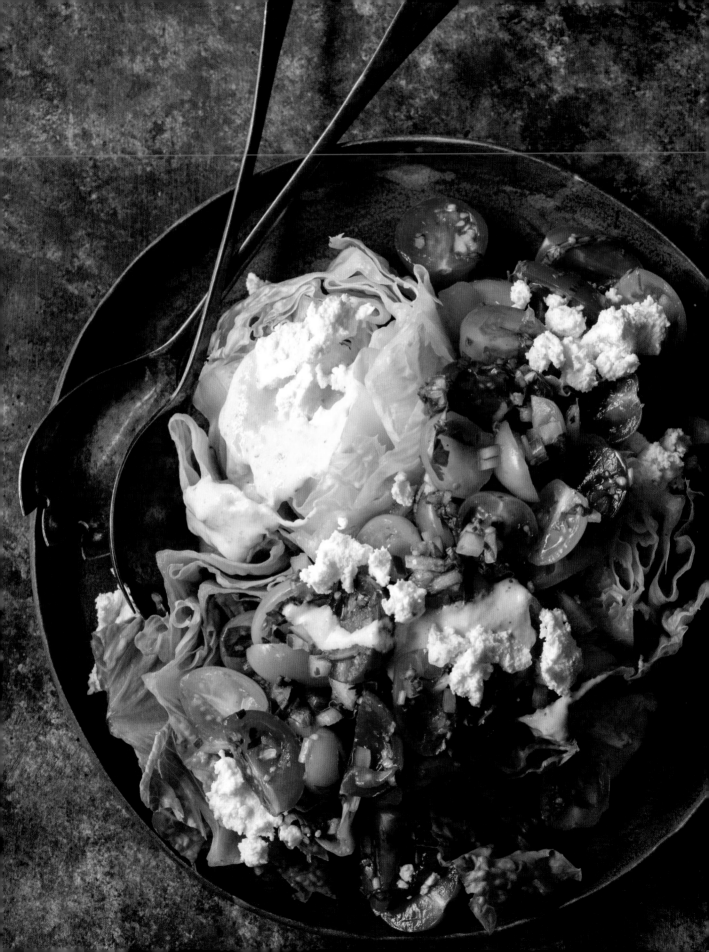

CONFETTI KOHLRABI SLAW

Serves 6

Vibrant, crunchy and bursting with big, bright flavors—not to mention color—this confetti kohlrabi slaw is not only pretty to look at, it's a joy to eat. Whip up a big batch, and enjoy it inside a Moroccan Pulled Pork Sandwich (page 103) or alongside our Indian-Spiced Fried Chicken (page 220). Cutting the veggies into even matchsticks might be tedious, but the results are worth it.

Vinaigrette:

4 tbsp extra virgin olive oil

Zest of 1 lemon

2 tbsp fresh lemon juice

1 tsp Dijon mustard

1 garlic clove, minced

Pinch of salt

Slaw:

½ cup thinly sliced kohlrabi

½ green apple, thinly sliced

½ cup thinly sliced carrot

½ cup thinly sliced purple cabbage

½ cup thinly sliced green cabbage

¼ cup thinly sliced daikon

¼ cup thinly sliced radish

¼ cup fresh cilantro (leaves and stems), finely chopped

¼ cup fresh mint, finely chopped

Make vinaigrette: In a small mason jar, combine olive oil, lemon zest and juice, Dijon, minced garlic and salt. Seal with the lid, and shake vigorously until emulsified. Refrigerate until ready to use.

Make slaw: In a large serving bowl, combine all of the salad ingredients.

Drizzle vinaigrette on salad and toss until well coated. Serve immediately, or cover and refrigerate for up to 3 days.

Styling Note:
We love the bold, bright look of this slaw. Pairing it with a blue bowl helped to accentuate the cool tones of the cabbage and apple.

Settings and Angle:
f/5
ISO 800
1/100 sec
90 degrees

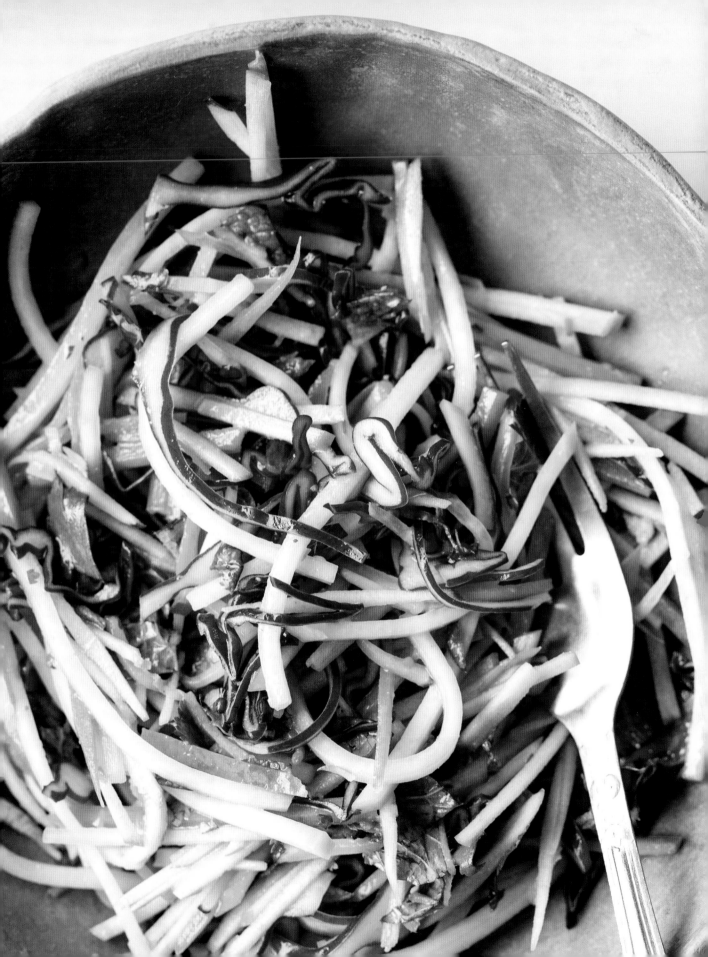

SHAVED BRUSSELS SPROUTS SALAD

Serves 4

Crunchy shaved Brussels sprouts, sweet oranges and creamy goat cheese make this one memorable salad. Try it with our Sweet and Sticky Chicken with Basil and Lime (page 215).

Vinaigrette:

4 tbsp extra virgin olive oil

2 tbsp fresh orange zest (about 1 orange)

Juice of ½ orange

2 tbsp red wine vinegar

Salt and pepper, to taste

Salad:

2 cups packed baby arugula

1 cup thinly shaved purple cabbage

1 cup thinly shaved Brussels sprouts

¼ cup thinly shaved red onion

¼ cup crumbled goat cheese

2 tbsp coarsely crushed pistachios

2 tbsp fresh mint leaves

1 small seedless orange, peeled and cut into bite-size pieces

Make vinaigrette: In a small mason jar, combine olive oil, orange zest and juice, red wine vinegar, and salt and pepper. Seal with the lid, and shake vigorously until emulsified.

Make salad: Layer salad ingredients on a serving platter, with mint leaves and orange pieces on top.

Drizzle vinaigrette on salad, and gently toss to combine. Serve immediately.

Tip: To thinly shave vegetables, use a mandoline for best results.

Styling Note: There's a lot going on in this salad, and it's important that all the ingredients be fully visible in the hero shot, without looking too primped or handled.

Settings and Angle: f/10 ISO 1600 1/100 sec 0 degrees

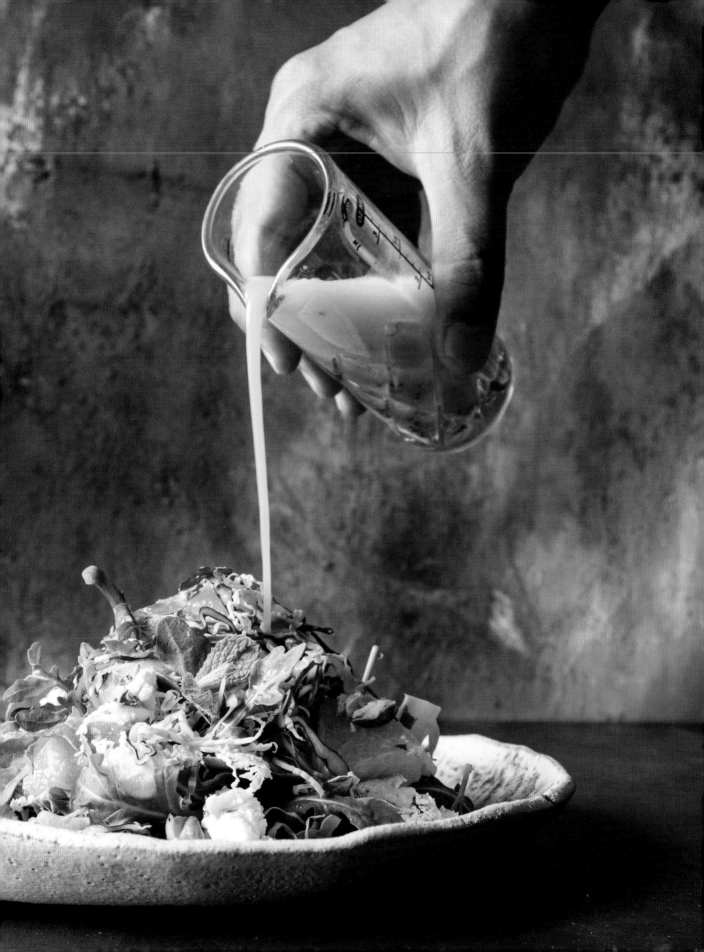

COUSCOUS SALAD WITH APPLES AND CRANBERRIES

Serves 4

This light, crisp salad pairs beautifully with just about anything, from our Shrimp and Chorizo Skewers with Grilled Lemons (page 152) to our BBQ Chimichurri Chicken (page 218).

Vinaigrette:

4 tbsp extra virgin olive oil

2 tbsp red wine vinegar

1 tsp Dijon or grainy mustard

½ tsp raw black sesame seeds

Pinch of salt and pepper

Salad:

½ cup couscous

⅔ cup vegetable broth

2 cups packed arugula

½ green apple, cored and thinly sliced (with mandoline)

Red onion, thinly sliced (with mandoline), to taste

½ cup unsweetened dried cranberries

¼ cup crumbled goat cheese

¼ cup toasted walnuts (optional; see Tip)

Make vinaigrette: In a small mason jar, combine olive oil, red wine vinegar, Dijon, black sesame seeds, and salt and pepper. Seal jar with lid and shake until emulsified.

Make salad: Prepare couscous according to the package instructions, substituting broth for the water. Fluff with a fork, and then transfer to a large bowl. Add arugula, sliced apple and onion, and cranberries.

Dress salad with vinaigrette, to taste, and toss together. Top with crumbled goat cheese and toasted walnuts (if using).

Tip: To toast walnuts, preheat oven to 350°F. Line a baking sheet with parchment paper. Spread out walnuts in an even layer. Bake, uncovered, for 4 to 6 minutes, until toasted and fragrant.

Styling Note:
When styling a salad, most times we'll leave the vinaigrette on the side. It helps keep the dish looking fresh for the camera, as dressing often wilts the greens.

Settings and Angle:
f/10
ISO 1250
1/100 sec
90 degrees

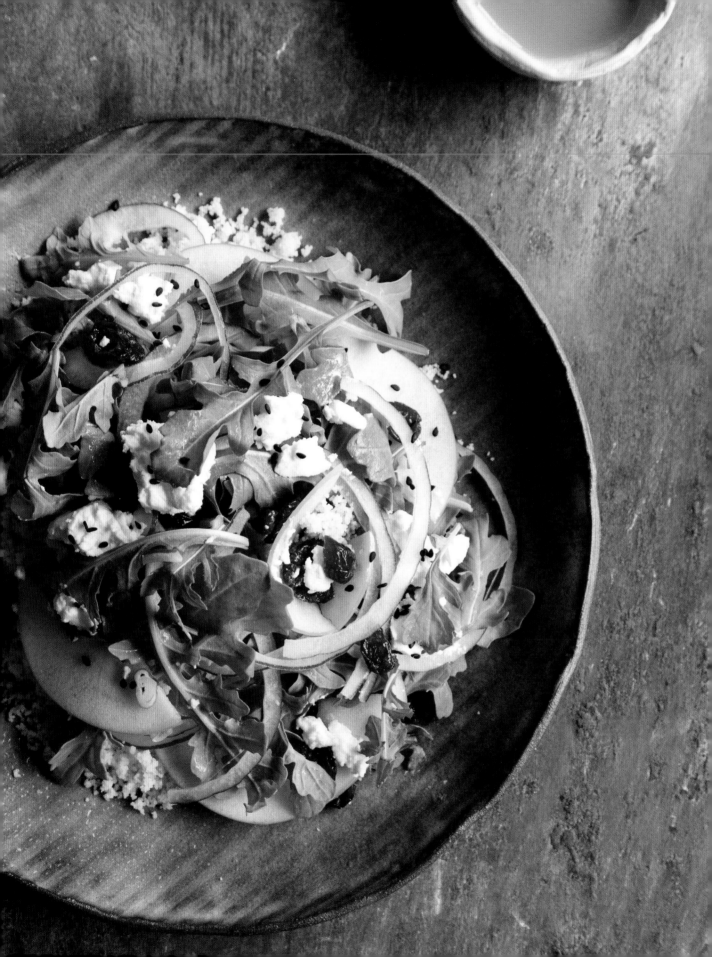

RED QUINOA, MANGO AND PURPLE CABBAGE SALAD

Serves 4

This recipe has been around our place for a while, and has a lot of memories attached to it. Whether we're making it for a party or a family gathering, it always fits the bill as a bright and crunchy bite. Packed with fresh herbs and a lively lime-based vinaigrette, this salad basically screams summer. Now, where's the patio?

Vinaigrette:

2 tbsp extra virgin olive oil
2 tbsp fresh lime juice
Pinch of salt

Salad:

1 cup red quinoa, rinsed and
    drained
1½ cups vegetable broth
1 cup thinly sliced purple cabbage
1 avocado, pitted, peeled and cubed
½ mango, peeled, pitted and cubed
2 green onions, sliced
1 tsp sesame seeds (raw or toasted)
½ cup roughly chopped fresh
    cilantro leaves
½ cup roughly chopped fresh
    mint leaves
½ cup roughly chopped fresh
    basil leaves
Flaky sea salt, to taste

Make vinaigrette: In a small mason jar, combine olive oil, lime juice and salt. Seal with the lid and shake vigorously until emulsified.

Make salad: Prepare quinoa according to the package instructions, substituting broth for the water. Fluff with a fork, and then transfer to a large bowl. Add prepared cabbage, avocado, mango, green onions, sesame seeds, cilantro, mint and basil. Season with salt.

Drizzle salad with vinaigrette and toss to evenly coat. Serve immediately, or cover and refrigerate for up to 24 hours before serving.

Styling Note: We've always loved the look of natural materials, and this is a perfect example.

Settings and Angle: f/5 ISO 400 1/100 sec 45 degrees

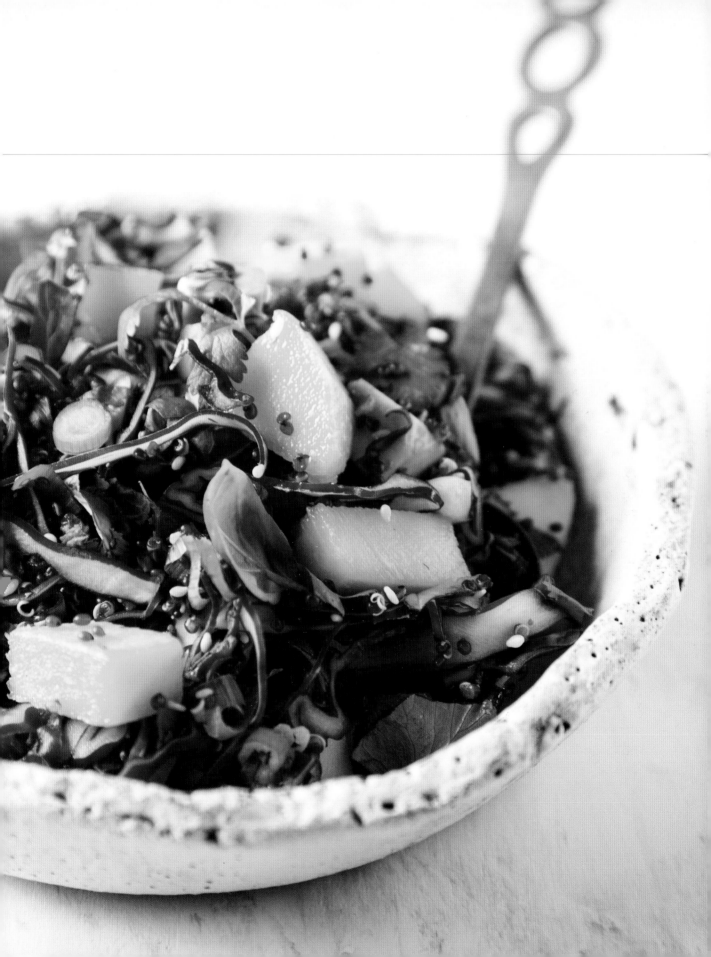

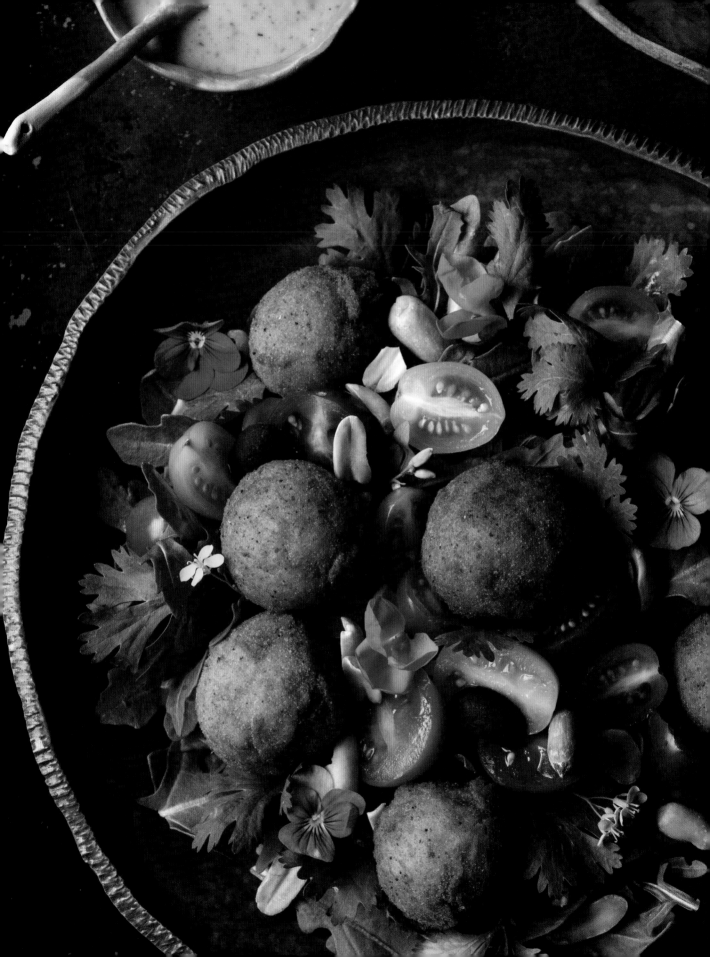

ARANCINI SALAD

Serves 4

We're not completely clear on the backstory of arancini, but one thing we do know for certain: they're damn delicious. Whatever the case, this humble "rice ball" has been synonymous with Southern Italian cuisine for centuries. If you have some leftover risotto hanging around, this is a perfect use for it. Our recipe omits the pricy addition of saffron, which is traditionally used, but if you're a formalist, do feel free to add a pinch to your broth.

Arancini:

1 tbsp neutral cooking oil
¼ cup diced onion
1 garlic clove, minced
1 cup arborio rice
1 tsp porcini mushroom powder
  (see Tip, page 24)
2 to 3 cups vegetable broth
½ cup peppered goat cheese
2 tbsp all-purpose flour
4 tbsp cold water
1 cup unseasoned breadcrumbs
Oil, for deep-frying

Make arancini: Heat cooking oil in a large pot on medium heat. Add onion and garlic, and cook, stirring frequently, for 2 to 3 minutes, until the onion begins to brown. Stir in rice and porcini mushroom powder. Add ¼ cup broth and cook, stirring constantly, until broth is nearly absorbed. Repeat, adding broth ¼ cup at a time, until the broth has been absorbed and the rice is fully cooked. You may not need to use a full 3 cups of broth. Add goat cheese, and stir until completely combined. Transfer mixture to a bowl and cover with plastic wrap.

Refrigerate for 1 to 2 hours, or overnight.

Using a ⅛-cup measure, shape chilled risotto into small balls. Place on a plate, loosely cover with plastic wrap and refrigerate until ready to fry.

(recipe continues on next page)

Styling Note:
Organic edible flowers are always an effortless way to enhance the look of a dish and inject an extra dose of color.

Settings and Angle:
f/11
ISO 3200
1/200 sec
90 degrees

(continued from previous page)

(continued from previous page)

Dressing:

3 tbsp extra virgin olive oil

2 tbsp fresh lemon juice

1 tsp Dijon mustard

5 black olives, pitted

1 garlic clove

Pinch of salt and pepper

Salad:

4 cups loosely packed baby arugula

1 cup cherry tomatoes, halved

¼ cup black olives, pitted and halved

⅓ cup fresh cilantro leaves

¼ cup roasted peanuts, roughly chopped

Organic edible flowers, to garnish (optional)

Prepare your breading station: In one small bowl, make a slurry by whisking together the flour and water. In another small bowl, place the breadcrumbs.

Dip each rice ball first into the slurry and then into the breadcrumbs, ensuring a nice, even coat. Return coated balls to plate.

In a large pot, heat oil until it reaches 350°F to 360°F. Working in batches, fry balls until golden brown, 2 to 3 minutes. Using a spider utensil or slotted spoon, transfer fried balls to paper towel or wire rack and let cool.

Make dressing: In a food processor, combine olive oil, lemon juice, Dijon, olives, garlic, salt and pepper. Blend until smooth.

Make salad: In a large bowl, toss all of the salad ingredients with dressing, to taste.

Serve salad topped with arancini, peanuts and edible flowers (if using).

Tip: Preparing your risotto the night before makes completing this recipe a breeze. Chill risotto for 1 to 2 hours before rolling into balls, then keep covered in the fridge until ready to bread and fry them.

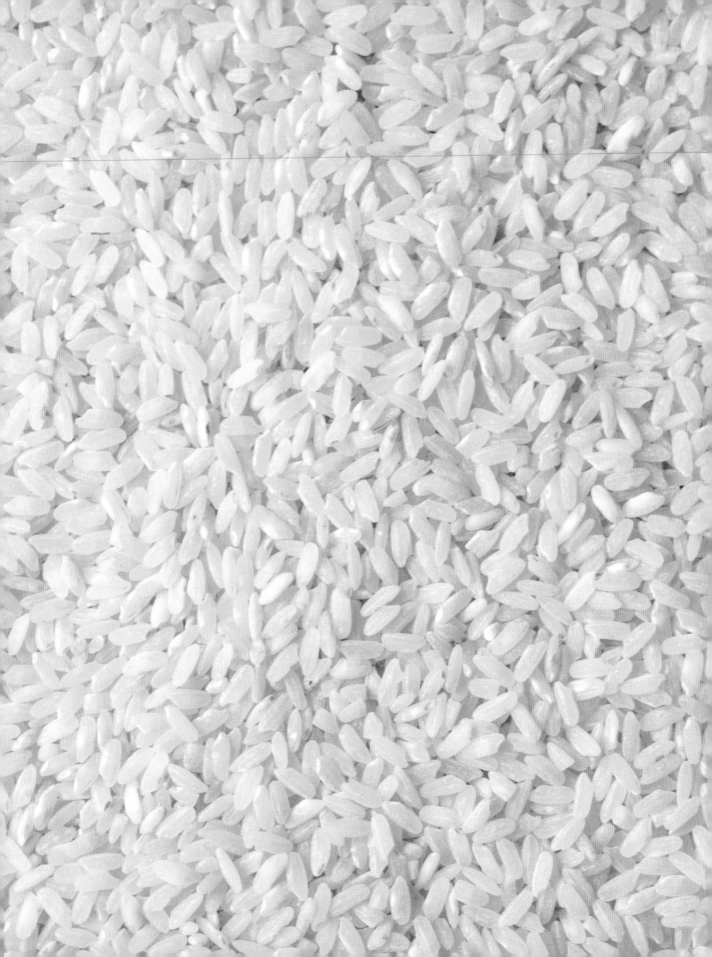

COLD SOBA NOODLE SALAD WITH KIMCHI AND BASIL

Serves 4

Kimchi fan? You've gotta give this one a try. This chilled soba noodle salad is a fermented food lover's dream and the perfect 10-minute meal.

2 large eggs

3.2 oz soba noodles (see Tip)

2 tsp soy sauce

1 tsp sesame oil

1 tsp fish sauce

Juice of 1 lime

1 tsp brown sugar

¼ cup roughly chopped kimchi

1 tbsp raw sesame seeds

1 green onion, white and green parts, sliced

6 large fresh basil leaves, chopped

Bring a small saucepan of water to a boil on high heat, then carefully submerge eggs. Cook for 7 minutes, then transfer eggs to a bowl of ice water. Let chill for 1 to 2 minutes. Peel eggs and set aside.

Bring another small saucepan of water to a boil. Cook soba noodles according to the package instructions. Drain and rinse noodles under cold water. Shake away any excess water, then transfer to a large bowl and set aside.

In a small jar, combine soy sauce, sesame oil, fish sauce, lime juice and brown sugar. Seal with the lid, then shake vigorously until emulsified. Set aside.

Add kimchi to the noodles, along with the sesame seeds and green onion. Toss with dressing. Serve topped with soft-boiled egg and basil.

Tip: Soba are Japanese noodles made of buckwheat flour, and are super low in fat and carbohydrates. If they're unavailable to you, try swapping them out for rice noodles.

Styling Note:
A bright blue bowl gives the shot nice color contrast. Extra sesame seeds and kimchi accentuate the ingredients.

Settings and Angle:
f/9
ISO 3200
1/100 sec
90 degrees

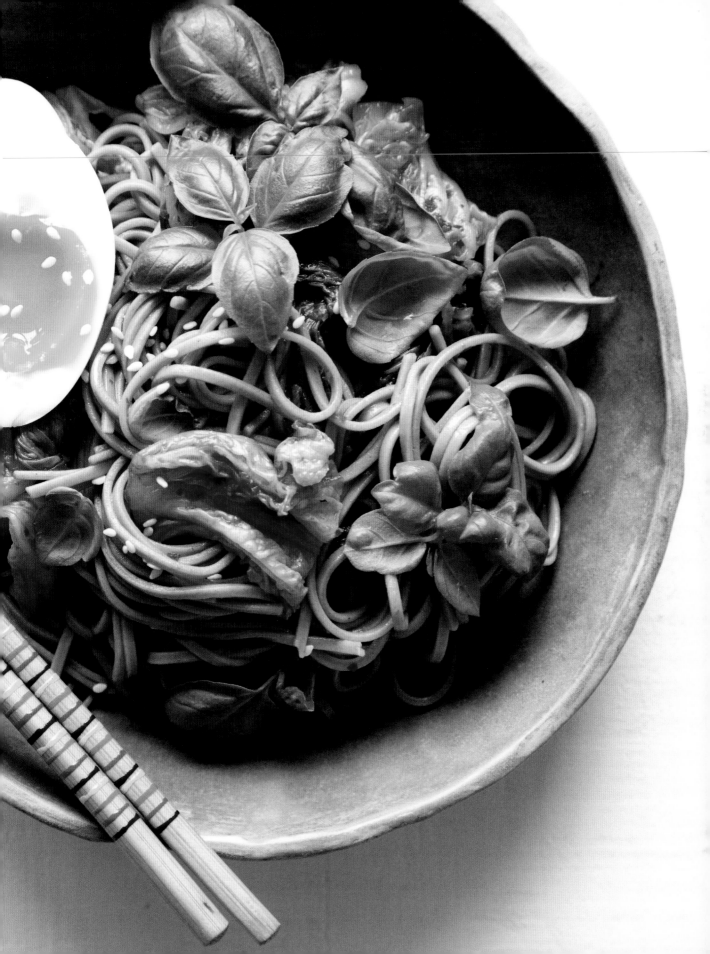

BALELA PANZANELLA SALAD

Serves 6 to 8

This is one of our favorite "big salads" to make any time of year, and it's perfect for larger get-togethers. A twist on a traditional Middle Eastern balela salad, our version incorporates crunchy homemade croutons and an enticing, creamy avocado-based dressing.

Salad:

1 cup canned black beans, rinsed and drained

1 cup canned chickpeas, rinsed and drained

½ cup diced red onion

½ cup grape tomatoes, halved

½ cup diced English cucumber

2 tbsp finely diced roasted red pepper

2 tbsp finely chopped sun-dried tomatoes (in oil)

½ cup finely chopped fresh cilantro (leaves and stems)

¼ cup crumbled soft unripened cheese (goat or feta cheese)

1 cup large croutons (see Tip)

Dressing:

1 avocado, pitted and peeled

2 tbsp fresh lemon juice

2 tbsp extra virgin olive oil

1 tbsp plain yogurt

1 garlic clove

Salt and pepper, to taste

Make salad: In a large serving bowl, combine black beans, chickpeas, red onion, grape tomatoes, cucumber, roasted red pepper, sun-dried tomatoes and cilantro. Set aside.

Make dressing: In a blender or food processor, combine avocado, lemon juice, olive oil, yogurt and garlic. Season with salt and pepper. Blend until completely smooth.

Add dressing to salad, and toss well. Top with crumbled cheese and crunchy croutons. Serve immediately.

Tip: Homemade croutons are a cinch to make, and are a great use for stale bread. Simply cut bread into 1-inch cubes, then drizzle with extra virgin olive oil and season with salt. Spread out on a baking sheet and bake in a 350°F oven for 8 to 10 minutes, until golden brown. Let cool completely before storing in an airtight container at room temperature for up to 6 weeks.

Styling Note: We love playing with negative space, and the colors in this salad look positively radiant paired with matte black plates and golden flatware.

Settings and Angle: f/9 ISO 3200 1/100 sec 90 degrees

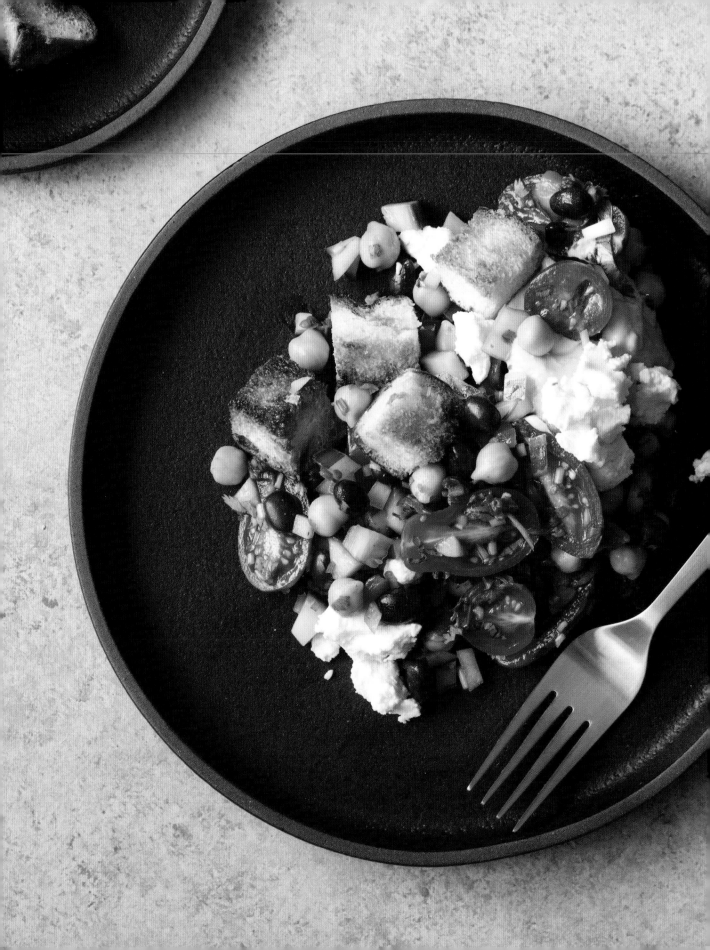

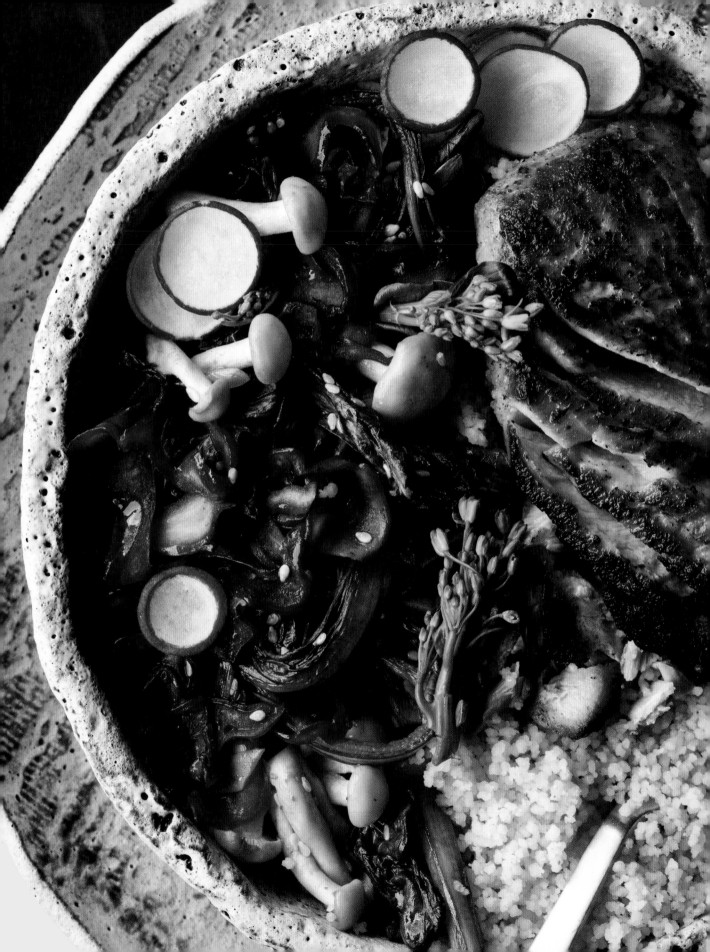

MISO MAPLE SALMON
WITH CHINESE VEGETABLES

Serves 2

*Vibrant, hearty, healthy bowls like this one are a necessity in our home —
the ideal lazy meal after a long day, without sacrificing flavor or nutrition.*

Marinade:

¼ cup pure maple syrup

2 tbsp fresh lemon juice

1 tbsp rice wine vinegar

2 tsp yellow miso paste

3 garlic cloves, minced,
  divided

Pinch of salt and pepper

2 x 5-oz spring salmon fillets,
  skin on

Sauce:

2 tbsp sesame oil

2 tbsp soy sauce

1 tsp sambal oelek

Juice of 1 lime

4 dashes fish sauce

1 tbsp toasted sesame seeds

Make marinade: In a small bowl, whisk together maple syrup, lemon juice, rice wine vinegar, miso paste, 1 minced garlic clove, salt and pepper. Stir until well combined. Transfer to a resealable bag and add salmon. Gently turn to coat and refrigerate for at least 30 minutes and up to 1 hour.

Make sauce: In a small bowl, combine sesame oil, soy sauce, sambal oelek, lime juice, fish sauce and sesame seeds. Stir well and set aside.

For serving: Cook couscous according to the package instructions, substituting broth for the water.

Heat 1 tsp cooking oil in a medium frying pan or skillet on medium-high heat. Remove salmon from marinade. Discard marinade. Cook salmon, skin-side down, for 6 to 7 minutes, until skin is golden and crisp. Flip, and cook the other side for 2 to 3 minutes, or to desired doneness. (If your cut of salmon is on the thinner side, adjust cooking time accordingly.) Transfer salmon to a side plate and set aside; reserve pan.

(recipe continues on next page)

Styling Note:
We wanted this shot to have an inviting quality, with the salmon slightly tucked into. Keep the flowering buds on the Chinese greens for beautiful color.

Settings and Angle:
f/10
ISO 4000
1/100 sec
90 degrees

(continued from previous page)

For Serving:

½ cup medium couscous

⅔ cup vegetable broth

2 tsp neutral cooking oil, divided

¼ cup sliced green onion

1 tsp minced peeled ginger

1 cup yu choy (see Tip)

1 cup shimeji mushrooms

1 cup thinly sliced purple cabbage

¼ cup sliced radishes

Heat the remaining 1 tsp cooking oil in the reserved pan on medium heat. Add green onion, ginger and remaining 2 minced garlic cloves, and cook for 1 to 2 minutes, stirring frequently. Add yu choy and mushrooms, and cook for another minute. Stir in cabbage and add the sauce. Reduce heat slightly, cover with a lid, and cook for 1 minute. Remove from heat. Divide couscous between bowls, and top with vegetables, radishes and salmon. Serve immediately.

Tip: Our recipe calls for yu choy, a leafy Chinese green, but bok choy or gai lan (Chinese broccoli) would also work well. We topped our bowl with salmon, but feel free to swap in any protein of your choice (tuna or hard-boiled eggs are both good options).

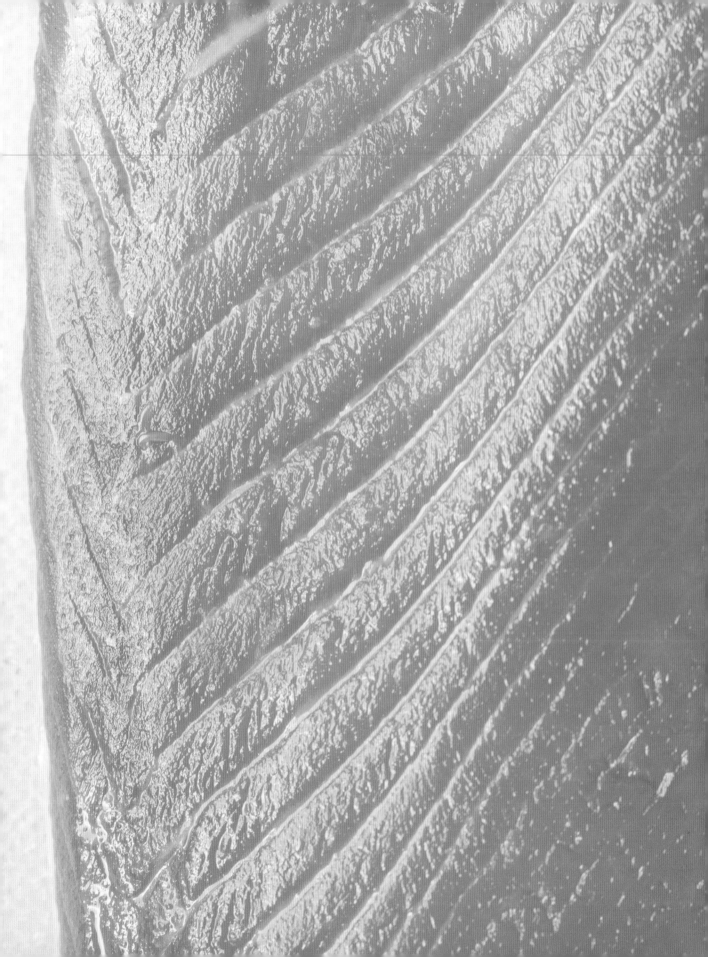

CHICKEN SALAD WITH STRAWBERRIES AND SUNFLOWER SEEDS

Serves 2

Strawberry season feels shorter and shorter each passing year on the west coast of Canada. But that doesn't stop us from gobbling up all the berries we can get our greedy little paws on when the season strikes. This recipe is another way to love strawberries, other than how we normally do: perched over the kitchen sink.

Salad:

2 boneless skinless chicken breasts

½ tbsp neutral cooking oil

Salt and pepper, to taste

2 cups packed baby arugula

¼ cup fresh cilantro leaves

¼ cup fresh basil leaves

4 strawberries, hulled and sliced

2 tsp toasted sunflower seeds,
  to serve

Vinaigrette:

2 tbsp extra virgin olive oil

2 tbsp lemon juice

1 tsp Dijon mustard

Pinch of flaky sea salt

Cook chicken: Drizzle chicken breasts with oil and season with salt and pepper. In a medium frying pan or skillet on medium-high heat, cook chicken for 5 to 7 minutes per side, until cooked through (it should reach an internal temperature of 165°F when tested with a meat thermometer). Set aside to cool slightly, and then cut into strips.

Make vinaigrette: In a small jar, combine olive oil, lemon juice, Dijon and salt. Seal with the lid and shake vigorously until emulsified.

In a medium bowl, toss together baby arugula, cilantro and basil. Divide between serving plates, then top with sliced strawberries and cooked chicken. Sprinkle with sunflower seeds. Drizzle with vinaigrette, and serve.

Styling Note:
This shot has a very natural, earthy palate that is easy on the eyes. The greens and blues in the props accentuate the food.

Settings and Angle:
f/10
ISO 3200
1/100 sec
45 degrees

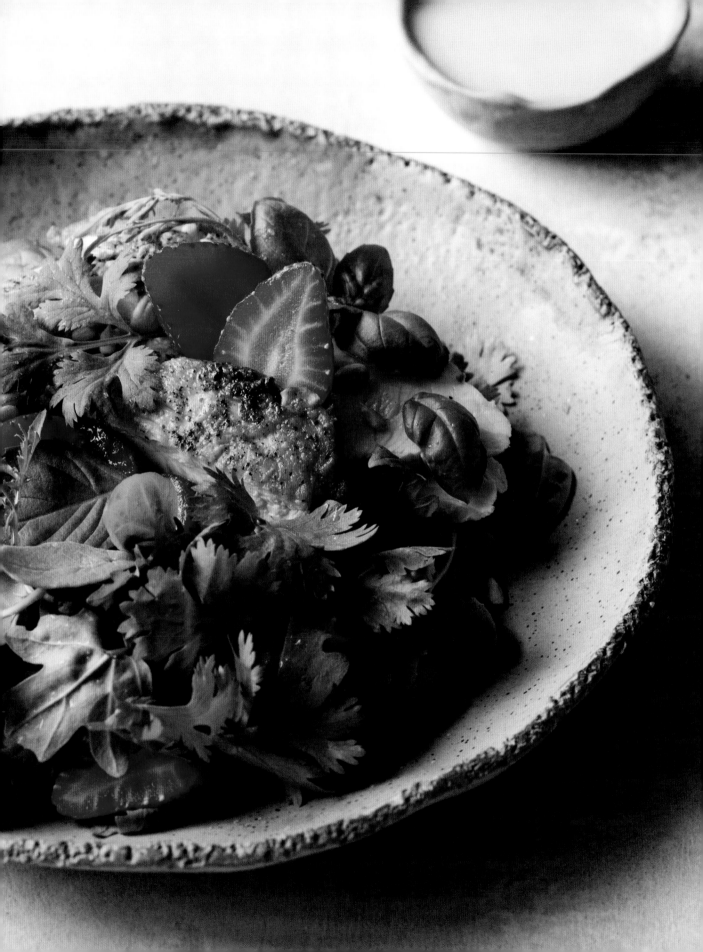

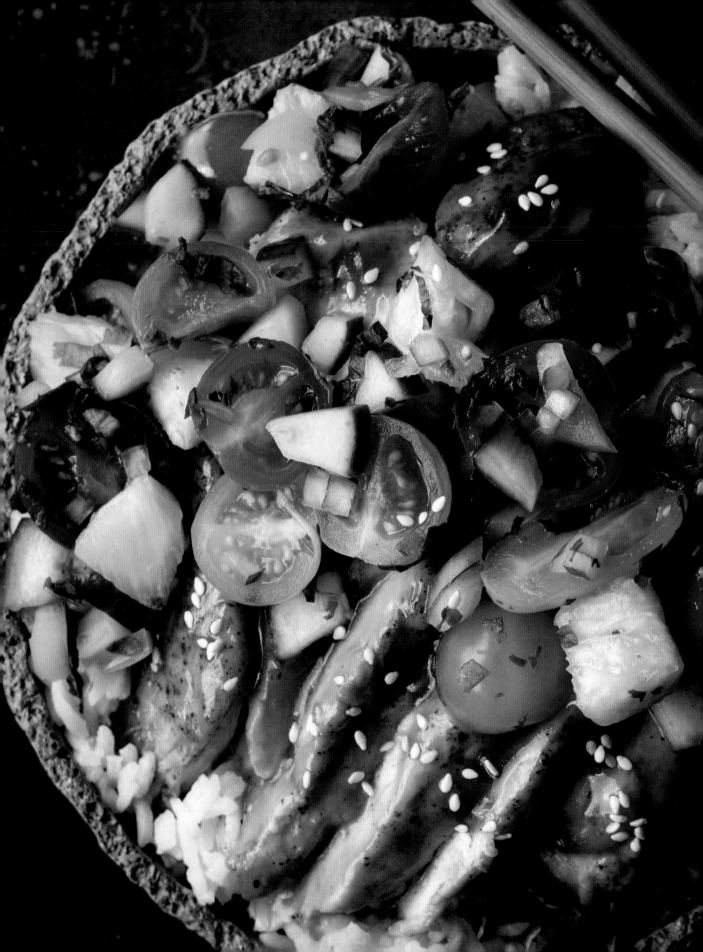

TERIYAKI CHICKEN SALAD BOWL

Serves 2

Forever on a quest to create alluring and functional meals, we stumbled on this headliner in our pure need to get dinner on the table. Because weeknights can be such a busy time, we'll often put any leftover pineapple salsa to work in our Lemon Pepper Grilled Chicken Wrap (page 88) for lunch the next day, or just eat as a dip with tortilla chips for a late-night snack.

½ cup long-grain white rice, rinsed and drained

2 boneless skinless chicken breasts

Salt and pepper, to taste

1 tsp neutral cooking oil

Pineapple Salsa:

1½ cups diced fresh pineapple

1 cup diced English cucumber

½ cup halved cherry tomatoes

½ cup diced yellow bell pepper

¼ cup diced red onion

⅛ cup roughly chopped mint leaves

2 tbsp roughly chopped cilantro leaves

Juice of ½ lime

Salt, to taste

In a small saucepan or rice cooker, cook rice according to the package instructions.

Make salsa: In a medium bowl, combine pineapple, cucumber, cherry tomatoes, yellow pepper, red onion, mint and cilantro. Add lime juice and season with salt. Toss together, taste and adjust seasoning, if needed. Set aside.

Cook chicken: Preheat oven to 375°F. Season chicken with salt and pepper. Heat oil in an ovenproof skillet on medium heat. Sear chicken for 1 to 2 minutes per side, until slightly golden. Transfer skillet to preheated oven, and bake chicken for 5 to 10 minutes, until cooked through (it should reach an internal temperature of 165°F when tested with a meat thermometer). Set aside.

(recipe continues on next page)

Styling Note: We used a vibrant mix of tomatoes to add an extra boost of color.

Settings and Angle: f/10 ISO 2500 1/100 sec 90 degrees

(continued from previous page)

Glaze:

2 tbsp soy sauce

1 tbsp liquid honey

1 tbsp chili oil

1 tbsp brown sugar

1 garlic clove, minced

1 tsp minced peeled ginger

1 tbsp cornstarch

½ cup water

For Serving:

1 cup finely sliced radicchio

Sesame seeds (raw or toasted),
  to garnish

Make glaze: In a small saucepan on medium heat, combine soy sauce, honey, chili oil, brown sugar, minced garlic and ginger, and bring to a simmer.

Meanwhile, in a small bowl, whisk together cornstarch and water. Add to pan and stir well. Cook for 4 to 5 minutes, stirring occasionally, until thickened to desired consistency (see Tip). Cut the cooked chicken into thick pieces, and brush generously with the glaze.

Divide rice between serving bowls, and top with glazed chicken, radicchio and pineapple salsa. Finish with sesame seeds, and serve immediately.

Tip: Cornstarch tends to work its magic pretty quickly. If you cook the glaze too long, it will become overly thick and gloopy.

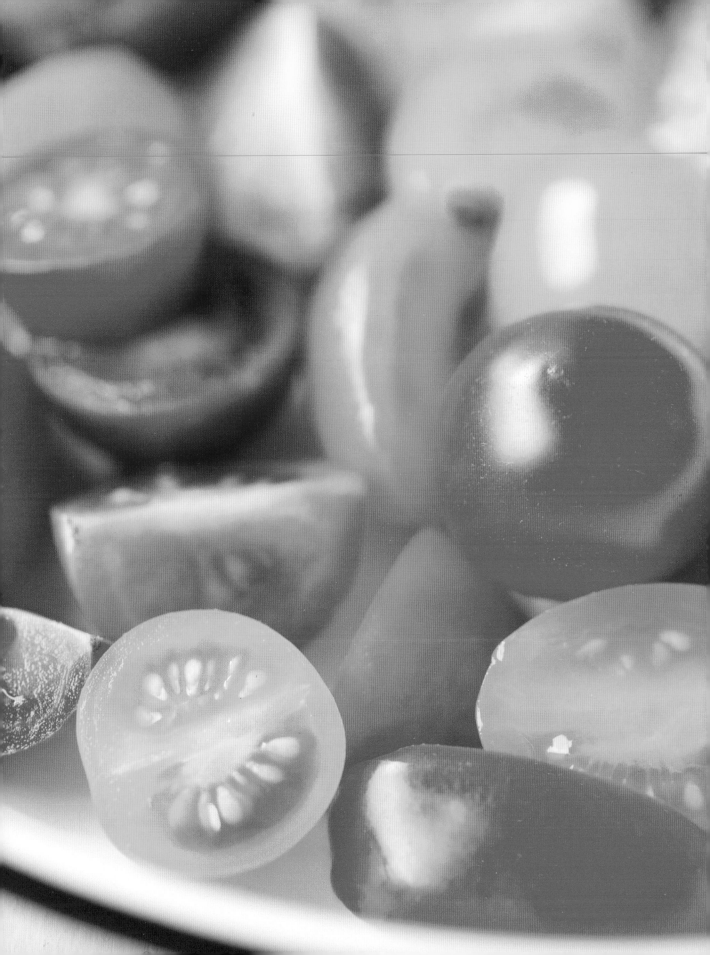

CHAPTER 5

SMALL PLATES AND COCKTAILS

Whisky-Spiked Olives

Broiled Feta with Chili Salt, Tomatoes and Basil

Warm Baked Brie with Fruit and Savory Granola

Blackberry, Brie and Arugula Crostini with Honey and Lavender

Fresh Nachos with Greek Yogurt and Watercress

Halibut Ceviche

Shrimp and Chorizo Skewers with Grilled Lemon

Greek-Style Lamb Sliders with Tzatziki and Tomato

Cucumber Ginger Fizz Cocktail

Whisky Tea Cocktail

Jalapeño Lime Margarita

Blueberry Pisco Sour

Kombucha Collins

Entertaining is something we've grown to love over the years, though our cramped city dwelling doesn't exactly allow for the largest crowds. It's all about quality over quantity, right? Intimate nights in with good friends, conversing, laughing and enjoying ourselves . . . it's always a good time, no matter how big (or small) the space. And it usually doesn't require anything more than some tasty bits and bites— and maybe a few bottles of good wine, for safe measure.

When we're eating with our friends, it's about the sharing experience. Smaller plates with substance; not too much of one thing. A tapas-like approach to dining. This is how we like to entertain, and we think a lot of people these days do too. A little of this, a little of that. Because variety is the spice of life, after all.

WHISKY-SPIKED OLIVES

Serves 4

Warmed olives always make for elevated, reliable party fare. They pair wonderfully with everything from wine, bubbly or maybe something a little stiffer, if you prefer (we're partial to our Whisky Tea Cocktail, page 158, in case you're curious). Here we've enhanced the olives' natural briny flavors with fresh herbs, garlic and some whisky, which brings a woody, caramelized note to the warm, buttery olives.

1 cup mixed marinated olives (with pits)

¼ cup peperoncino peppers

¼ cup sweet drop peppers (or pearl onions)

2 sprigs thyme, leaves only

1 sprig rosemary, leaves only

Lemon peel (one 3- to 4-inch x ½-inch piece)

1 garlic clove, crushed

Pinch of salt (optional)

1 oz whisky

In a small frying pan or skillet on medium heat, combine olives, peperoncino, sweet drop peppers, thyme, rosemary, lemon peel, crushed garlic and salt (if using). Let everything warm through for 2 to 3 minutes, stirring occasionally. Stir in whisky, remove pan from heat and set aside, covered, for 1 minute. Discard lemon peel and garlic clove, and serve immediately.

Styling Note: Opt for a Mediterranean olive mix for more vibrancy and texture.

Settings and Angle:
f/16
ISO 2000
1/40 sec
45 degrees

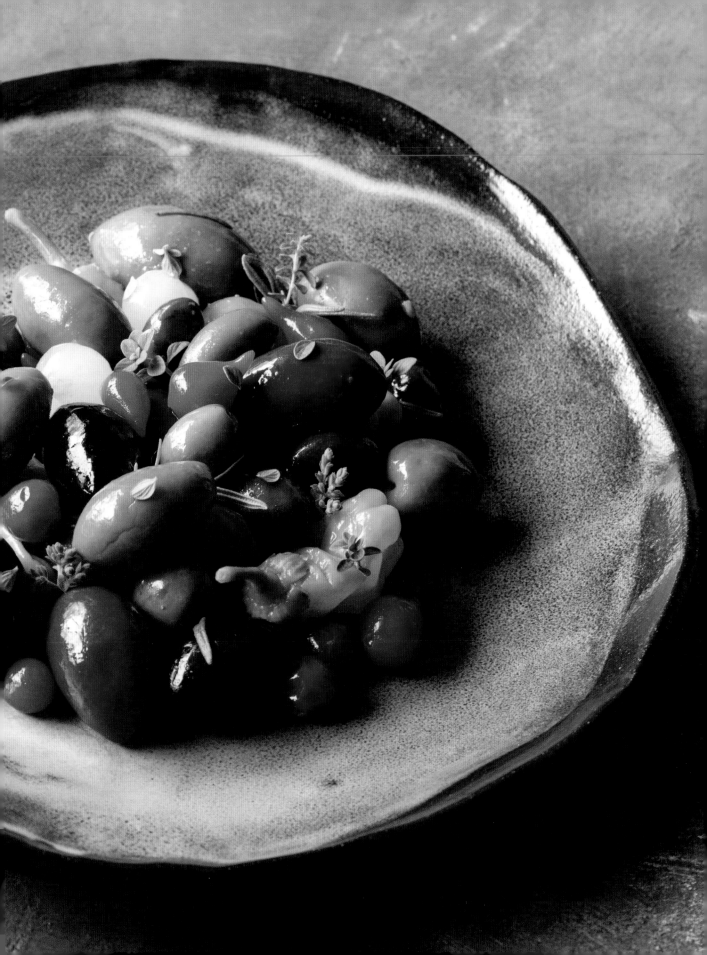

BROILED FETA WITH CHILI SALT, TOMATOES AND BASIL

Serves 4

Super simple yet decidedly elegant, this is the ultimate last-minute appetizer. Use Macedonian feta if you can; with its soft, creamy texture enhanced by the heat, it spreads beautifully on a crispy cracker or toasted baguette. Just don't pick feta that is too fresh — it will crumble under the heat, leaving you with a tasty but messy dish.

8 oz feta cheese, cubed

½ tsp extra virgin olive oil

½ tsp Chili Salt (page 24)

½ tsp freshly ground black pepper

1 to 2 sprigs thyme, leaves only

½ tsp neutral cooking oil

½ cup grape or cherry tomatoes, halved

Salt and pepper, to taste

Fresh basil leaves, to serve

Toasted baguette slices, to serve

Preheat oven to 400°F.

Place feta in a medium baking dish. Drizzle with olive oil, then season with chili salt, black pepper and thyme leaves. Toss gently to coat. Bake on top rack in preheated oven for 10 minutes. Switch to broil for an additional 8 to 10 minutes, until feta is golden brown and a little bubbly (keep a very close eye on it and adjust time as needed; our timing is merely an estimate and it can vary from oven to oven).

Meanwhile, heat cooking oil in a small frying pan or skillet on medium heat. Sauté halved tomatoes, along with salt and pepper, for 1 to 2 minutes, or just until softened.

Arrange feta on a serving dish and top with cooked tomatoes and basil. Serve immediately with toasted baguette slices.

Styling Note:
Feta cheese brings to mind the Mediterranean, and this ocean-blue plate is the ideal pairing. Broiling the feta adds gorgeous color and rustic charm.

Settings and Angle:
f/8
ISO 4000
1/100 sec
90 degrees

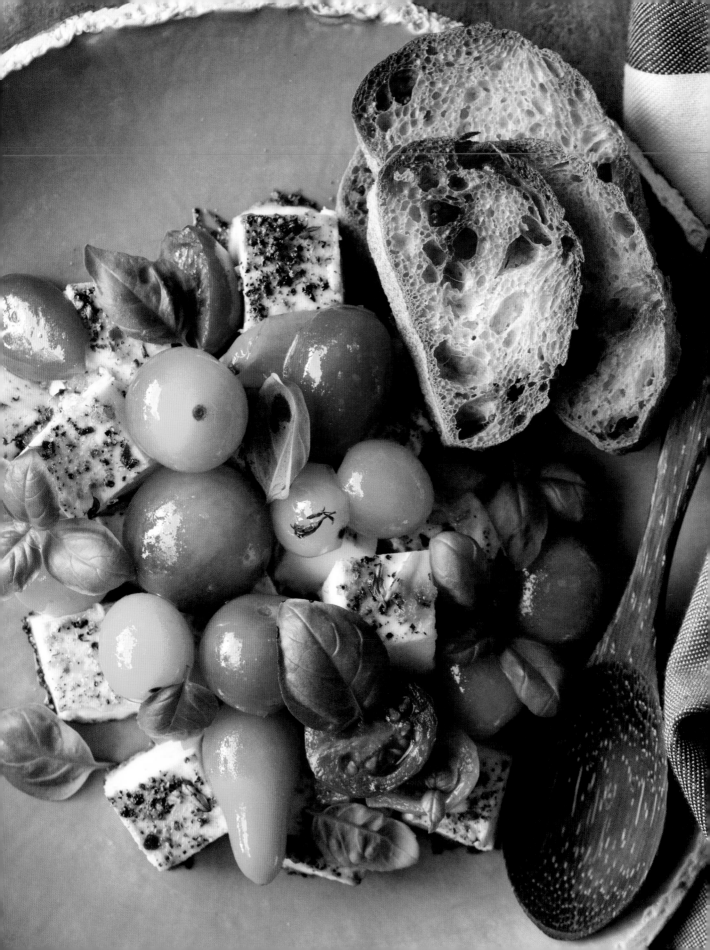

WARM BAKED BRIE WITH FRUIT AND SAVORY GRANOLA

Serves 4

Every time we make a batch of this savory granola, we have to stop ourselves from inhaling the whole tray. Paired with ooey-gooey, warm baked brie (triple-cream all the way, y'all), and topped with luscious, fresh cherries and strawberries, this is one toothsome snack that might just be too good to share.

¼ cup extra virgin olive oil

2 tbsp pure maple syrup

2 tsp balsamic crema (see Tip)

½ tsp smoked paprika

4 dashes fish sauce

1 cup large-flake rolled oats

2 tbsp sliced almonds

2 tbsp crushed walnuts

1 tbsp flax seeds

1 tsp raw black sesame seeds

1 tbsp raw white sesame seeds

1 wheel triple-cream brie cheese

1 cup fruit of your choice, to serve (we use local cherries and strawberries)

Crackers or bread, to serve

Preheat oven to 325°F. Line a 15- x 12-inch baking pan with nonstick foil.

In a small bowl, whisk together olive oil, maple syrup, balsamic crema, smoked paprika and fish sauce. Add oats, sliced almonds, crushed walnuts, flax seeds and both sesame seeds, and stir until well incorporated. Spread mixture evenly in prepared baking pan. Bake in preheated oven for 30 to 35 minutes, until golden brown. Remove granola from oven (leave oven on) and set aside to cool.

Wrap brie in foil and bake for 15 to 20 minutes. Discard foil and carefully transfer brie to a serving dish, along with the savory granola, fresh fruit and crackers.

Tip: Balsamic crema is reduced balsamic vinegar and has a rich, syrupy consistency. You can find it in most grocery stores, or make your own by simmering balsamic vinegar on medium heat until it's reduced by about half. Keeps in an airtight jar for up to 3 months.

Styling Note: We wanted the brie to be the star of the shot, surrounded by a bounty of in-season fruit, granola and crackers.

Settings and Angle: f/10 ISO 3200 1/100 sec 90 degrees

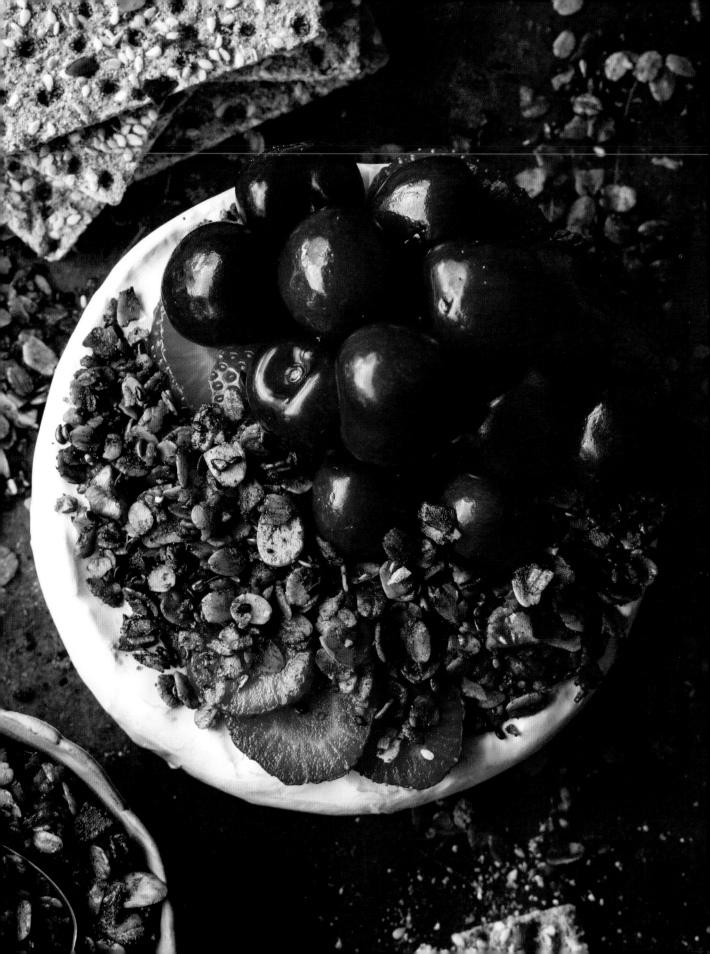

BLACKBERRY, BRIE AND ARUGULA CROSTINI WITH HONEY AND LAVENDER

Serves 4 to 6

In our opinion, toast has always been, and forever will be, one of life's simple pleasures. Humble or haute (and everything in between), is there really anything you can't make better with a glorious slice of toasted bread? We think not.

1 baguette, sliced on a
  diagonal
1 wheel triple-cream brie
  cheese, cut into wedges
1½ to 2 cups loosely packed
  baby arugula
1 pint blackberries
¼ cup liquid honey
Organic lavender flowers,
  to garnish (optional)

Preheat oven to 375°F.

Arrange baguette slices in a single layer on a baking sheet. Bake in preheated oven for 8 to 9 minutes, until golden brown.

Spread a wedge of brie on each piece of toast, and top with arugula and blackberries. Drizzle with honey and garnish with lavender flowers (if using).

Styling Note:
This shot is a good example of how keeping things clean and simple can often work to great effect.

Settings and Angle:
f/11
ISO 1000
1/100 sec
10–20 degrees

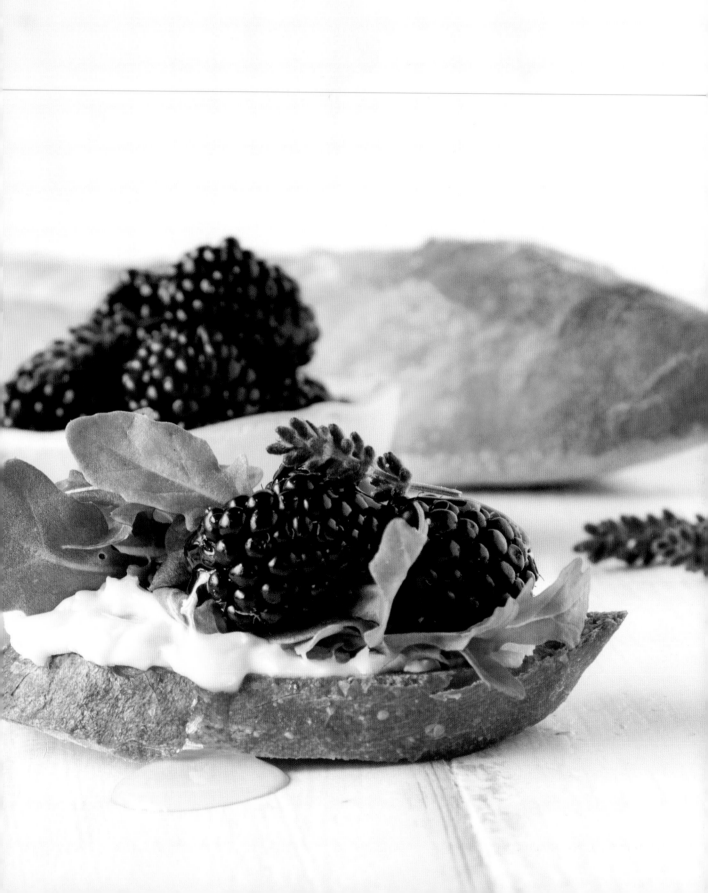

FRESH NACHOS WITH GREEK YOGURT AND WATERCRESS

Serves 4

Nachos have been one of Adrian's favorite foods since, well, forever. Our lighter take on this classic means you really can enjoy them without all those greasy, heavy toppings. We like to make our own chips (using packaged fresh corn tortillas) — it's quick and adds a ton of character to the dish.

6 to 8 small fresh yellow corn tortillas

2 tsp neutral cooking oil

Salt, to taste

⅓ cup ricotta salata or pecorino cheese

2 tbsp pitted Kalamata olives

2 tbsp thinly sliced red onion

1 jalapeño pepper, thinly sliced (optional; see Tip)

Several cherry tomatoes, sliced

¼ cup watercress or other fresh tender greens (see Tip), leaves only

¼ cup plain Greek yogurt

Preheat oven to 375°F. Set aside a baking sheet.

Brush the corn tortillas with oil and season with salt. Cut each tortilla into eight wedges, and arrange in a single layer on the baking sheet. Bake in preheated oven for 4 to 5 minutes, until golden brown and slightly crisp.

Remove the baking sheet from the oven. Top tortilla chips with the ricotta salata, olives, and sliced red onion and jalapeño (if using). Return the pan to the oven and bake for another 2 to 3 minutes. Remove from oven and finish with cherry tomatoes, watercress and dollops of yogurt. Serve immediately.

Tips: If you like your peppers hot, feel free to leave in the seeds; if not, remove the membrane and seeds.

Watercress can vary in quality. If it doesn't look up to par, opt for another robust tender green, such as arugula, frisée or dandelion.

Styling Note:
Shots at this angle are about ensuring the viewer can see each ingredient. We built the nachos with a "front side" for the camera and propped extra chips underneath to add height.

Settings and Angle:
f/11
ISO 4000
1/100 sec
10–20 degrees

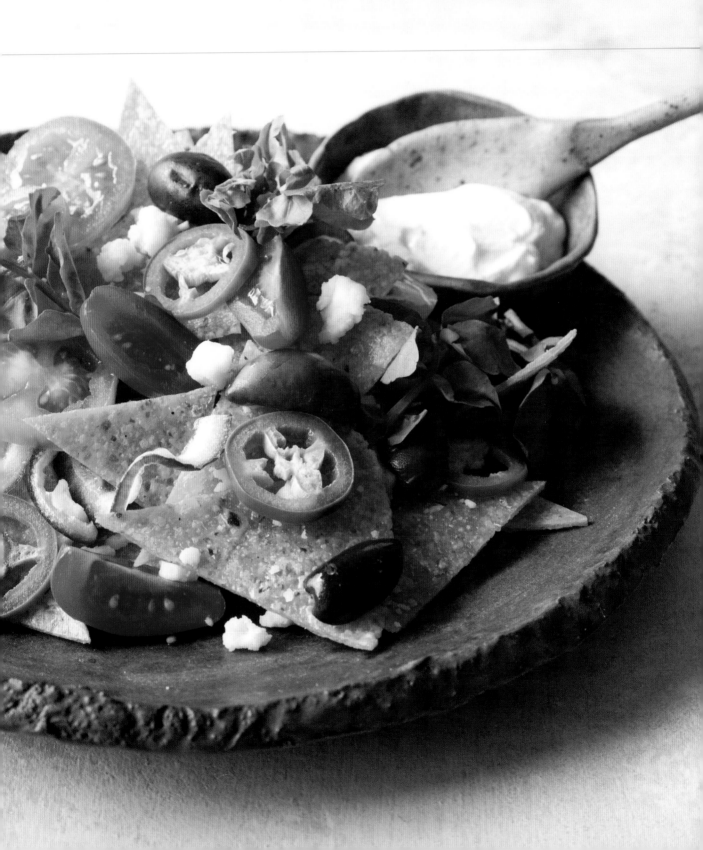

HALIBUT CEVICHE

Serves 4

Ceviche is a great dish to serve to small crowds, because it seems like it's especially difficult to prepare, when it really couldn't be easier. Be sure to get your hands on a good-quality piece of halibut, as you'll be eating it fairly rare. Either served in a shot glass or more family-style, it's always a crowd-pleaser!

1 lb fresh wild halibut, cut into 1-inch cubes

½ cup chopped yellow bell pepper

½ cup chopped red bell pepper

⅔ cup chopped red onion

⅔ cup chopped fresh cilantro

½ cup chopped fresh mint

2 serrano peppers, seeded and diced

Juice of 2 grapefruits

1 tbsp finely grated lime zest

Tortilla or plantain chips, to serve

In a medium bowl, combine halibut and chopped bell peppers, red onion, cilantro, mint and serrano peppers. Gently stir in grapefruit juice and lime zest. Let sit for a minimum of 5 minutes but no longer than 30 minutes. Serve with tortilla or plantain chips.

Styling Note:
We opted for a clean, white presentation so the colors of the ceviche would really sparkle. This is an old DIY background we made years back, which helps create a distressed, natural look.

Settings and Angle:
f/8
ISO 4000
1/100 sec
90 degrees

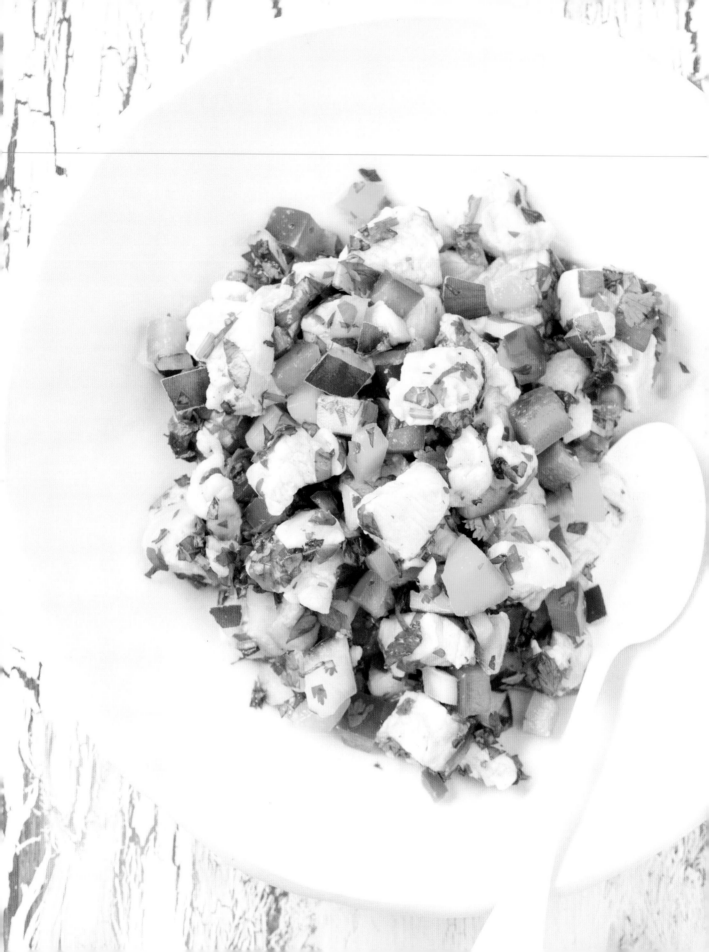

SHRIMP AND CHORIZO SKEWERS WITH GRILLED LEMON

Serves 4

Who doesn't love barbecue season? This is such a speedy dinner, but damn, is it ever tasty. It's really all about the grilled lemons, which add an intense kiss of sweet and sour that lifts everything up. This has become one of our staples at home, and once you taste 'em for yourself, you'll see why.

2 x 3-oz Spanish chorizo, cut into ½-inch-thick pieces

½ lb medium shrimp, peeled and deveined

1 cup chopped red onion (1-inch pieces)

1 cup chopped yellow bell pepper (1-inch pieces)

1 cup chopped green bell pepper (1-inch pieces)

1 to 2 tbsp neutral cooking oil

1 to 2 tbsp Sweet and Smoky Spice Rub (page 28)

1 lemon, cut into 8 wedges

Soak 8 wooden skewers for 2 to 3 hours before assembling dish. Preheat barbecue to medium-high.

Alternate threading the soaked skewers with chorizo, shrimp, red onion and bell peppers. Drizzle with oil and dust with spice rub.

Place the skewers and lemon wedges on the preheated grill. Grill the lemon wedges for 3 to 4 minutes, until they've taken on some nice grill marks. Grill the skewers for 5 to 6 minutes per side, until shrimp are pink, fully cooked and slightly charred.

Squeeze grilled lemons over skewers and enjoy.

Styling Note: We wanted a nice, tight crop on this shot, really focusing in on the bright, vivid, summer-inspired colors of this dish.

Settings and Angle: f/4 ISO 250 1/100 sec 45 degrees

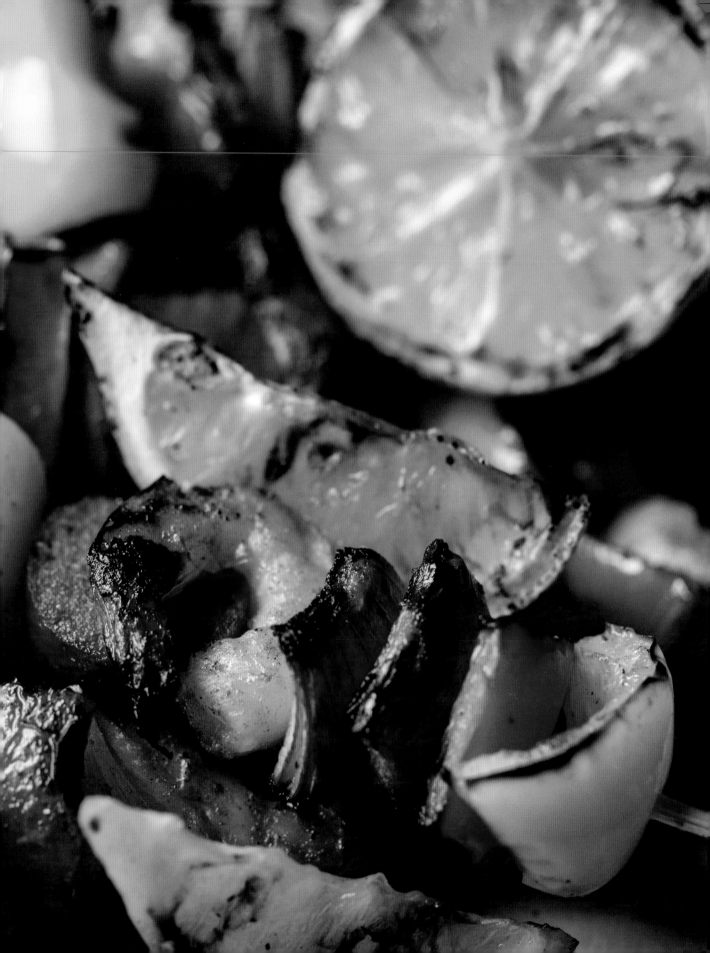

GREEK-STYLE LAMB SLIDERS WITH TZATZIKI AND TOMATO

Serves 4

Having friends over for some bites? These sliders are a great way to keep things casual, while still having everyone think you went to a ton of effort.

Tzatziki:

½ cup plain Greek yogurt

¼ cup grated English cucumber

¼ tsp garlic powder

Zest of ½ lemon

1 tsp fresh lemon juice

½ tbsp chopped fresh dill

¼ tsp each salt and pepper

Sliders:

1 lb ground lamb

½ cup diced onion

2 garlic cloves, minced

¼ cup finely chopped fresh flat-leaf parsley

½ tsp each salt and pepper

1 tbsp neutral cooking oil

2 roma tomatoes, sliced

8 to 10 small dinner rolls, to serve

Make tzatziki: Place yogurt in a colander lined with cheesecloth or double-layered paper towel. Place colander over a bowl and refrigerate for 12 hours to drain excess liquid.

Transfer drained yogurt to a medium bowl, and add cucumber, garlic powder, lemon zest and juice, dill, and ¼ tsp each salt and pepper. Stir well and set aside.

Make sliders: In a large bowl, combine lamb, onion, garlic, parsley, and ½ tsp each salt and pepper. Using your hands, shape into 8 to 10 small patties (each about 2½ x 2½ inches).

Heat oil in a large frying pan or skillet on medium heat. Cook lamb patties for 2 to 3 minutes per side, until golden brown and cooked through (they should reach an internal temperature of 160°F when tested with a meat thermometer). Transfer patties to a plate lined with paper towel to absorb any excess oil.

Split buns and top each with a lamb patty. Garnish with tzatziki and tomato slices, and secure with toothpicks, if desired.

Styling Note:
Sliders are meant for a crowd, so we couldn't photograph just one.

Settings and Angle:
f/10
ISO 3200
1/100 sec
0 degrees

CUCUMBER GINGER FIZZ COCKTAIL

Serves 1

This cooling vodka-cucumber-spiked beverage is the ultimate refresher on a hot day. We're big fans of ginger beer, which is widely available these days. We've infused cucumber right into our vodka in this recipe, but if time (or patience) eludes you, simply blend the cucumber and vodka together in a blender, and strain. It won't be quite as potent, but it will do the job in a pinch.

2 oz cucumber-infused vodka
  (see headnote; recipe follows)
1 cup ginger beer
Slice English cucumber,
  to garnish
Sprig of mint, to garnish

Fill a mug with ice. Pour cucumber-infused vodka over top. Add ginger beer and garnish with a thick slice of cucumber and a sprig of mint.

CUCUMBER-INFUSED VODKA
Makes 1 cup

1 cup vodka
½ cup grated English
  cucumber

In a mason jar, combine vodka and cucumber. Cover with the lid and let infuse in a cool, dark place for up to 48 hours. Strain and refrigerate in an airtight jar for up to 2 weeks.

Styling Note:
Styling drinks is really
all about the glassware.
We used a traditional Moscow
Mule mug for this shot, which
lent itself well to the style of
the cocktail but did pose
a challenge for
reflections.

Settings
and Angle:
f/5
ISO 2000
1/250 sec
10–20 degrees

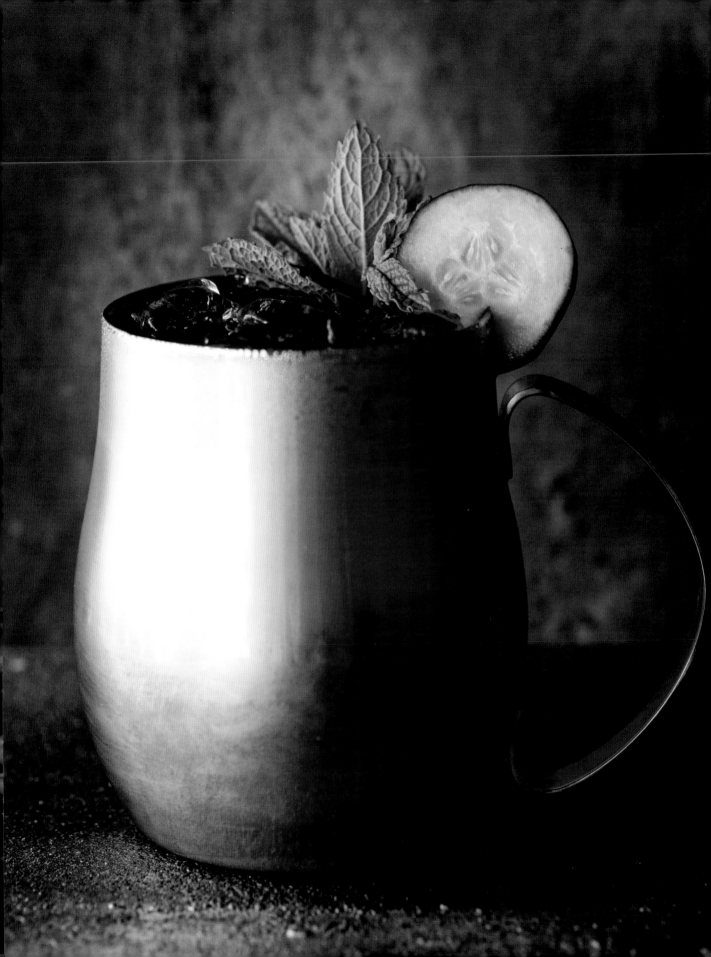

WHISKY TEA COCKTAIL

Serves 1

The only problem with this cocktail is that it might be a little too easy to drink! This officially brings a whole new meaning to "teatime."

2 oz whisky

½ oz lemon simple syrup (recipe follows)

6 fresh mint leaves + extra to garnish

Ice cubes, to serve

½ cup strong-brew black tea (see Tips)

Lemon slice, to garnish

In a glass or mug, muddle the whisky, lemon simple syrup and 6 mint leaves together. Fill the glass with ice, add chilled brewed black tea and stir well. Garnish with a fresh mint sprig and lemon slice.

Tips: For your tea, opt for something full-bodied and robust. Ours contained notes of ginger, cardamom and pink berries.

To brew tea: In a teapot, combine 2 cups boiling-hot water with 4 tsp loose-leaf tea. Let steep for 5 to 7 minutes, then add 2 cups cold water. Strain and refrigerate until completely cool before using.

LEMON SIMPLE SYRUP
Makes about 1 cup

1 cup granulated sugar

½ cup water

1 lemon, sliced

In a small saucepan, combine sugar and water, and bring to a boil. Add lemon slices, then reduce heat and simmer for 5 minutes. Remove pan from heat and let sit for 30 minutes before discarding lemon slices. Let cool completely. Keeps, refrigerated, in a sealed jar for up to 3 months.

Styling Note:
These handsome mugs were perfect for this drink, offering a slightly hefty look.

Settings and Angle:
f/4.5
ISO 1000
1/100 sec
45 degrees

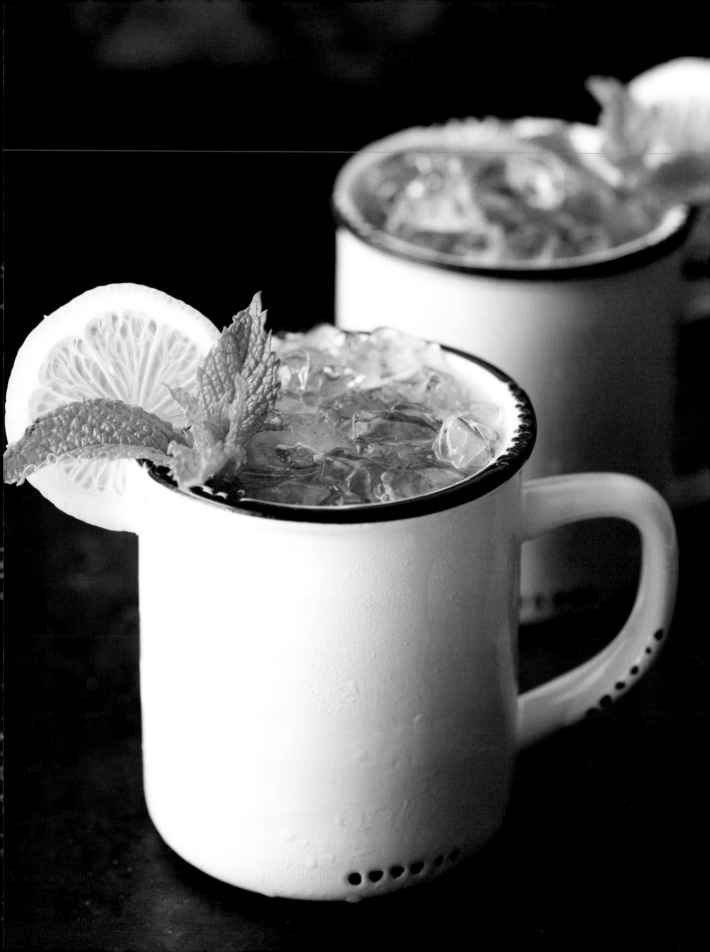

JALAPEÑO LIME MARGARITA

Serves 2

We like our margarita hot and spicy, how 'bout you? Our recipe blends the entire lime right into the mix, and then simply strains out the pulp and skin, leaving an intense, pure citrus flavor we can't get enough of.

Lime wedge
Chili Salt, for rim (page 24)
Ice cubes, to shake and serve
2 oz Jalapeño Lime Tequila
  (see headnote; recipe follows)
1 oz Cointreau or Grand Marnier
Juice of ½ lime

Run lime wedge around the rim of each of two glasses. Place chili salt on a small plate, in an even layer. Dip rims of glasses into the salt to coat. Carefully fill glasses with ice.

Fill a cocktail shaker with ice. Add jalapeño lime tequila, Cointreau and lime juice. Cover and shake vigorously, then divide evenly between glasses. Enjoy.

JALAPEÑO LIME TEQUILA
Makes about 1 cup

1 jalapeño pepper
1 whole organic lime (carefully washed)
1 cup tequila

In a blender or food processor, combine the jalapeño, lime and tequila, and blend until smooth. Using a fine-mesh sieve, strain mixture into a mason jar (discard solids). Use immediately.

Tip: By incorporating the jalapeño right into the tequila, the results are supremely spicy. This is definitely not a drink for the faint of heart!

Styling Note:
This drink's electric hue seemed appropriate for a white backdrop. We adored the glassware we selected for this shoot, and ended up buying a set for ourselves. Hazards of the job!

Settings and Angle:
f/5.6
ISO 1250
1/100 sec
10–20 degrees

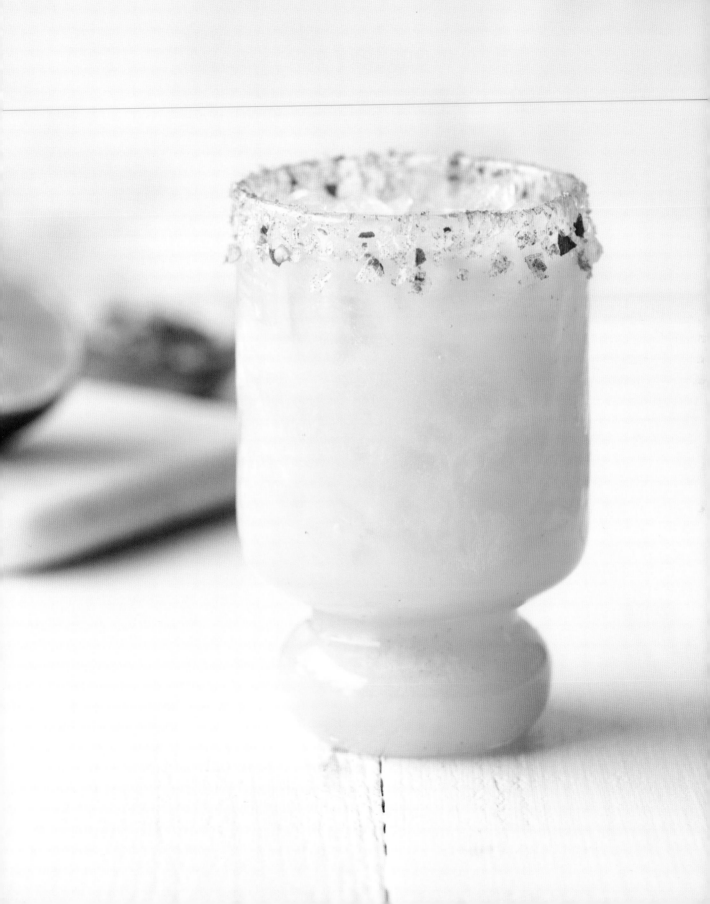

BLUEBERRY PISCO SOUR

Serves 1

Pisco sours are always a fun cocktail to sip on, and here we've amped it up a notch with a blueberry simple syrup. We use Chilean pisco, which is slightly sweeter than its Peruvian counterpart without being cloying.

Ice cubes, to shake
2 oz pisco
1 oz blueberry simple syrup
  + extra for garnish (recipe follows)
Juice of ½ lime
1 large egg white

Fill a cocktail shaker with ice. Add pisco, blueberry simple syrup, lime juice and egg white. Cover and shake until the shaker has frosted and your fingertips are slightly numb (this might sound dramatic, but it's important to shake vigorously to get the egg white to really foam up). Strain into a glass. Using a dropper (see Tip), garnish the top with 5 dots of blueberry simple syrup, then run a toothpick right through the centers to create a heart-shaped effect.

Tip: You can find droppers in pharmacies and gourmet supply stores.

BLUEBERRY SIMPLE SYRUP
Makes about 2 cups

1 cup hot water
1 cup frozen blueberries
¾ cup packed brown sugar
Juice of 1 lime

In a small saucepan on medium heat, combine hot water, blueberries and brown sugar. Bring to a boil, reduce heat and cook, stirring frequently, until sugar is dissolved and berries begin to burst, about 10 minutes. Using a fine-mesh sieve, strain into a mason jar (discard solids). Add lime juice, stir and let cool completely before using. Keeps in the refrigerator for up to 3 months.

Styling Note:
This dapper, gold-rimmed glass was begging for a dazzling cocktail, wouldn't you agree?

Settings and Angle:
f/6.3
ISO 2000
1/125 sec
45 degrees

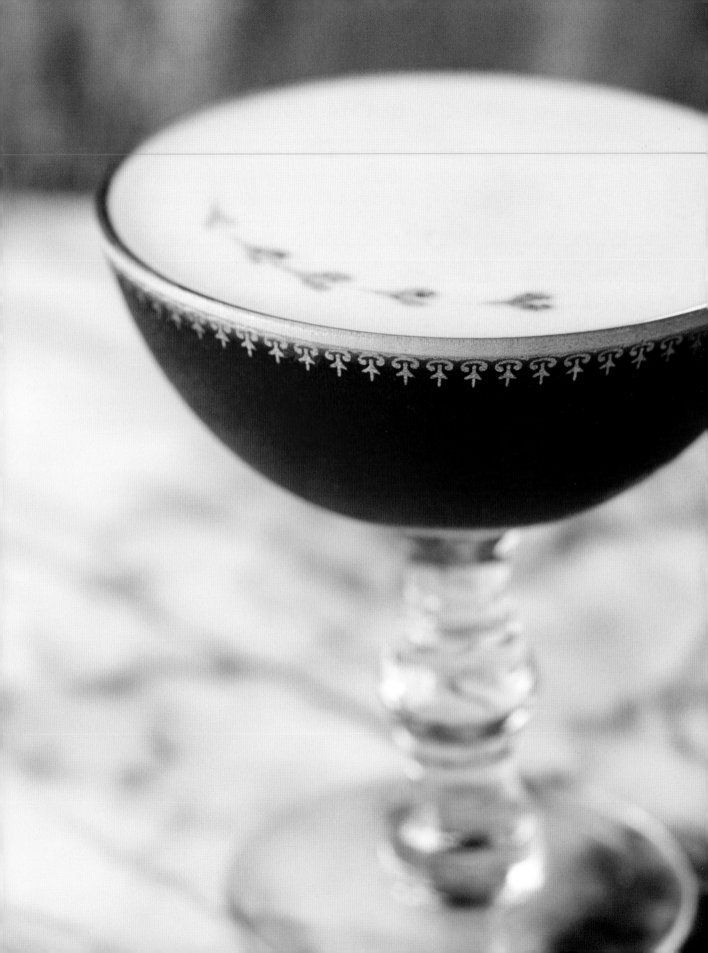

KOMBUCHA COLLINS

Serves 1

A twist on the classic Tom Collins cocktail, our version substitutes kombucha for the sparkling water or club soda. Using a flavored kombucha like rose and hibiscus adds a splendid pink hue, but feel free to customize with whatever is available to you.

Ice cubes, to serve

1 cup kombucha (we used rose and hibiscus)

2 oz gin

Juice of ½ lemon

Lemon peel, twisted, to garnish

Fill a glass with ice. Add kombucha, gin and lemon juice. Stir well. Garnish with lemon twist, and serve.

Styling Note:
We loved the way this drink had an almost swirled, marbled effect as the kombucha was being added to the glass, so an action shot seemed appropriate.

Settings and Angle:
f/10
ISO 3200
1/100 sec
10–20 degrees

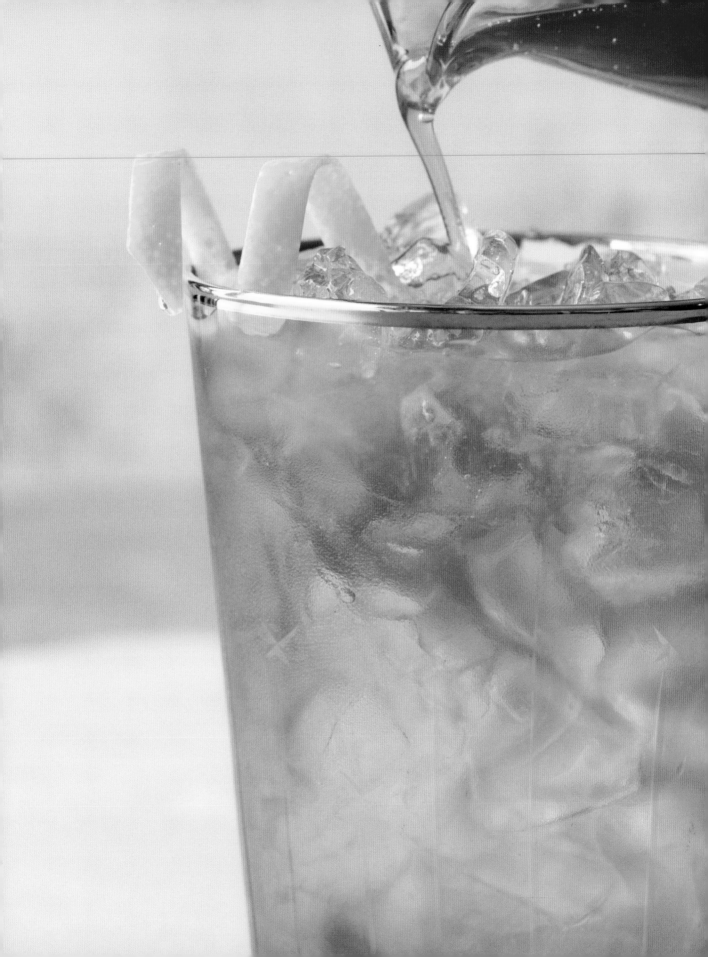

CHAPTER 6

VEGETABLE LOVE

It was Yotam Ottolenghi's *Plenty* and *Plenty More* that changed the way we look at vegetables. No longer were they an afterthought, filling up a corner of the plate. In his world, they took center stage and demanded full attention. Ottolenghi makes vegetables sexy, quite frankly, and his cookbooks inspired us to actually get into the kitchen and cook. We learned to truly love the art of vegetarian food, finally grasping what brilliant little flavor-vessels vegetables can be.

We want this chapter to evoke the idea that vegetables can indeed be the main event, without any frills or gimmicks. No, we aren't vegetarian, but we do aspire to eat a more plant-based diet, and have made gains in the last few years by simply being more aware of what we're consuming.

Some of these dishes are larger and can be enjoyed as a main, while others would work well together as a family-style meal. However you choose to enjoy them, we hope that you find them as comforting and nourishing as we do.

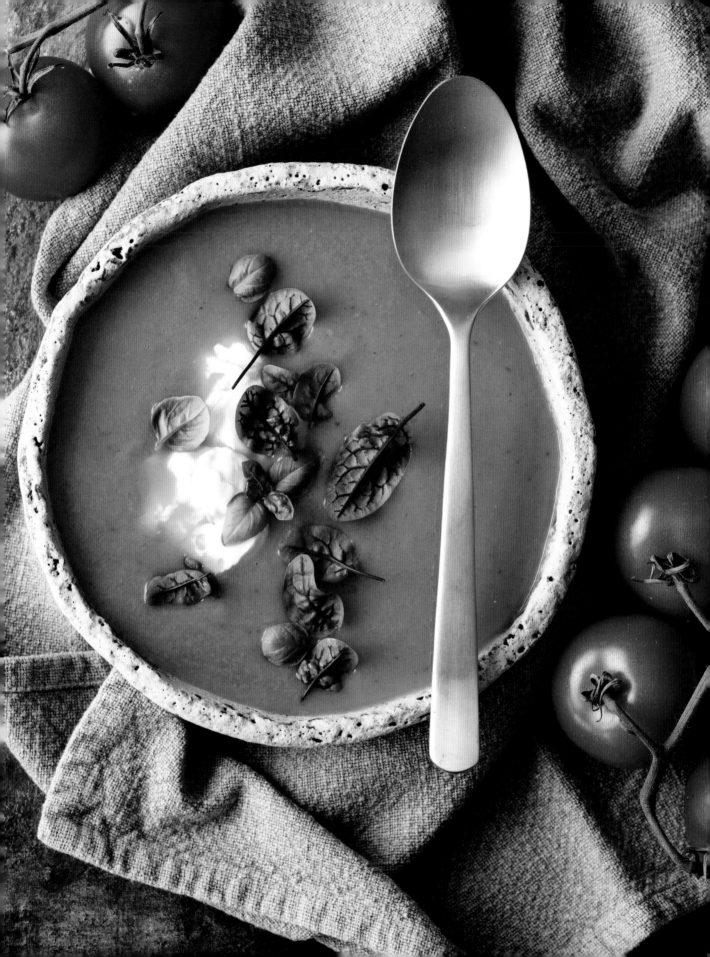

BLISTERED TOMATO SOUP

Serves 2

When you think of comfort food, what comes to mind? For us, it's a good old-fashioned homemade soup and sandwich, which give us all the nostalgic feels. Try pairing this with our Veggienormous Sandwich (page 96) or Hummus Veggie Wrap (page 90) and make it a full meal.

10 to 12 medium tomatoes
  on the vine

2 tbsp extra virgin olive oil

1 tsp dried thyme

1 tsp dried rosemary

1 tbsp neutral cooking oil

1½ cups chopped onion

2 garlic cloves, chopped

½ tsp salt

2½ cups vegetable broth

⅓ cup finely grated Parmigiano-
  Reggiano cheese

Crème fraîche or plain Greek yogurt,
  to serve (optional)

Fresh basil and sorrel leaves,
  to garnish (optional)

Preheat oven to 400°F. Line a baking sheet with foil.

Slice an "X" in the bottom of each tomato and place on prepared baking sheet. Drizzle with olive oil. Sprinkle with thyme and rosemary. Toss tomatoes until well coated.

Roast in preheated oven for 30 minutes, then broil for another 15 to 20 minutes, until slightly charred on top. Keep a close eye on the tomatoes so they don't burn completely—this definitely isn't the time to leave the room for a phone call!

Meanwhile, heat cooking oil in a soup pot on medium heat. Sauté onion and garlic for 4 to 5 minutes, until the onion is translucent. Season with salt.

(recipe continues on next page)

Styling Note:
We wanted this shot
to look comfortable yet
elegant, so we incorporated
props in the background. A
soft cotton napkin and fresh
tomatoes offer an air of
casualness to the
scene.

Settings
and Angle:
f/7.1
ISO 1600
1/100 sec
90 degrees

(continued from previous page)

Transfer the roasted tomatoes to the pot with the onion and garlic and stir well. Add broth. Bring to a simmer. Add Parmigiano-Reggiano, and stir until the cheese has melted.

For a super-smooth consistency (which we prefer), transfer the mixture to a blender and blend until completely smooth. For a chunky soup, you can use an immersion blender, and blend until it reaches your desired consistency.

Divide soup between serving bowls. Top with a dollop of crème fraîche (if using) and fresh basil and sorrel (if using).

Tip: You can make this soup ahead of time. It'll keep in the refrigerator for 3 days.

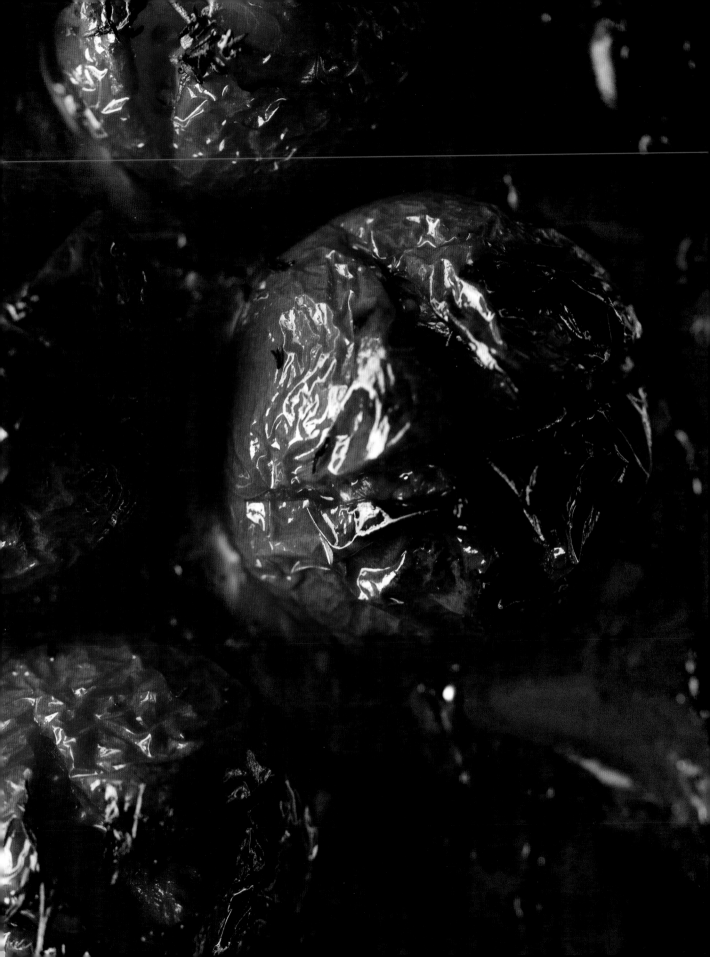

BEET AND BUTTERCUP SQUASH SOUP

Serves 4

This is one of the world's simplest soup recipes, and among the most visually enticing. The magical pink color of the blended beets and squash is sure to have you swooning. Completely dairy-free and vegan-friendly, this five-ingredient meal can't be beat on a chilly evening.

4 cups roughly chopped buttercup squash (unpeeled)

2 cups roughly chopped beets (unpeeled)

1 can (14 oz) coconut milk

2 cups vegetable broth (room temperature)

Salt, to taste

Pea shoots, to garnish (optional)

Steam vegetables. We use a pressure cooker to cook our vegetables until tender (it takes 20 to 25 minutes), but if you don't have one, feel free to use whatever method you prefer (see Tip).

In a small saucepan on medium heat, warm up coconut milk, just until it begins to simmer. Remove from heat and set aside (see Tip).

Once vegetables are steamed, remove and discard the skins from the beets and squash. Place flesh in a blender, then add warmed coconut milk and vegetable broth. Season with salt. Blend until completely smooth. Serve, topped with pea shoots (if using).

Tips: To steam your veg in a pot and steam basket, fill the basket with vegetables, then add enough water to cover the bottom of the pot without touching the basket. Bring the water to a boil and cook the veg until fork-tender.

It's important to use warmed coconut milk in this recipe. If the coconut milk is too cold, you risk curdling the mixture in the blender.

Styling Note: Garnishes, while not always necessary, can elevate a dish as every-day as soup into something a little more special.

Settings and Angle: f/4.5 ISO 1600 1/100 sec 45 degrees

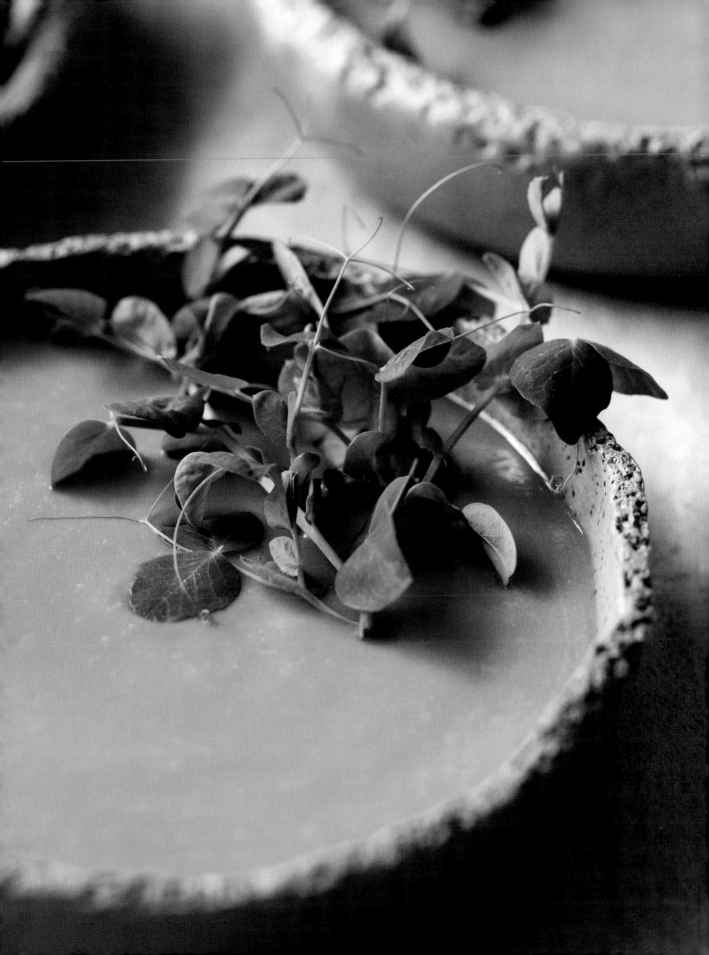

ROASTED VEGETABLE GAZPACHO

Serves 6 to 8

Chilled soups are a great way to cool down in the summer months, and this roasted vegetable gazpacho is a wonderful way to clear out the crisper, too.

1 cup chopped red bell pepper

1 cup chopped yellow bell pepper

1 cup chopped onion

2 cups chopped tomato, in large chunks

1 tbsp neutral cooking oil

Salt, to taste

1 cup passata

1 cup water

1 cup chopped English cucumber

¼ cup fresh cilantro leaves, roughly chopped

Toppings:

Baby tomatoes, halved

English cucumber, diced

Extra virgin olive oil

Lemon Petal Salt (page 24)

Preheat oven to 375°F. Line a 13- x 9-inch baking pan with parchment or nonstick foil.

Place chopped bell peppers, onion and tomatoes on prepared baking pan. Drizzle with oil. Season with salt. Bake in preheated oven for 30 to 40 minutes, stirring occasionally, until vegetables are tender and golden.

Carefully transfer vegetables to a blender, working in batches if necessary. Add passata, water, cucumber and cilantro. Blend on high speed until completely smooth. Refrigerate for at least 2 hours before serving.

Divide gazpacho among serving bowls. Top with halved baby tomatoes and diced cucumber, drizzle with olive oil and sprinkle with lemon petal salt.

Tip: Make this ahead of time and refrigerate for up to 1 week.

Styling Note:
The contrast between the dark background and light props adds mystery to a shot. We garnished this soup with an off-center, free-style approach.

Settings and Angle:
f/10
ISO 4000
1/100 sec
90 degrees

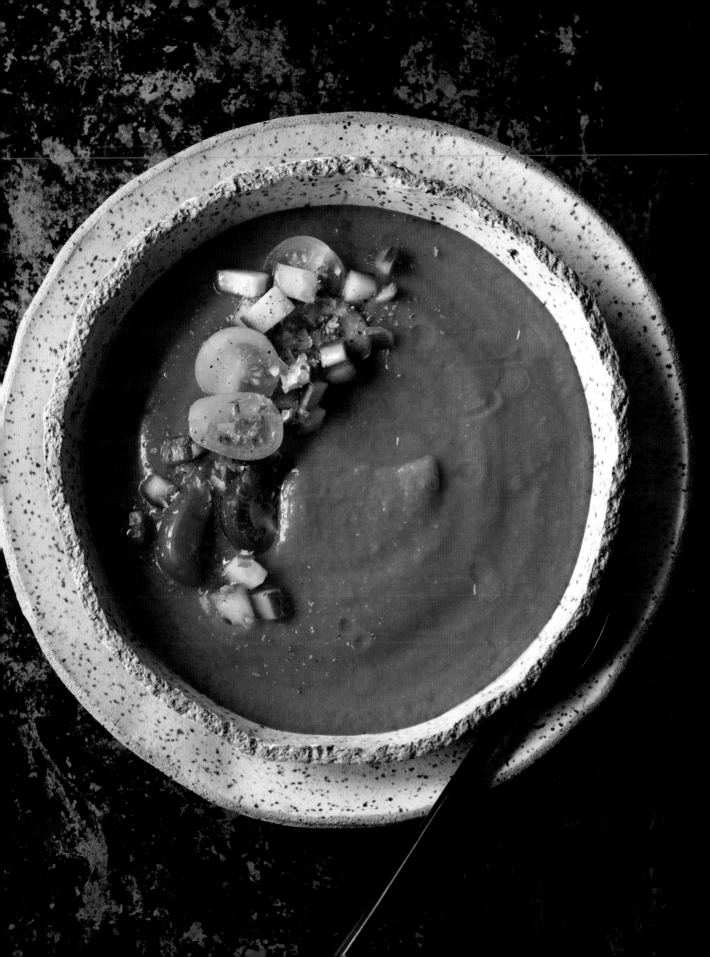

CORN THREE WAYS

Each toppings recipe makes enough for 2 ears of corn

Few things are more enjoyable to eat in the summer than barbecued corn, wouldn't you agree? We've taken things to the next level by preparing three different flavor boosters. Each one has a dynamic, bold taste that perfectly enhances the natural sweetness of the corn.

Mexican Topping:

1 tbsp Classic 30-Second
   Mayonnaise (page 31)

1 tbsp sour cream

1 tsp ancho chili powder

Juice of ½ lime

1 tbsp finely chopped cilantro leaves

1 garlic clove, minced

Korean Topping:

2 tbsp Classic 30-Second
   Mayonnaise (page 31)

2 tbsp finely chopped kimchi

½ tsp gochujang (red chili paste)

Black sesame seeds, to garnish

Japanese Topping:

2 tbsp Classic 30-Second
   Mayonnaise (page 31)

1 tsp shichimi togarashi

½ tsp sesame oil

Furikake, to garnish

6 ears of corn, shucked and
   halved crosswise

1 tbsp neutral cooking oil

In three small bowls, combine all of the ingredients for each topping, except for the garnishes.

Preheat barbecue to medium-high. Brush corn with oil, and barbecue for 2 to 3 minutes per side, until cooked through. Some charred parts help give it character (and flavor!), but be sure to keep your corn moving on the grill so it doesn't burn.

Brush grilled corn with prepared topping and add garnishes. Serve immediately.

Tip: Prepare the toppings ahead of time so you have more time to enjoy with guests.

Styling Note:
With some of the corn yet to receive its luscious toppings, this shot feels a bit "unfinished." Showing something in process like this can give the shot a more natural atmosphere.

Settings and Angle:
f/10
ISO 3200
1/160 sec
90 degrees

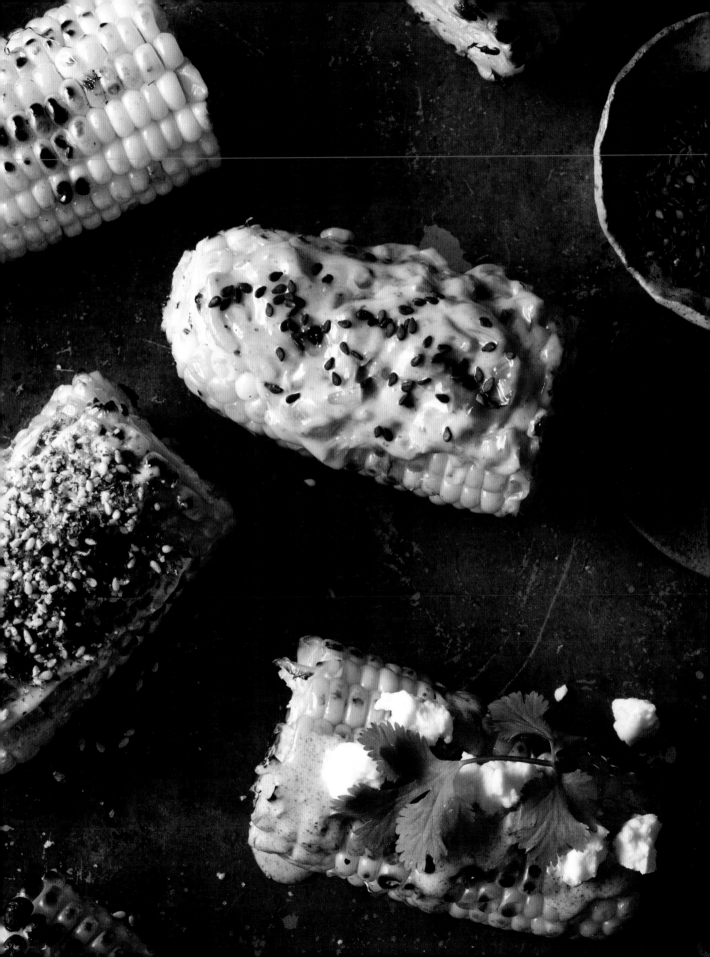

ROASTED RADISHES
AND TOMATOES

Serves 4

We were wary of roasting radishes, but they turn tender and sweet in the oven, and retain a slight crunch that we adore.

12 to 16 radishes, greens
   trimmed and reserved

1 cup cherry tomatoes

1½ tsp neutral cooking oil, divided

½ tsp chili flakes

⅛ tsp salt

2 tbsp minced peeled
   ginger

2 tsp liquid honey

2 tsp fish sauce

1 tsp soy sauce

Juice of 1 lime

1 garlic clove, minced

2 tbsp water

Preheat oven to 375°F. Line a baking sheet with nonstick foil.

Spread radishes and tomatoes on prepared baking sheet in a single layer, keeping everything snugly together. Drizzle with 1 tsp oil. Season with chili flakes and salt, and toss together. Bake in preheated oven for 20 to 30 minutes, until you begin to hear the radishes whistle and crackle. They should be tender to the touch, yet still moderately firm. The tomatoes will be blistered, and some of their juices will have spilled out onto the pan. Remove from heat and set aside.

Heat the remaining ½ tsp oil in a medium frying pan or skillet on medium heat. Add minced ginger and sauté for 1 minute. Stir in the honey, fish sauce, soy sauce, lime juice and minced garlic, and cook for another 2 to 3 minutes. Add the water and reduce the heat to medium-low. Cook for another 1 to 2 minutes, until reduced by about half. Add reserved radish greens and turn off heat. Cover frying pan, and let greens cook for another 1 to 2 minutes, until wilted.

To the frying pan with the greens, add the cooked radishes and tomatoes and toss to combine. Transfer to a serving dish, and enjoy.

Styling Note:
Using a combination of breakfast and Easter radishes gives this dish both color and shape.

Settings
and Angle:
f/10
ISO 5000
1/100 sec
90 degrees

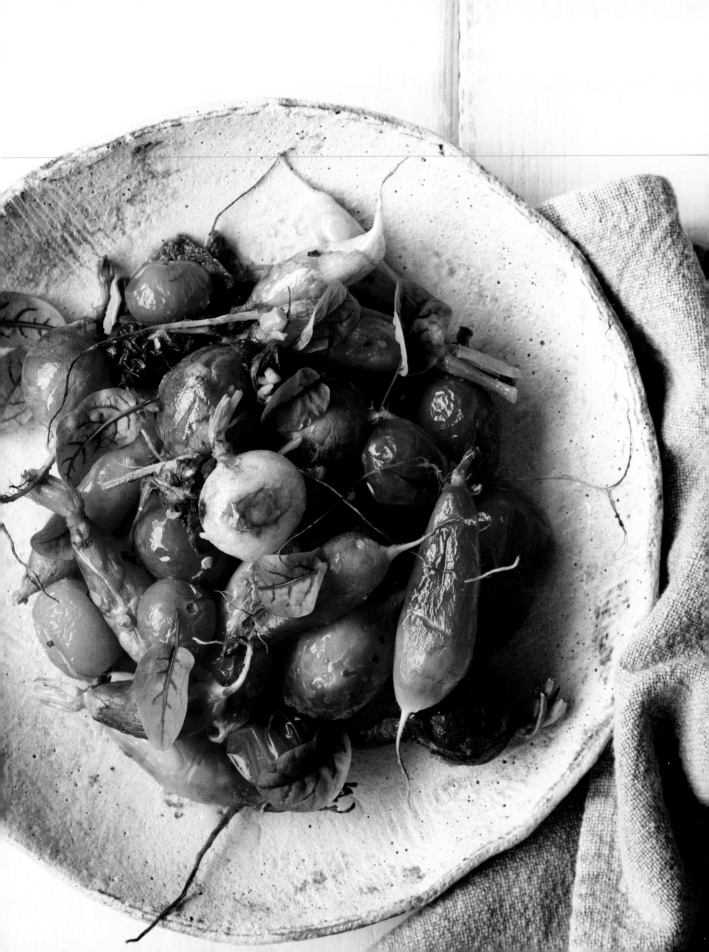

INDIAN-SPICED SQUASH

Serves 2

Robust and full of bold spice, this is a luxurious and unfussy way to enjoy squash. Double the recipe to make a big batch — you'll probably want seconds.

1 tsp flaky sea salt

1 tsp freshly ground black pepper

¼ tsp garlic powder

¼ tsp chili powder

1 tsp smoked paprika

¼ tsp ground coriander

¼ tsp ground cardamom

¼ tsp ground ginger

1 butternut squash, peeled, seeded and cubed

1½ cups cherry tomatoes

1 tbsp neutral cooking oil

¼ cup crumbled Macedonian feta cheese

Yogurt Sauce:

1 cup plain Greek yogurt

1 tsp fresh lemon juice

1 cup roughly chopped fresh cilantro (leaves and stems)

Pinch of salt

Fresh mint leaves, torn, to serve

Dukkah (page 26), to serve

Preheat oven to 375°F. Line a 13- x 9-inch baking pan with nonstick foil.

Combine all of the seasonings and spices in a small bowl.

Place squash and tomatoes on prepared baking pan and drizzle with oil. Add spices and gently toss together until well coated. Bake in preheated oven for 1 hour, stopping at the 40-minute mark to add the feta cheese.

Make sauce: Meanwhile, in a food processor, combine yogurt, lemon juice, cilantro and salt. Blend until smooth.

Transfer the roasted squash and tomatoes to individual serving plates. Top with cilantro yogurt sauce, and garnish with mint and dukkah.

Styling Note:
This is another older background that we still love using from time to time. It's actually made by layering silver paint and rock salt, which gives it an interesting texture.

Settings and Angle:
f/10
ISO 1600
1/100 sec
90 degrees

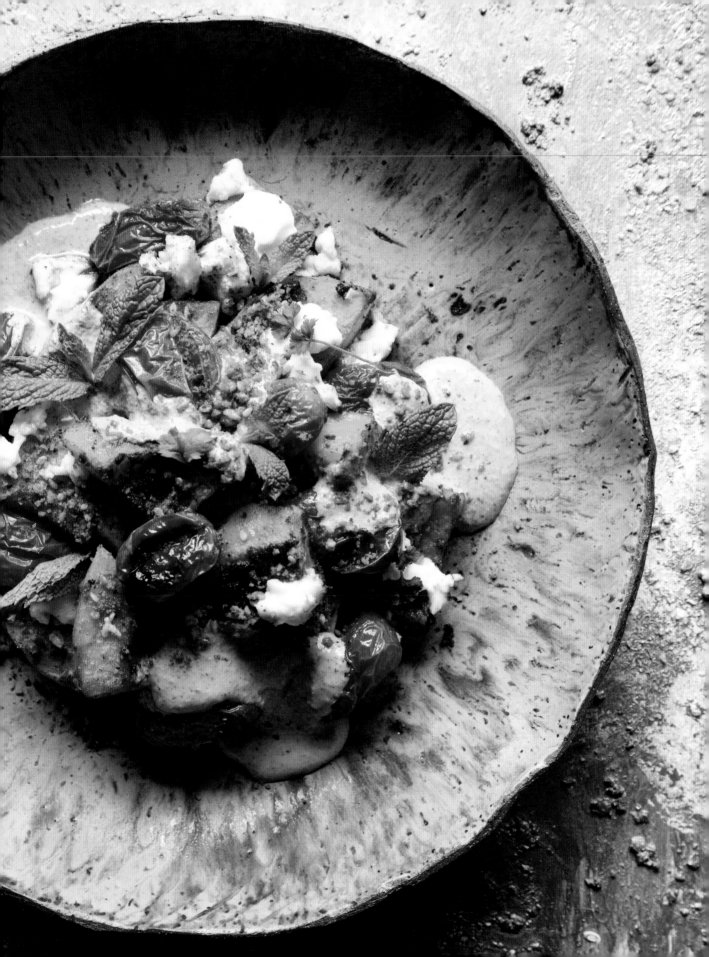

BAKED SWEET POTATOES

Serves 4

Sweet potatoes never looked so dressed up! We used toppings like roasted corn and pea shoots here, but feel free to choose whatever suits you to create something unique, colorful and nutritious.

4 sweet potatoes

1 tbsp olive oil, divided

Salt, to taste

1 ear of corn, shucked

½ cup pea shoots

Radish slices, to garnish

Sour cream or plain Greek yogurt, to serve

Preheat oven to 400°F. Set aside a baking sheet.

Poke sweet potatoes a few times with a fork. Place on the baking sheet, drizzle with most of the olive oil, and season with salt. Bake in preheated oven for 40 to 45 minutes, until fork-tender.

Brush corn with remaining oil, and sprinkle with salt. Grill corn, turning occasionally, until slightly charred, 3 to 5 minutes (we like to use a barbecue, but if you have a grill pan, that will work, too). Remove from heat and let cool slightly.

Using a sharp knife, remove all the corn kernels from the cob (you should end up with about 1 cup). Discard cob.

Slice potatoes lengthwise without fully dividing, and top with corn, pea shoots and radish slices. Serve with sour cream or Greek yogurt.

Styling Note:
We shot this on one of our favorite vintage baking sheets, which has a natural worn patina that can only be earned with time.

Settings and Angle:
f/10
ISO 4000
1/100 sec
90 degrees

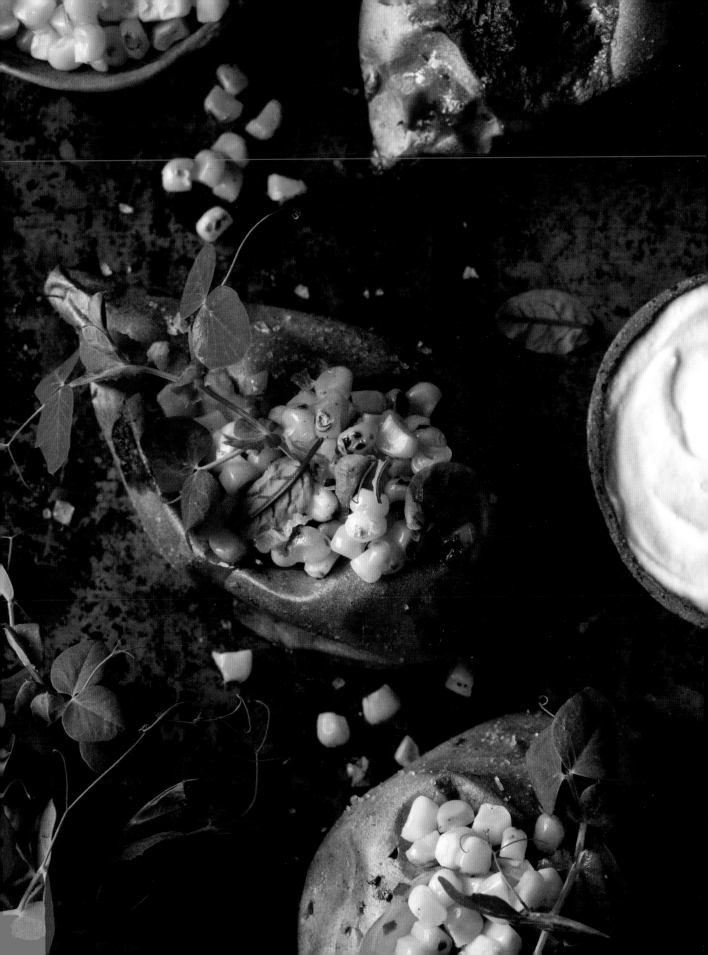

ROASTED FIVE-SPICE CAULIFLOWER

Serves 4

Cauliflower absolutely loves spice. Here we've roasted the whole head with smoky cayenne, black pepper and Chinese five-spice. The heat is tempered by a pea mint dip, a bright and flavorful partner to cool things down. We'd definitely advise making them together.

1 head of cauliflower, cut into large florets

2 tbsp neutral cooking oil

1 tsp ground ginger

1 tsp flaky sea salt

½ tsp cayenne pepper

¼ tsp Chinese five-spice powder

¼ tsp freshly ground black pepper

¼ tsp garlic powder

Raw black sesame seeds, to garnish

Pea Mint Dip:

1 cup frozen peas

2 tbsp fresh lemon juice

1 tbsp extra virgin olive oil

10 fresh mint leaves

1 garlic clove, minced

Preheat oven to 375°F. Line a baking sheet with parchment paper. In a medium bowl, toss together the cauliflower florets, oil, ginger, salt, cayenne, Chinese five-spice, black pepper and garlic powder.

Spread seasoned cauliflower evenly on prepared baking sheet. Bake in preheated oven for 20 to 25 minutes, stirring occasionally, until golden and tender.

Make dip: Bring a small saucepan of water to a boil. Cook peas for 1 minute, just until they turn bright green. Drain in a colander and run under cold water to stop the cooking process.

In a blender or food processor, combine cooked peas, lemon juice, olive oil, mint and minced garlic. Blend until completely smooth.

Serve roasted cauliflower with dip family-style, or get a little fancier by plating it as a first course. Sprinkle with black sesame seeds. Enjoy.

Styling Note: Get inspiration online for plating techniques. For a refined approach, less is more.

Settings and Angle: f/13 ISO 1250 1/100 sec 90 degrees

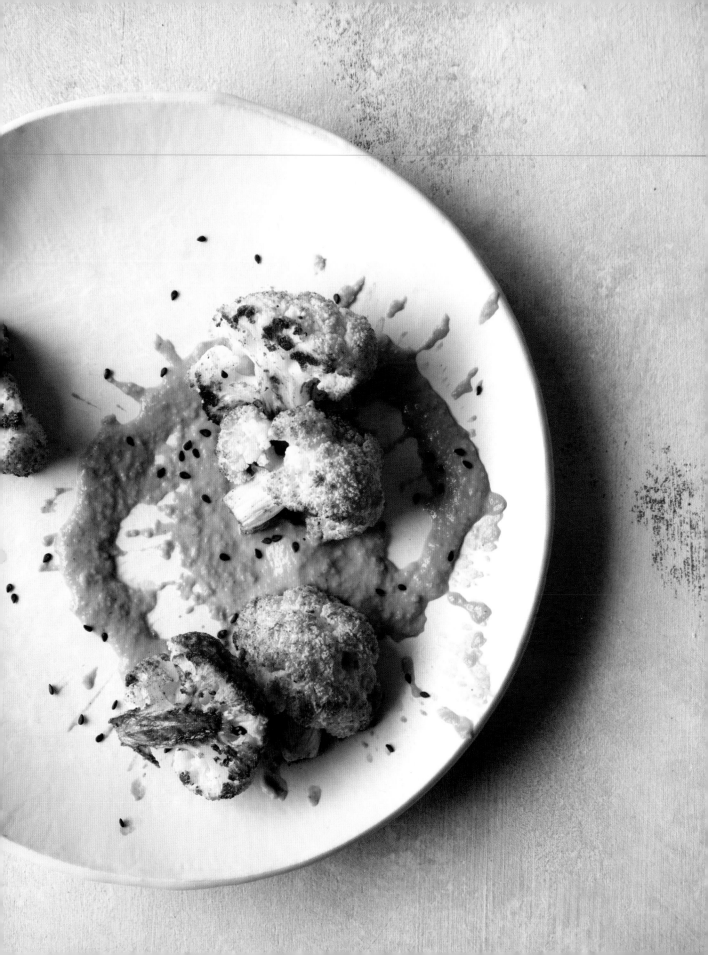

ORZO-STUFFED TOMATOES WITH MOZZARELLA AND BASIL

Serves 4

When tomatoes are at their finest, we usually are too. Use larger-sized tomatoes — the bigger the better — so they can withstand being packed full of this delicious orzo stuffing and then baked to perfection. This is one of those intimate, cozy dinners that goes great with a big healthy side (like our Watermelon and Cucumber Salad with Herb Vinaigrette, page 106) or perhaps even just a nice glass of Merlot.

1 tbsp neutral cooking oil

1 cup diced red onion

1 cup diced red bell peppers

Pinch of salt

1 cup shiitake mushrooms, finely chopped

½ tbsp finely chopped fresh rosemary

2 garlic cloves, minced

1 cup orzo pasta

2 cups vegetable broth

1 cup finely grated Parmigiano-Reggiano cheese

½ cup unseasoned panko breadcrumbs

8 large tomatoes (see Tip, page 188)

Torn mozzarella cheese, to garnish

Fresh basil leaves, to garnish

Preheat oven to 375°F.

Heat oil in a large frying pan or skillet on medium heat. Add onion and red peppers, and sauté for 2 to 3 minutes, until softened. Season with salt. Add mushrooms, rosemary and garlic, and cook for 1 to 2 minutes. Add orzo, and cook, stirring, until the orzo is slightly toasted, about 2 minutes. Add broth and bring to a gentle boil. Reduce the heat, cover with a lid, and cook for 8 minutes, stirring occasionally, or until the broth has been absorbed. Add Parmigiano-Reggiano and breadcrumbs, and stir until incorporated. Remove from heat.

(recipe continues on page 188)

Styling Note:
We love how dark food photography can still be bright and colorful. We played with the shadows a bit here, using black fill cards to give the photo an enhanced, richer appearance.

Settings and Angle:
f/5.6
ISO 500
1/125 sec
45 degrees

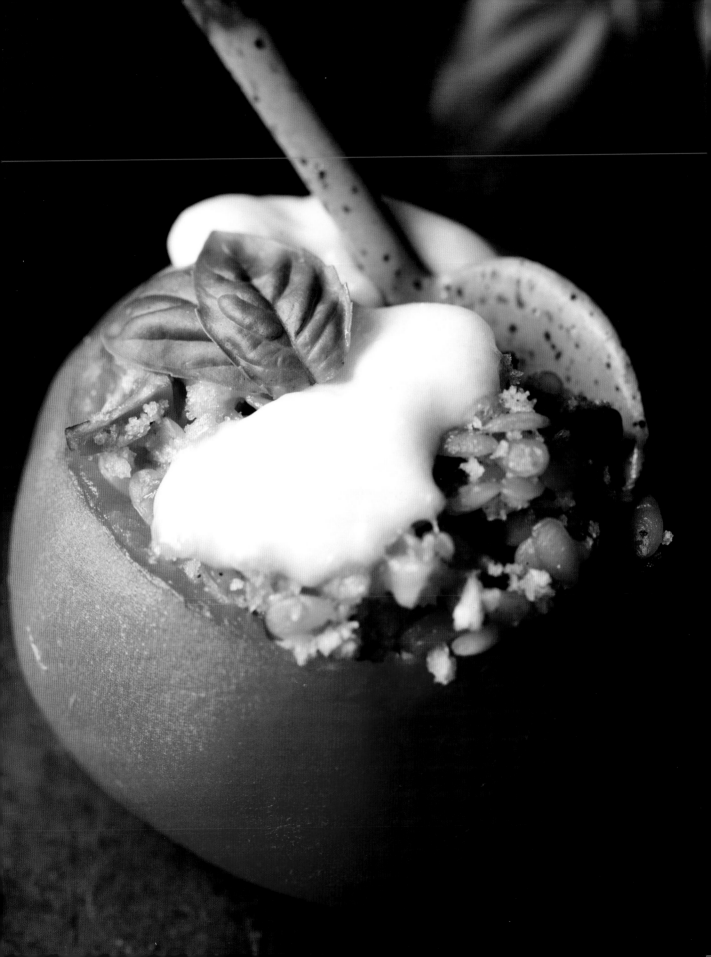

(continued from page 186)

Using a spoon, hollow out the tomatoes (be careful to leave the bottoms intact). Stuff each tomato with an equal amount of the orzo mixture. Place in a lightly oiled baking dish. Bake in preheated oven for 20 to 25 minutes, until tops are slightly golden and bubbly.

Remove the baking dish from the oven and top the tomatoes with torn mozzarella. Return to the oven, and set oven to broil. Broil for 2 to 3 minutes, just until cheese melts. Top with fresh basil and serve.

Tip: We recommend using beefsteak tomatoes. They tend to be firm enough to hold up to stuffing and rarely split open while baking.

HEIRLOOM TOMATO
PHYLLO TART

Serves 8 to 10

Phyllo works so well as a quick tart base, mostly because of how forgiving it is. It can tear and get messy, but somehow it all works out in the end. Brilliant, really. Because tomatoes are pretty much the star of the show here, we'd definitely suggest you make this one when they're at their prime. Use heirlooms if available, but if not, don't sweat it. With a resilient and delicate crust, this is one to impress guests with . . . or maybe to enjoy all by yourself (just kidding!).

½ cup fresh ricotta cheese

½ cup mascarpone cheese

1 large egg yolk

2 tbsp fresh lemon zest

1 tsp fresh thyme leaves

1 tsp flaky sea salt

10 sheets of phyllo pastry, thawed if frozen

¼ cup olive oil or melted butter

½ lb assorted heirloom tomatoes, cut into ½-inch-thick slices

2 to 3 tbsp balsamic crema (see Tip, page 144)

¼ cup fresh basil leaves, to garnish

Preheat oven to 375°F. Line a large baking sheet with parchment paper.

In a medium bowl, mix together ricotta, mascarpone, egg yolk, lemon zest, thyme and salt. Stir until well combined, then set aside.

Using a pastry brush, coat each layer of phyllo pastry with olive oil, stacking one on top of the other on the prepared baking sheet until you have 10 layers.

Spread the ricotta and mascarpone filling across the center of the top layer, leaving a 1-inch border all around. Top with a single layer of sliced tomatoes. Fold up the edges of the phyllo, all the way around. Brush the top edges with a bit more oil. Bake in preheated oven for 35 to 40 minutes, until golden brown around the edges.

(recipe continues on next page)

(continued from previous page)

Transfer to a wire rack and let cool for 5 to 10 minutes (see Tip). Drizzle with balsamic crema and top with fresh basil. Cut into squares and serve.

Tip: If any excess liquid remains on top of your tart after baking, do not fear! Simply blot it with clean paper towel to remove.

Styling Note:
The tomatoes we used for this shoot were so darn gorgeous, we almost couldn't bear to cut them up. This tart is photogenic all by itself, so we kept things minimal and unfussy.

Settings and Angle:
f/10
ISO 1600
1/100 sec
90 degrees

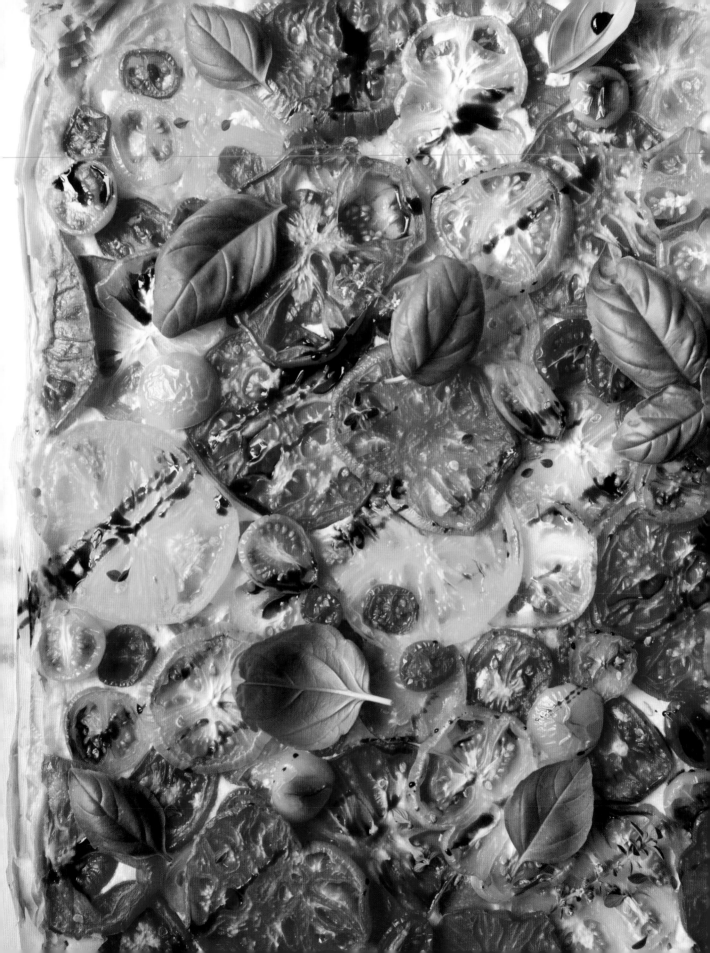

BRAISED YAMS WITH CHIMICHURRI, EGGS AND DUKKAH

Serves 2

This dish is simple to make yet so packed with intense flavor that it proves once and for all that easy food can indeed be supremely satisfying. The dukkah really helps bring things to the next level, with its spicy and crunchy hit helping lift up the sweetness of the yams. Once you've got it stashed away in your pantry, you'll likely be sprinkling it on everything.

Chimichurri:

3 tbsp olive oil

Juice of ½ lime

1 cup roughly chopped
  fresh flat-leaf parsley
  (leaves and stems)

½ cup roughly chopped fresh
  cilantro (leaves and stems)

1 garlic clove, minced

Pinch of salt

Eggs and Braised Yams:

2 large eggs

½ tbsp neutral cooking oil

½ cup diced red onion

Salt, to taste

2 cups diced yams
  (unpeeled)

1 tbsp water

Dukkah, to serve
  (page 26)

Make chimichurri: In a food processor, combine olive oil, lime juice, parsley, cilantro, minced garlic and salt. Blend until smooth. Set aside.

Boil eggs: Bring a small saucepan of water to a boil on high heat. Carefully submerge the eggs, and cook for 7 minutes. Drain, then transfer eggs to a bowl of ice water for 2 to 3 minutes. Peel, and set aside.

Braise yams: Meanwhile, heat oil in a medium saucepan on medium heat. Add onion, and cook for 2 to 3 minutes, stirring occasionally. Season with salt. Add diced yams, toss together and cook for another 1 to 2 minutes, just until slightly browned. Add water, then cover with a lid and cook for 1 minute. Add chimichurri, then gently toss together. Remove from heat. Taste for seasoning, and adjust if needed.

Serve braised yams with boiled eggs, halved. Finish with a sprinkle of dukkah.

Styling Note:
We wanted to play off the homey vibe of the dish. The orange and yellow hues contrast nicely with the dark background and bowl.

Settings and Angle:
f/8
ISO 3200
1/100 sec
45 degrees

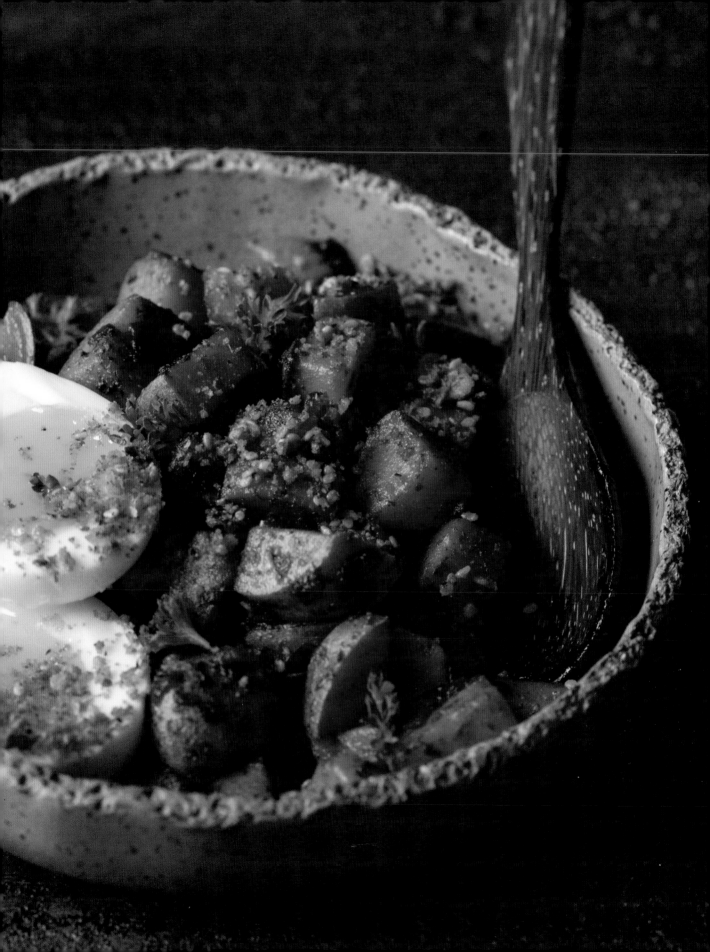

COMPANY

We understand the need for time-saving recipes, but to be perfectly honest, we find being in the kitchen relaxing (most of the time, anyway). As such, we tend not to rush. Preparing food is an expression of love, many would say, and we definitely believe most good things take time. Food should be no different, right?

That's not to say we want to spend all day fussing over a recipe. Whether we're cooking a larger informal meal for friends, family or just ourselves, we like to be enjoying our time with one another, not be stuck slaving over a hot stove or stressing over a difficult, intricate technique we feel the need to master for the first time.

Many of our recipes in this chapter have components that can be easily prepped ahead of time, meaning time saved on the day of the gathering and, ultimately, more enjoyment with those we love.

SHRIMP, PINEAPPLE AND CASHEW RICE PILAF

Serves 4

Every home cook needs a dependable rice dish, and this one is our go-to. It makes for a great midweek meal, mostly because it uses so many ingredients we usually have hanging around our kitchen. We like to keep a bag of frozen shrimp on hand for these exact occasions, but if it's in season and readily available, fresh is best.

1 tbsp unsalted butter

½ cup diced onion

1 tsp minced peeled ginger

1 garlic clove, minced

1 cup long-grain white rice

1 tsp sambal oelek

2 cups chicken broth

¼ cup unsalted cashews, roughly chopped

½ lb frozen or fresh shrimp, peeled and deveined

1 cup diced bell pepper (any color)

1 cup diced fresh pineapple

Salt and pepper, to taste

¼ cup roughly chopped fresh cilantro (leaves and stems)

In a large saucepan on medium heat, melt butter. Add onion, ginger and garlic, and sauté for 2 to 3 minutes, until onion is tender. Add rice and sambal oelek, and stir well. Cook, stirring frequently, until the rice is slightly toasted, about 5 minutes.

Add broth and bring mixture to a boil. Reduce heat and simmer for 15 to 20 minutes, covered, stirring every 5 minutes or so.

About 2 to 3 minutes before the rice is done, add cashews, shrimp, bell pepper and pineapple. Cook for another 2 minutes or so, until the shrimp is cooked through (they should appear pink and be slightly firm to the touch). Season with salt and pepper. Add cilantro, stir through, and serve.

Tip: Use fresh pineapple, if at all possible. We find the canned variety really doesn't have much flavor, and isn't worth buying.

Styling Note: Black and gold are two distinct colors that add a touch of luxury to any table setting.

Settings and Angle: f/10 ISO 2500 1/100 sec 90 degrees

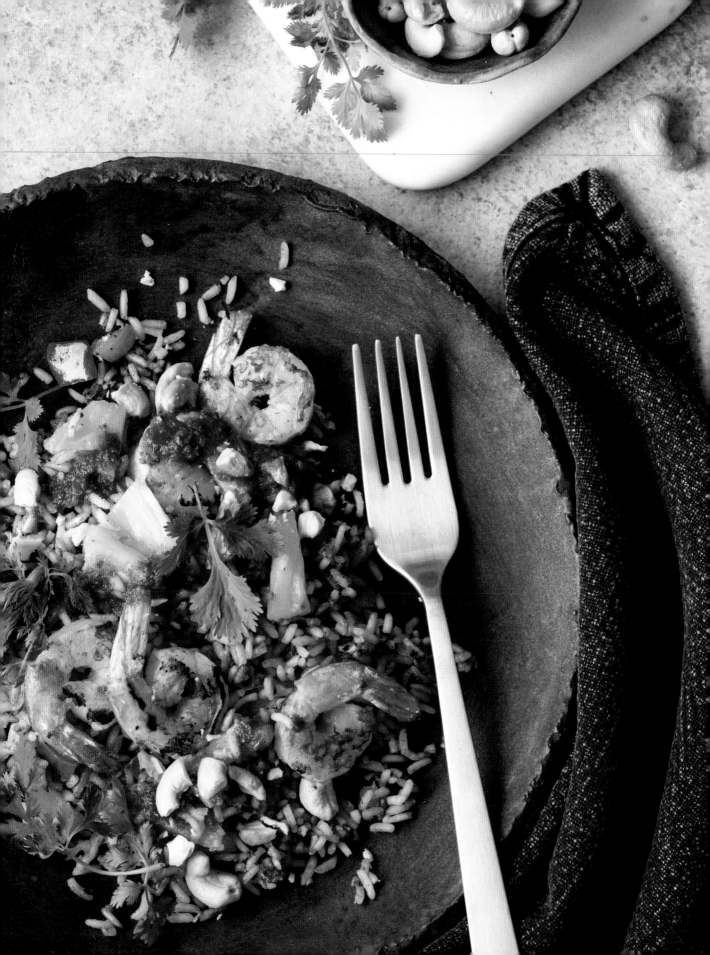

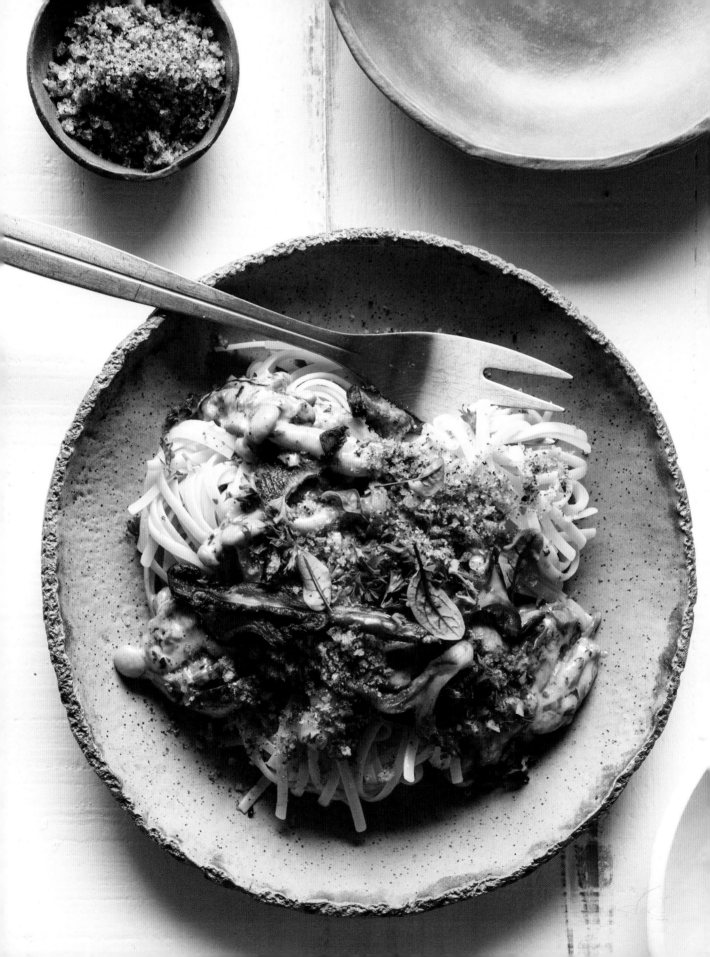

CREAMY MUSHROOM LINGUINE WITH PANGRITATA

Serves 4 to 6

A gratifying meal can take many forms, and this creamy linguine topped with crispy pangritata (toasted breadcrumbs) makes company feel right at home.

2 thick slices of sourdough bread

Extra virgin olive oil

Flaky sea salt, to taste

7 oz dried linguine pasta

½ tsp butter

½ tsp neutral cooking oil

½ cup chopped onion

1 garlic clove, minced

1 tsp porcini mushroom powder (see Tip, page 24)

3 cups sliced mixed mushrooms (we used oyster, shimeji and shiitake)

¾ cup whipping (35%) cream

¼ cup minced fresh flat-leaf parsley + 1 tbsp for garnish

Sorrel, to garnish

Preheat oven to 375°F. Set aside a baking sheet.

Drizzle bread with olive oil and season with flaky sea salt. Arrange in a single layer on the baking sheet, and bake in preheated oven for 5 to 7 minutes, until golden brown and crispy. Let cool at room temperature for 10 to 15 minutes. Transfer toasted bread to a food processor and blend to a relatively fine breadcrumb consistency. Set aside.

Bring a large pot of salted water to a boil. Cook linguine according to package instructions. Drain pasta, reserving 2 tbsp of starchy water.

In another large pot, melt butter with cooking oil. Add onion, and cook for 1 to 2 minutes. Stir in minced garlic and porcini powder, and cook for another 2 minutes. Add mushrooms, and cook for 5 to 7 minutes, stirring occasionally. Add whipping cream and reserved starchy water. Cook until reduced to a thick, saucy consistency, about 5 minutes. Add ¼ cup parsley, and stir well.

Toss cooked pasta with sauce. Serve topped with toasted breadcrumbs (pangritata), parsley and sorrel.

Styling Note:
You can serve individual portions with the sauce on top or toss it all together, family-style.

Settings and Angle:
f/7.1
ISO 2500
1/100 sec
90 degrees

SPAGHETTI WITH SHRIMP, WILTED GREENS AND SUN-DRIED TOMATOES

Serves 4

Impressing a crowd shouldn't mean you require a bunch of ingredients overflowing your refrigerator. Speedy pasta dishes are the go-to when there's not much to work with and we just want something simple to serve to friends in a pinch. We like to use fresh shrimp here, but frozen thawed will work just fine.

10½ oz dried spaghetti pasta

1 tbsp extra virgin olive oil + extra for finishing

½ cup sun-dried tomatoes, finely chopped

1 garlic clove, minced

Salt and pepper, to taste

½ lb fresh pink shrimp, peeled and deveined

3 cups loosely packed arugula

Fresh basil leaves, to garnish (optional)

Bring a large pot of salted water to a boil. Cook spaghetti according to the package instructions. Drain pasta, reserving 2 tbsp starchy water.

Meanwhile, heat olive oil in a large frying pan or skillet on medium heat. Add sun-dried tomatoes and minced garlic. Cook for 3 to 4 minutes, stirring frequently so as not to let the garlic burn, until tomatoes are tender and garlic is golden brown. Season with salt and pepper.

Add shrimp to the pan. Cook for 1 to 2 minutes per side, until the shrimp turns pink and opaque. Add arugula, followed by the cooked pasta and a spoonful or two of the reserved starchy water. Drizzle with olive oil, and toss everything together. Serve with basil (if using).

Styling Note:
We wanted to give the impression of a group table setting. The blue, green and gray hues of the dishes play off the colors of the pasta beautifully.

Settings and Angle:
f/8
ISO 4000
1/100 sec
90 degrees

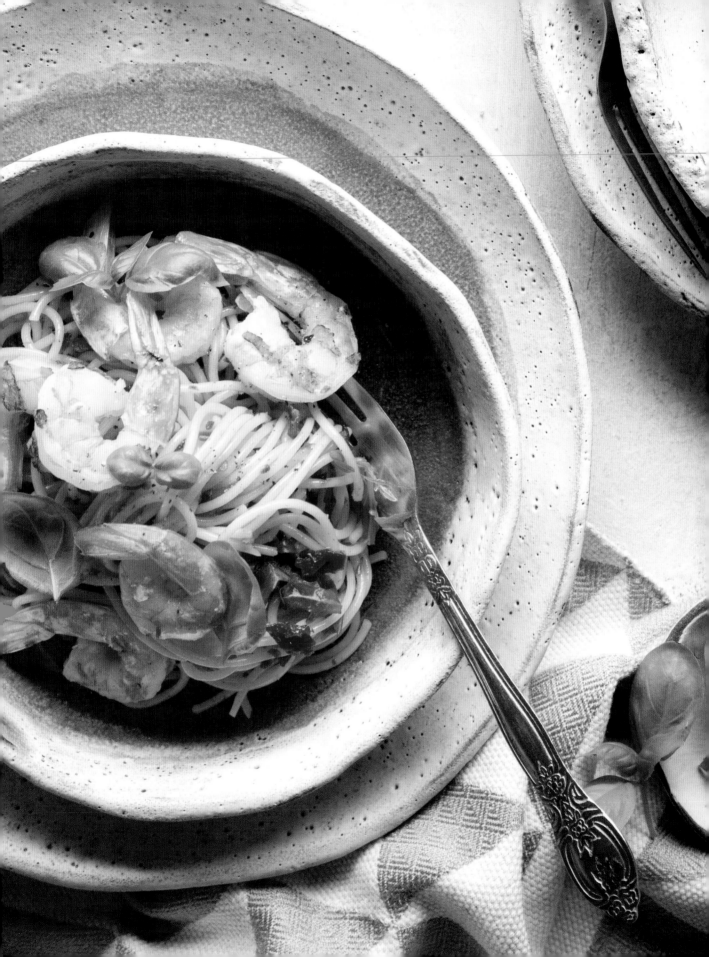

PERFECT PIZZA DOUGH

Makes enough for two 14-inch pizzas

Once we figured out how easy it was to make pizza at home, we were hooked. Our pizza dough recipe will become a staple we know you'll return to again and again. For an extra-crispy crust, prepare the dough the day before using and refrigerate overnight. On the pages that follow, we've provided three of our favorite ways to top pizza. Enjoy!

1 cup warm water

2 tsp granulated sugar, divided

2¼ tsp active dry yeast

2¼ cups all-purpose flour

1 tsp salt

Oil, for the bowl

In the bowl of a stand mixer, combine water, 1 tsp sugar and the active dry yeast. Let stand for 10 minutes, or until the water is foamy and yeast is activated.

Meanwhile, in a separate medium bowl, whisk together flour, salt and remaining 1 tsp sugar. Add to bowl with yeast. Using the dough hook attachment, mix on medium speed for 10 minutes, or until a pliable dough ball forms and the sides of the mixer are clean. Remove dough and coat bowl with a little oil. Return dough to the oiled bowl, cover with a clean kitchen towel and let rise in a warm, draft-free place until doubled in size, about 1 hour.

Punch down the dough and divide into two equal portions. Shape each portion into a small ball. Let dough rest, covered, for 10 minutes before stretching out and covering with your favorite toppings.

Styling Note: Styling dough can be a little dull, so we livened up the scene with other ingredients.

Settings and Angle: f/10 ISO 4000 1/100 sec 90 degrees

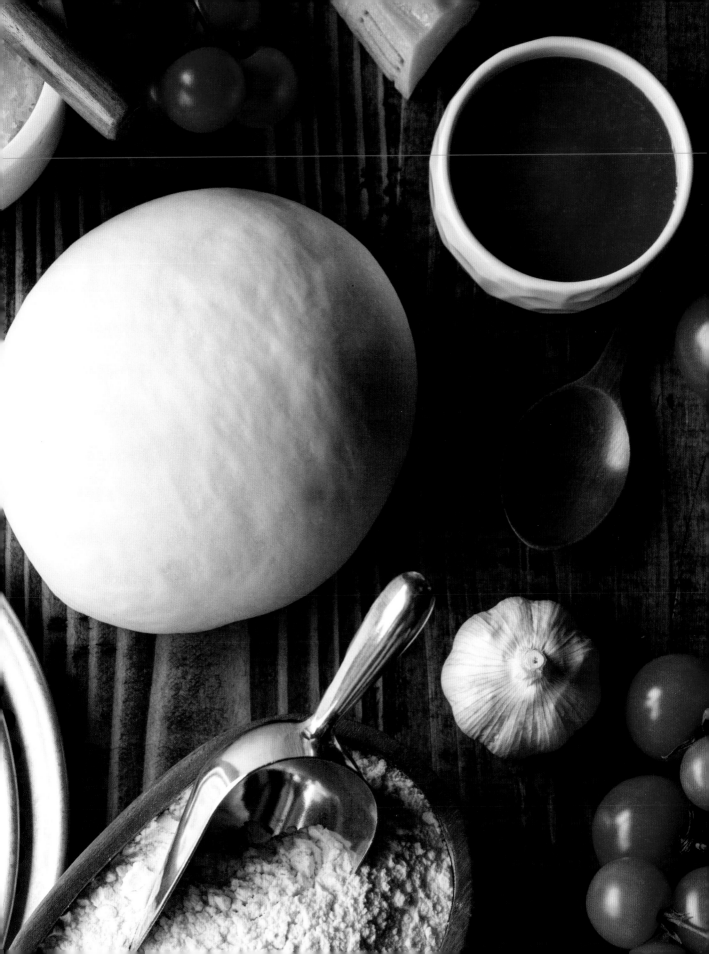

SPRING VEGETABLE PIZZA

Makes one 14-inch pizza

This pizza is like an ode to spring.

1 portion (½ batch) Perfect Pizza
   Dough (page 202)

Sun-dried Tomato Pesto:
(Makes about 1 cup)
2 cups packed fresh basil leaves
½ cup finely grated Parmigiano-
   Reggiano cheese
¼ cup whole walnuts
¼ cup sun-dried tomatoes in oil
¼ extra virgin olive oil
2 tbsp fresh lemon juice
½ tsp salt

Toppings:
3 thick asparagus spears,
   shaved
2 radishes, sliced
¼ cup crumbled feta cheese
½ cup watercress, to garnish
½ cup assorted greens, to
   garnish
Fresh basil and sorrel, to
   garnish

Prepare pizza dough.

Make pesto: In a small blender or food processor, combine all of the pesto ingredients and blend until completely smooth. Transfer to a bowl, cover and refrigerate until needed.

Assemble pizza: Preheat oven to 450°F. Grease a pizza pan or baking sheet and set aside. Stretch dough out to desired pizza-base size and place on prepared pan. Spread an even layer of sun-dried tomato pesto over the dough, leaving some room around the edge for the crust (you will have some left over; save for another dish). Top with shaved asparagus and radishes. Finish with crumbled feta.

Bake in preheated oven for 20 to 25 minutes, until the edges start to brown. Remove from oven and let rest on pan for 2 to 5 minutes.

Top with watercress, greens, basil and sorrel. Serve and enjoy.

Tip: If you can, make your dough the day before you plan to use it. The extended proof time results in an ultra-crispy, airy crust.

Styling Note:
The vintage cooling
rack and dried chili
flakes give this shot an
effortless, just-out-
of-the-oven
look.

Settings
and Angle:
f/10
ISO 4000
1/100 sec
90 degrees

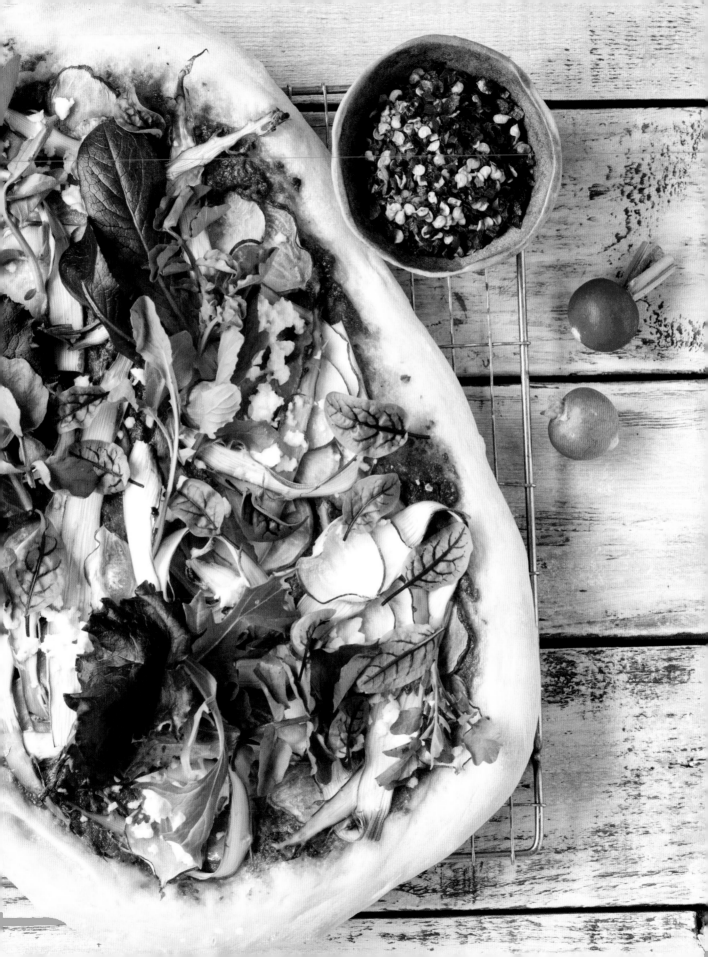

SPICY HAWAIIAN PIZZA WITH PROSCIUTTO

Makes one 14-inch pizza

This reinvention of the classic Hawaiian has it shining in a whole new light!

1 portion (½ batch) Perfect Pizza Dough (page 202)

Pizza Sauce:

½ cup passata

1 tbsp sambal oelek

½ tsp chili flakes

Toppings:

¼ cup thinly sliced red onion

¼ cup sliced green bell pepper

3½ oz Prosciutto di Parma, thinly sliced

¼ cup chopped fresh pineapple

1½ to 2½ oz fior di latte cheese

Fresh basil leaves, to garnish

Prepare pizza dough recipe.

Prepare sauce: In a small bowl, combine passata, sambal oelek and chili flakes.

Assemble pizza: Preheat oven to 450°F. Grease a pizza pan or baking sheet and set aside. Stretch dough out to desired pizza-base size and place on prepared pan. Spread sauce evenly over the dough, leaving room around the edge for the crust. Top with red onion, green pepper, prosciutto and pineapple.

Bake in preheated oven for 15 to 20 minutes, until slightly golden and crisp. Remove pan from oven and top pizza with chunks of fior di latte. Return to oven for 2 to 5 minutes, until cheese has melted.

Remove from oven and let rest on pan for 1 to 2 minutes. Sprinkle with basil. Serve and enjoy.

Tips: Use fresh pineapple if possible. The canned stuff doesn't compare.
   If you prefer a milder pizza, simply cut the quantity of sambal oelek in half and omit the chili flakes.

Styling Note:
Slice the peppers crosswise into rounds, instead of the usual strips, to add character to your pizza.

Settings and Angle:
f/10
ISO 4000
1/100 sec
90 degrees

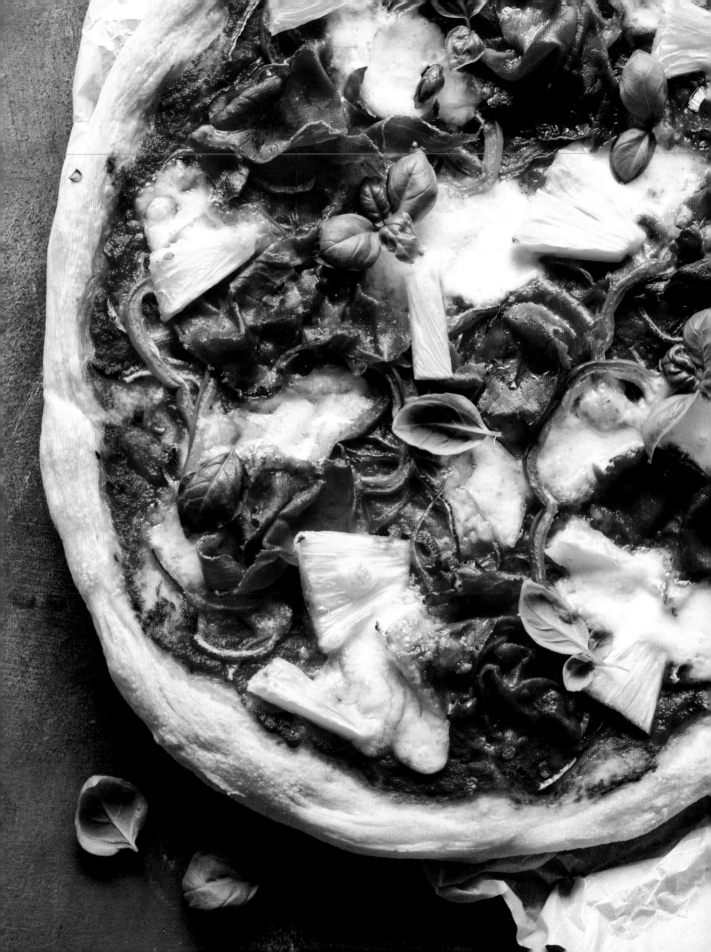

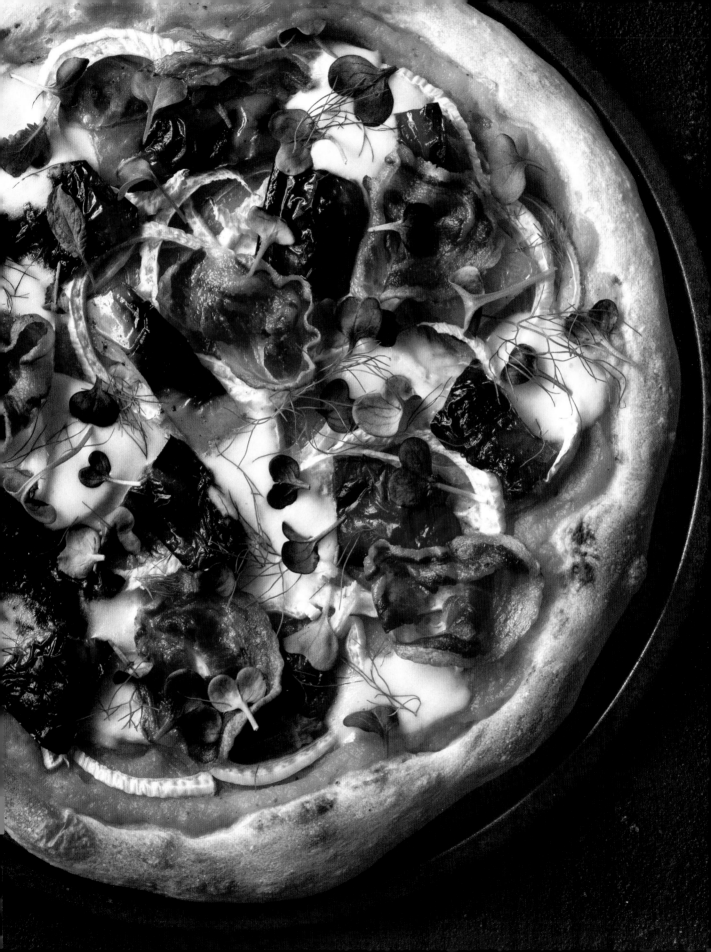

BUTTERNUT SQUASH PIZZA

Makes one 14-inch pizza

Butternut squash is one of those vegetables that is often overlooked but is actually a very versatile ingredient. In the past, we've used it in everything from mac 'n' cheese to a tart filling. But we prefer it this way: as a creamy, luscious base for this delectable winter-inspired pizza.

1 portion (½ batch) Perfect Pizza Dough (page 202)

Butternut Squash Purée:

1 medium butternut squash, halved and seeded

1 tbsp extra virgin olive oil

2 tsp Herbed Salt (page 24)

2 garlic cloves

Prepare pizza dough.

Make purée: Preheat oven to 400°F. Line a baking sheet with parchment paper.

Score the flesh of the butternut squash and drizzle with olive oil. Sprinkle with herbed salt. Tuck a garlic clove inside each squash half and place cut-side down on the prepared baking sheet. Bake in preheated oven for 30 minutes, or until fork-tender. Remove from oven and let cool at room temperature for 5 to 10 minutes. Using a large spoon, carefully scoop out the cooked squash and garlic and transfer to a food processor. Blend until completely smooth. Set aside until needed.

(recipe continues on next page)

Styling Note: Pizza naturally lends itself to being shot at 90 degrees, for a bird's-eye view of all the tasty toppings.

Settings and Angle: f/9 ISO 3200 1/100 sec 90 degrees

(continued from previous page)

Toppings:

⅓ cup red bell pepper

⅓ cup yellow bell pepper

⅓ cup green bell pepper

¼ fennel bulb, thinly sliced

3½ oz pancetta, thinly sliced

½ cup fior di latte cheese

Microgreens, to garnish
  (optional)

Fennel fronds, to garnish

Grill peppers: Heat your barbecue or grill pan to medium-high. Grill bell peppers on all sides until they're nice and charred. Transfer to a cutting board and cut into large pieces, discarding seeds and veins. Set aside.

Assemble pizza: Preheat oven to 450°F. Grease a pizza pan or baking sheet and set aside.

Stretch dough out to desired pizza-base size and place on prepared pan. Spread the butternut squash purée over the dough, leaving room around the edge for the crust. Top with charred bell peppers, sliced fennel and pancetta. Bake in preheated oven for 15 to 20 minutes, until the crust is golden and crispy.

Remove the pan from oven and top pizza with torn chunks of fior di latte. Bake for another 2 to 3 minutes, until cheese is melted. Remove from oven and top with microgreens (if using) and fennel fronds. Let cool for 1 to 2 minutes before serving.

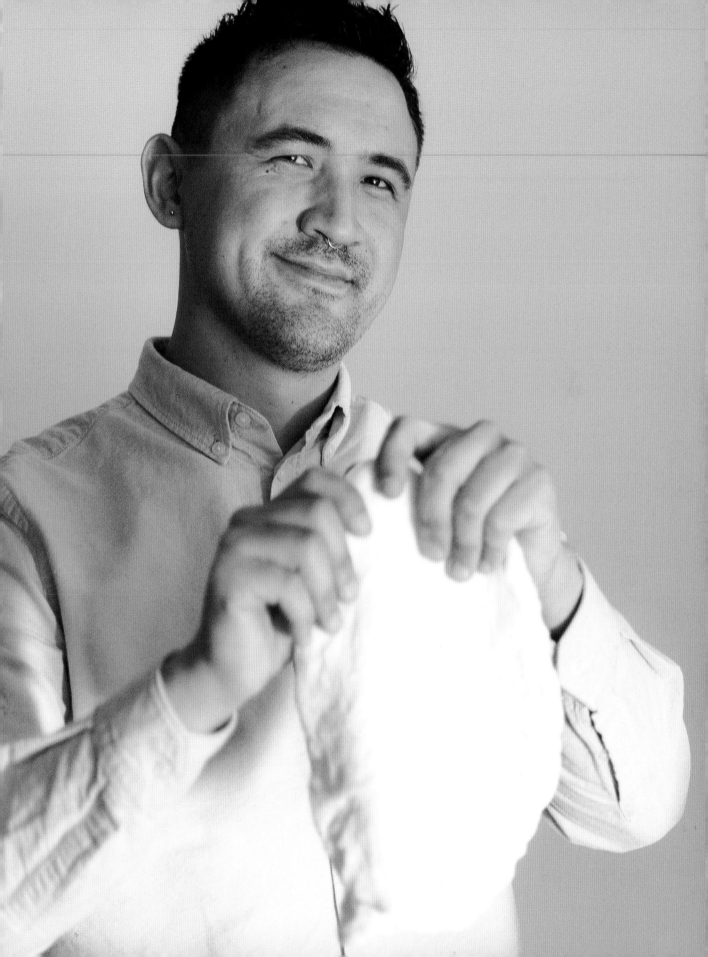

THE FOOD GAYS BURGER

Serves 4

You know the kind of burger you gotta roll up your sleeves for? The kind that requires copious amounts of napkins? Those are our kind of burgers. The best are usually made with freshly ground meat, but if you're not into doing that yourself, be sure to buy from a reputable butcher because the quality of the meat really does make all the difference.

Burger:

½ lb lean ground beef

½ lb lean ground pork

½ tsp garlic powder

½ tsp cayenne pepper

½ tbsp sweet paprika

½ tsp salt

½ tsp freshly ground black
  pepper

1 cup shredded cheddar
  cheese

4 burger buns, split

Toppings (optional):

Red onion, sliced

Tomato, sliced

Lettuce

Classic 30-Second Mayonnaise
  (page 31)

Mustard

Ketchup

In a large bowl, combine all of the burger ingredients, except the cheese, and mix until well incorporated.

Using your hands, make 8 meatballs. Flatten each ball between two pieces of parchment paper. To the center of 4 of the patties, add a good pinch of shredded cheese. Top with the remaining patties and pinch the edges together to seal in the cheese.

Preheat your barbecue or large frying pan to medium-high. Grill burgers, flipping as needed, until fully cooked (a meat thermometer will read 145°F for home-ground meat; 160°F for store-bought). Toast the buns.

Assemble each burger to your liking using your choice of toppings. We like ours with a thick slice of red onion, tomato, lettuce, mustard and mayo.

Tip: Use organic lean ground beef and pork, if possible. Keep in mind that if the meat is too lean, the burger will lack that juicy quality we all crave.

Styling Note:
This bad boy was
begging for a close-
up, no plate required.
Sometimes the food
speaks for itself.

Settings
and Angle:
f/10
ISO 3200
1/100 sec
0 degrees

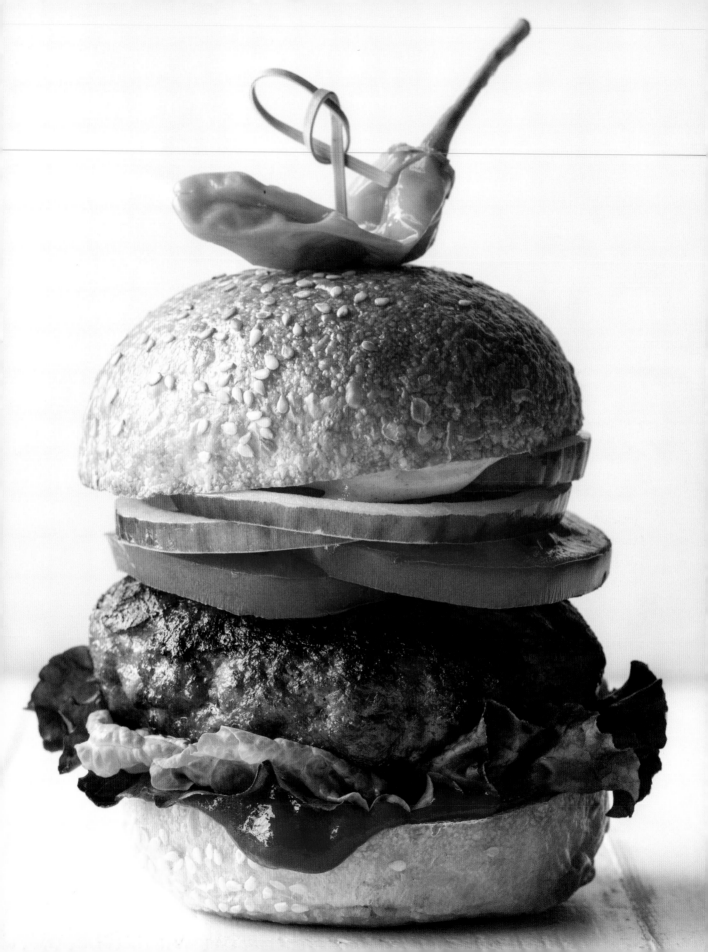

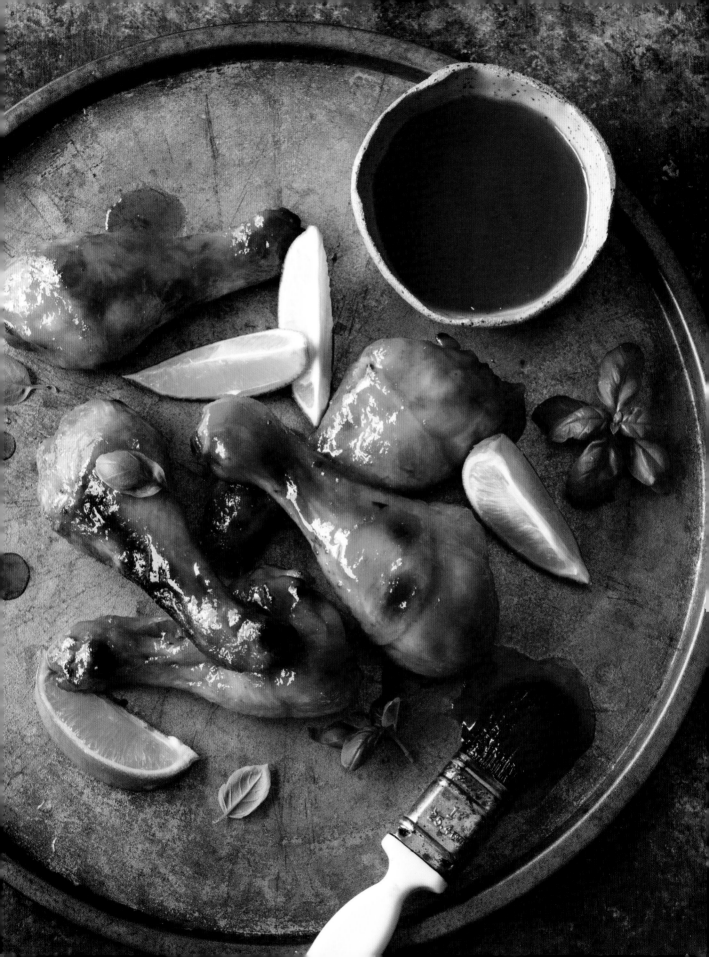

SWEET AND STICKY CHICKEN WITH BASIL AND LIME

Serves 4

Do you like it hot? And maybe a little sticky? We don't blame you — there's nothing better than getting your hands dirty while feasting. Paired with a gooey, irresistible glaze, this chicken goes well with a cooling salad, like our Grilled Cantaloupe Salad with Burrata and Asparagus (page 108).

8 chicken drumsticks and thighs
  (4 of each), skin-on
1 tsp neutral cooking oil
Salt, to taste
6 tbsp Sriracha sauce
5 tbsp liquid honey
2 tbsp unsalted butter
2 tsp sesame oil
1 tsp fish sauce
Zest and juice of 1 lime
  + 1 additional lime cut
  into wedges for garnish
½ cup fresh basil leaves
  (optional)

Preheat oven to 375°F. Line a baking sheet with nonstick foil or parchment paper.

Arrange chicken on prepared baking sheet and drizzle with cooking oil. Season with salt. Bake in preheated oven for 30 minutes, or until chicken is golden (but not cooked through).

Meanwhile, in a small saucepan on medium heat, combine Sriracha, honey, butter, sesame oil, fish sauce, lime zest and juice, and salt to taste. Bring to a boil, reduce heat and simmer for 8 to 10 minutes, until the sauce has reduced and thickened. Remove from heat, and divide the sauce between two small bowls. Let cool at room temperature.

(recipe continues on next page)

Styling Note:
Rather than piling
up the drumsticks in a
basket, we've given
them room to show
their glorious red
sauce.

Settings
and Angle:
f/10
ISO 3200
1/100 sec
90 degrees

(continued from previous page)

Remove chicken from oven (reserve pan), and transfer to a large bowl. Pour in one bowl of sauce, and gently toss chicken until well coated. Transfer to the reserved pan.

Increase oven temperature to 400°F. Bake chicken for another 10 to 15 minutes, until deep golden brown and it has reached an internal temperature of 165°F when tested with a meat thermometer. Remove the pan from the oven. Carefully transfer cooked chicken to a clean large bowl, add remaining glaze and toss to coat.

Serve chicken garnished with lime wedges and basil (if using).

Tip: Have napkins and a bowl of warm lemon water on hand for your guests, who'll undoubtedly appreciate it after enjoying these babies!

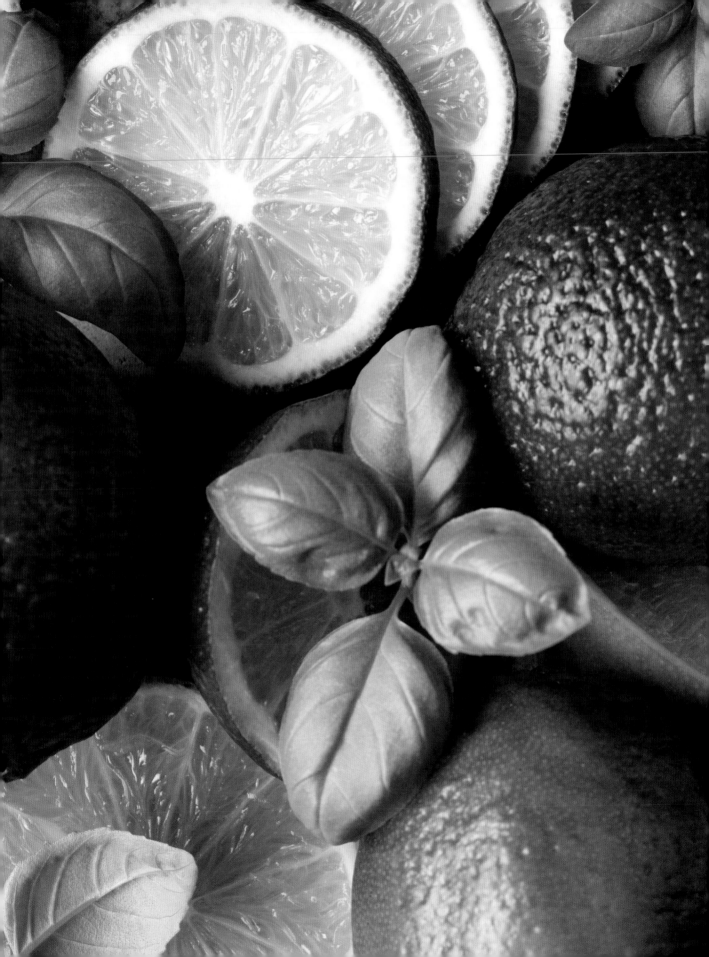

BBQ CHIMICHURRI CHICKEN

Serves 4

As you might have guessed already, we like our greens, especially herbs. Here we thought we'd showcase one of our most frequently used: cilantro. If you're not a fan, just give this a try and tell us you don't love it. Its strong flavor is balanced perfectly by the addition of basil, parsley and a nice kick of jalapeño.

1 cup roughly chopped fresh cilantro (leaves and stems)

½ cup fresh basil leaves

¼ cup fresh flat-leaf parsley leaves

1 jalapeño pepper

2 garlic cloves, minced

¼ cup olive oil

3 tbsp red wine vinegar

4 whole chicken legs (or 4 drumsticks + 4 thighs)

In a blender, combine cilantro, basil, parsley, jalapeño, minced garlic, olive oil and red wine vinegar. Blend until smooth. Transfer half of the chimichurri to a resealable bag; reserve the other half in an airtight container and refrigerate until needed.

Add chicken to bag with chimichurri, seal and turn to coat. Refrigerate for at least 8 hours (and up to 24 hours).

Heat barbecue or grill pan to medium-high. Cook marinated chicken, basting with the reserved chimichurri and turning occasionally, for 15 to 20 minutes, until it reaches an internal temperature of 165°F when tested with a meat thermometer. Serve immediately.

Tip: The longer you let the chicken marinate, the more rewarding the outcome.

Styling Note:
We thought it would be fun to capture the grilling process on our barbecue. It turned out to be our favorite shot, showing that being spontaneous with your photography can pay off.

Settings and Angle:
f/7.1
ISO 1250
1/100 sec
45 degrees

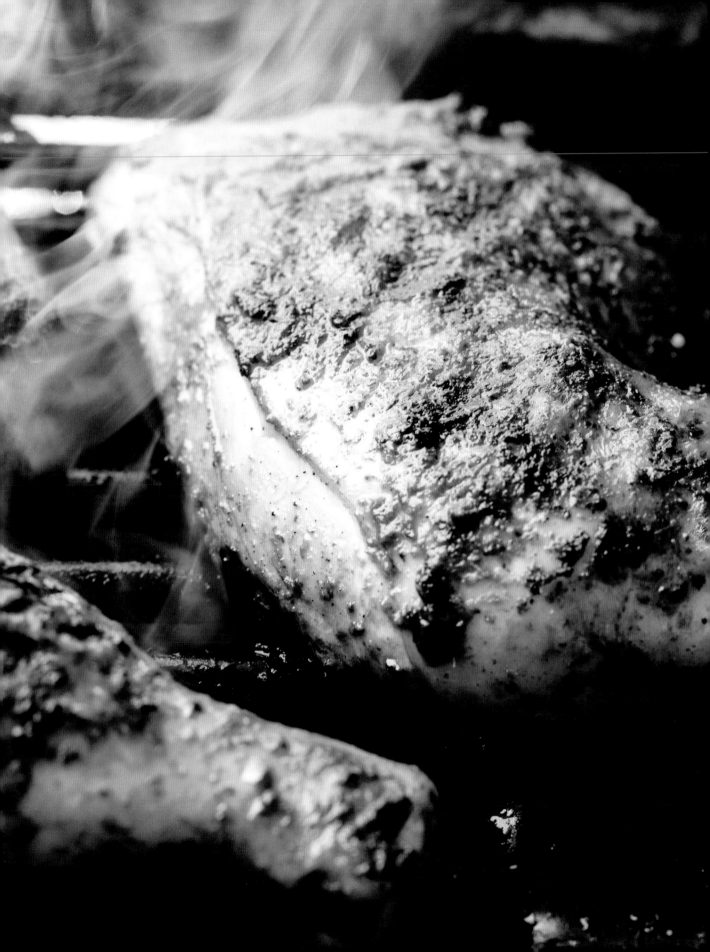

INDIAN-SPICED FRIED CHICKEN

Serves 4

Crispy on the outside and moist on the inside, this Indian-spiced fried chicken is fragrant and decadent — everything fried chicken should be. With a light yogurt-based coating, it develops a seductive outer crust once fried, and pairs exquisitely with a drizzle of cilantro yogurt. Try pairing it with our Confetti Kohlrabi Slaw (page 112).

Marinade:

1 cup plain Greek yogurt

2 garlic cloves, minced

2 tbsp fresh lemon juice

1 tbsp curry powder

1 tbsp hot paprika

1 tsp ground cumin

½ tbsp salt

½ tsp freshly ground black
   pepper

6 chicken legs

Sauce:

½ cup plain Greek yogurt

1 tsp fresh lemon juice

1 cup roughly chopped fresh
   cilantro (leaves and stems)

Pinch of salt

Oil, for deep-frying

Coating:

2 cups all-purpose flour

2 tsp baking powder

½ tsp salt

Make marinade: In a small bowl, whisk together yogurt, minced garlic, lemon juice, curry powder, paprika, cumin, salt and pepper. Transfer to a resealable bag, and add chicken. Seal, turn to coat and refrigerate for at least 8 hours (and up to 24 hours). Let rest at room temperature for 15 minutes before using.

Make sauce: In a blender or food processor, combine sauce ingredients and blend until completely smooth. Refrigerate until ready to use.

Make chicken and coating: In a large pot, heat oil to about 350°F. Meanwhile, in another resealable bag, combine flour, baking powder and salt. Add marinated chicken, seal bag and turn to coat.

Carefully add coated chicken to oil, and cook until golden brown and crispy (internal temperature should register 165°F or higher when tested with a meat thermometer). Serve immediately with the sauce. Enjoy.

Styling Note:
We kept things simple and clean to highlight the beautifully crisp texture of the chicken. The slightly aged, natural look of the ceramics adds a rustic, vintage quality.

Settings and Angle:
f/10
ISO 1000
1/80 sec
90 degrees

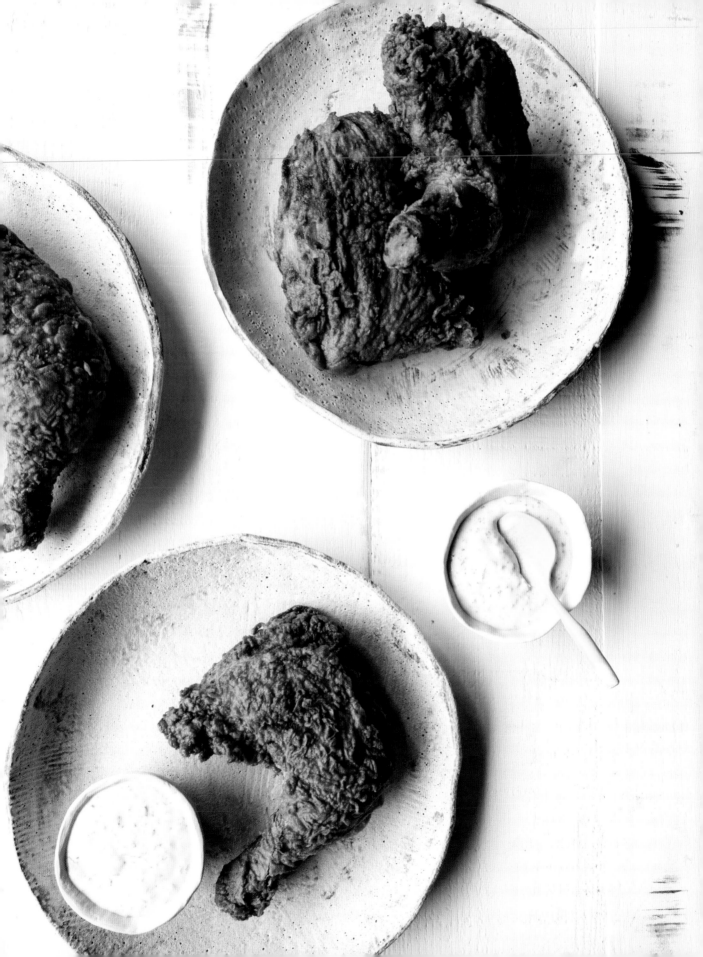

SMOKED SALMON SUSHI CONES

Makes 10 small cones

Sushi is so much fun to make at home, but many people find it intimidating. Not to fear! That's why sushi cones are so fantastic, because you don't need 10 years as a professional sushi chef to pull it off. Our recipe uses fresh smoked salmon (which, for many, tends to be more accessible than sushi-grade fish), but feel free to swap it out with whatever you'd like.

2 cups sushi rice

5 tbsp sushi seasoning (seasoned rice vinegar)

5 nori sheets (7 x 4 inches)

7 oz smoked salmon, thinly sliced

1 cup sliced English cucumber (matchsticks)

1 cup sliced carrot (matchsticks)

Japanese mayonnaise

Soy sauce, to serve

Cook sushi rice according to the package instructions. Add sushi seasoning, and, using a wooden spoon, stir to mix well. Transfer rice to a platter or tray, and set aside until rice has completely cooled.

Cut or split nori sheets in half. Working with one sheet at a time, place the nori widthwise, shiny-side down, on a clean work surface. Add 1 tbsp or so of rice, just slightly right of center on the bottom half of the nori. Spread rice evenly over just the bottom half, then top evenly with the sliced salmon, cucumber and carrot. Finish with a dollop of Japanese mayo.

Lift the bottom left corner of the nori up and over the fillings, and continue rolling towards the top corner of rice, wrapping fillings tightly into a cone shape. Set aside, seam-side down, and repeat with remaining nori and fillings. Serve immediately with soy sauce.

Tip: Rolling your cones may take one or two tries, but you'll soon get the hang of it.

Styling Note: The bright orange salmon was begging for a close-up.

Settings and Angle: f/6.3 ISO 2000 1/89 sec 45 degrees

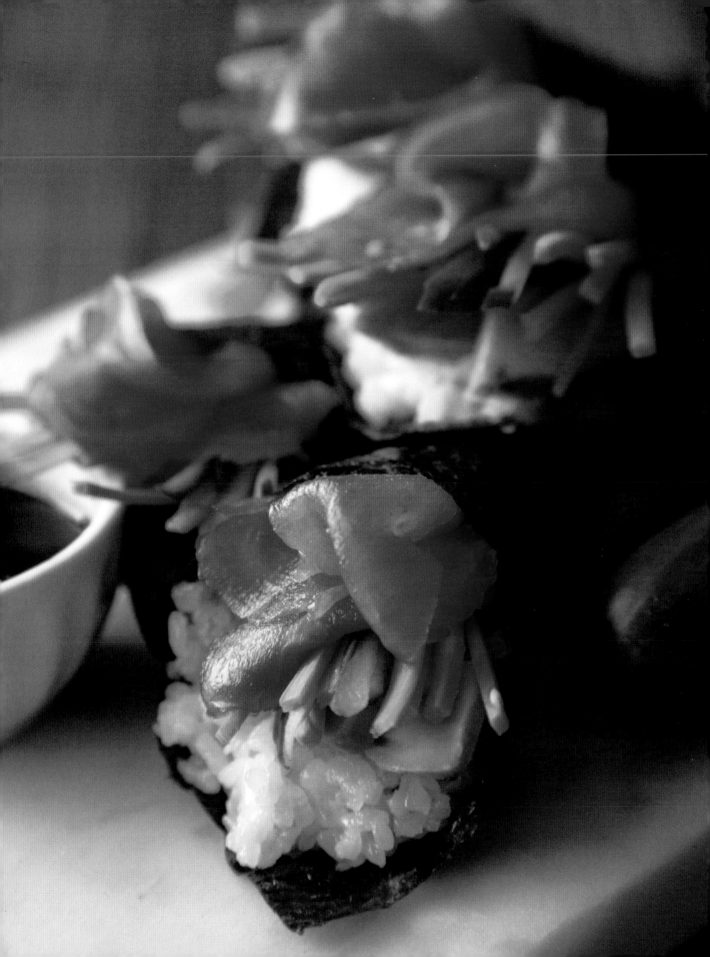

GRILLED SQUID
WITH CHILI AND MINT

Serves 4

Blue tiles, a cool ocean breeze and a gleaming-white pied-à-terre are just a few things that come to mind when making this dish, which is essentially the closest we'll be getting to an exotic vacation anytime soon.

1 tsp neutral cooking oil

¼ cup finely diced shallot

2 garlic cloves, minced

1 to 2 red chilies, sliced

Pinch of salt

1 lb fresh squid, cleaned
   and cut into ½-inch rings

1 tsp fresh lemon juice,
   to finish

Fresh mint leaves,
   to garnish

Heat oil in a medium frying pan or skillet on medium-high heat. Add shallot, and cook for 1 to 2 minutes, until slightly softened. Add garlic, red chilies and salt, and cook, stirring frequently, for another minute. Add squid, and sauté for 2 to 3 minutes, until springy and golden. Drizzle with lemon juice. Garnish with mint leaves and serve.

Tip: Grilled squid is effortless to prepare and doesn't require a whole lot to elevate it into something special—just take care to not overcook it, or it will turn into rubber bands.

Styling Note:
A monochromatic
setting can still offer
a sense of drama. This
background and plate
combo is one of our
personal favorites.

Settings
and Angle:
f/10
ISO 3200
1/100 sec
90 degrees

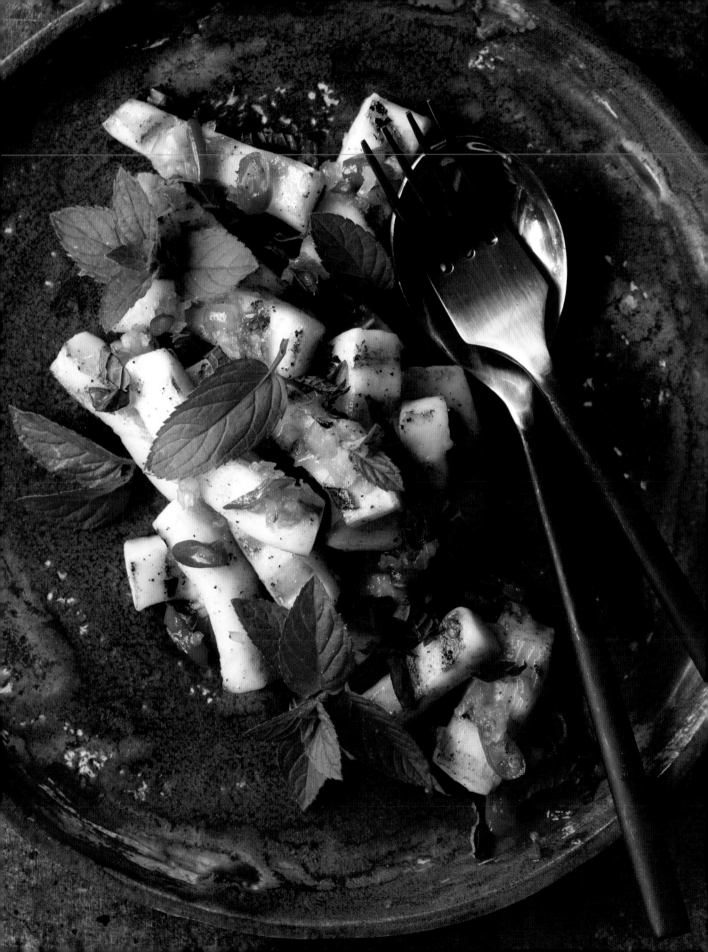

CHAPTER 8

SWEETS

Real Fruit Ice Pops

Roasted Raspberry and Beet Sorbet

Peach and Brown Butter Ice Cream

Sage, Lime and Vanilla Bean Ice Cream

Chocolate Mint Cupcakes with Sour Cream Frosting

Chocolate Cherry Skillet Brownies

Toasted Coconut Mango Mousse Cake

No-Bake Boozy Blueberry Cheesecake

Apple, Cinnamon and Beet Crumble

Classic Lemon Tart

Pavlovas with Lime Curd, Berries and Mint

Definite perks come with having a trained baker in the household, so it's a good thing neither of us has a *massive* sweet tooth, otherwise we'd have a big problem on our hands.

For this book, we wanted to create desserts that aren't cloying and that could act as a nice palate cleanser to end a meal. Whether it's our Sage, Lime and Vanilla Bean Ice Cream (page 234) or Pavlovas with Lime Curd, Berries and Mint (page 253), we think you'll find that this collection of not-too-sweet recipes is perfect for just about any occasion.

Dessert doesn't have to be complicated to be sophisticated or lick-the-spoon delicious. Most of the recipes in this chapter are simple enough for even the most novice baker to pull off.

REAL FRUIT ICE POPS

Each recipe makes 4 ice pops

It really doesn't get easier than this. Real fruit purées are a great way to make ice pops — an icy, sweet treat that we still love as adults. These are an ideal way to curb those sugar cravings when they hit, and since you know exactly what went into them, you won't feel bad about having two.

Strawberry Kiwi:

1 cup puréed strawberries

1 cup puréed yellow kiwi

1 tbsp liquid honey (optional)

Plum Apricot:

1 cup puréed black plum

1 cup puréed apricot

1 tbsp liquid honey (optional)

Blueberry Cantaloupe:

1 cup puréed blueberry

1 cup puréed cantaloupe

1 tbsp liquid honey (optional)

In a blender or food processor, combine ingredients for chosen flavor and blend until smooth.

Divide purée evenly among ice pop molds. Insert sticks. Freeze for 12 to 24 hours, until hardened. Enjoy.

Tip: For an ombré effect, as in the photograph, don't combine the fruit purées, but pour in one and then the other. Freeze as directed.

Styling Note: Shooting with ice not only looks cool, it helps keep the ice pops nice and frozen for the camera.

Settings and Angle: f/10 ISO 2500 1/100 sec 90 degrees

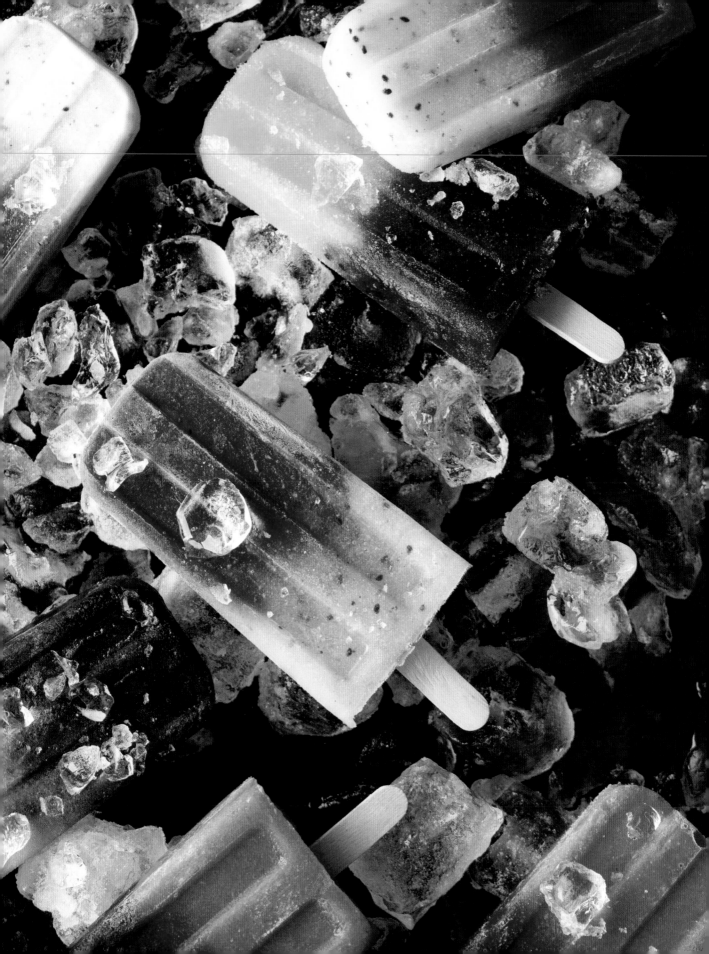

ROASTED RASPBERRY AND BEET SORBET

Makes about 1 cup

Sorbet is a light and satisfying way to wrap up any dinner party. It's elegant, and offers a bit of refinement without coming off stuffy or uptight. This one combines roasted raspberries and beets — the perfect marriage of tart and earthy.

4 cups raspberries
1 cup peeled and diced beets
1 tbsp neutral cooking oil
1 cup warm water
¼ cup liquid honey
½ tsp salt
¼ to ⅓ cup fresh lemon juice

Preheat oven to 400°F. Line a 13- x 9-inch baking pan with nonstick foil.

In a medium bowl, toss together raspberries, beets and oil. Pour into prepared pan. Keep everything grouped together in the pan, or the juices from the raspberries will leach out and parts will burn. Cover pan with foil and roast in preheated oven for 30 to 40 minutes, until the beets are soft and tender. Remove the pan from the oven and let cool for 5 to 10 minutes.

Transfer roasted raspberries and beets to a blender and purée. While blending, add water, honey and salt. Blend until smooth. Pour the mixture through a fine-mesh sieve into a bowl (discard solids). Add lemon juice and stir well. Refrigerate for 1 hour, or until chilled. Pour the mixture into an ice-cream maker. Churn according to the manufacturer's instructions.

Tip: This is a small-batch recipe, as homemade sorbets don't keep well in the freezer.

Styling Note:
We used an espresso cup as a serving vessel here, a simple yet inventive way to reinforce the intentionally small portion size of this dessert.

Settings and Angle:
f/7.1
ISO 2000
1/100 sec
0 degrees

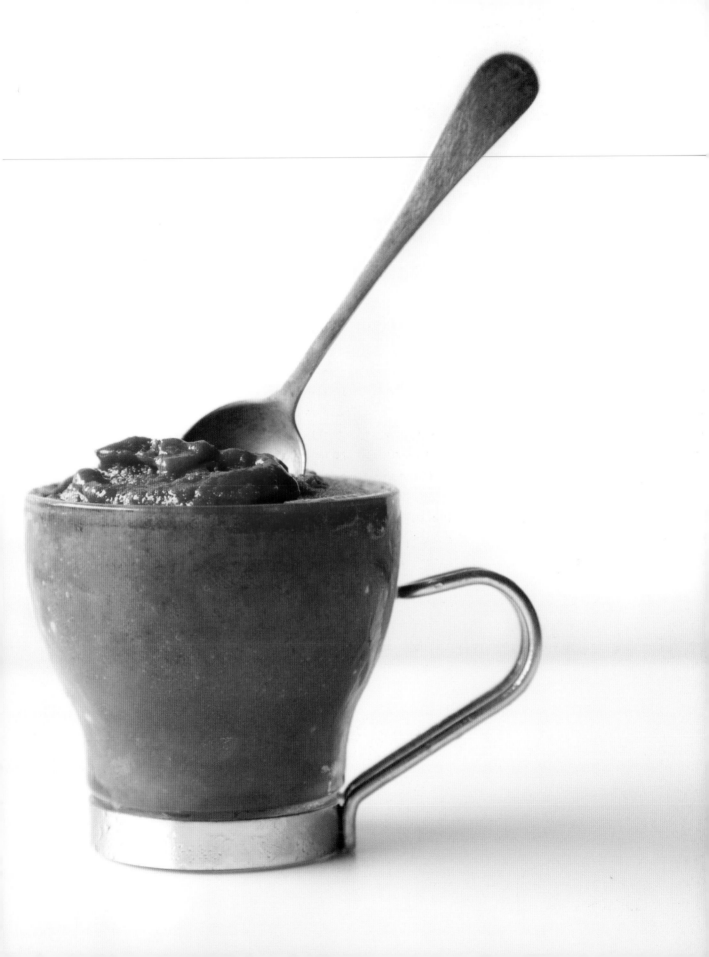

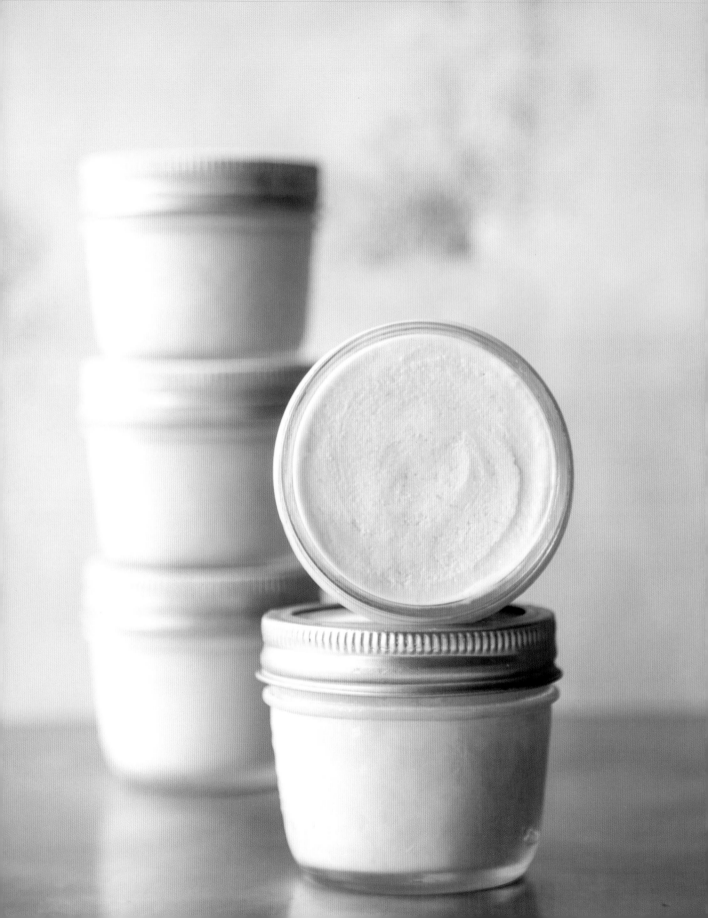

PEACH AND BROWN BUTTER ICE CREAM

Makes about 2 pints

You might be thinking brown butter in ice cream sounds a little crazy, but the nutty flavor pairs absolutely perfectly with peach, and together it's a total home run. Make this during the summer at the peak of peach season, when the fruit is incredibly ripe and fragrant.

2 cups whipping (35%) cream

⅔ cups whole milk

½ cup unsalted butter

½ cup + 2 tbsp granulated sugar

6 large egg yolks

½ tbsp pure vanilla extract

1 cup peeled and sliced peaches (fresh or frozen, thawed and drained; see Tip)

Styling Note:
For something a little different, we stored the ice cream in small mason jars, which are perfect for individual servings.

Settings and Angle:
f/4
ISO 500
1/100 sec
0 degrees

In a medium saucepan on medium heat, combine cream and milk. Bring just to a gentle simmer. Set aside.

Meanwhile, in a small frying pan or skillet on medium-high heat, melt butter, swirling the pan for 3 to 5 minutes, until the butter has browned.

In a medium mixing bowl, whisk together the browned butter and sugar until smooth. Add egg yolks and whisk until well incorporated. While whisking constantly, gradually add ¼ cup of the warmed milk mixture at a time, mixing well after each addition.

Transfer mixture to a large pot and heat on medium heat, stirring frequently with a wooden spoon, until the mixture thickens, 10 to 15 minutes. When the mixture can coat the back of the spoon, pour through a fine-mesh sieve into a bowl (discard solids). Let cool at room temperature for 30 minutes. Stir in vanilla. Cover and refrigerate for 12 to 24 hours, until you're ready to churn.

In a blender, blend peaches until completely smooth. Stir peach purée into the chilled ice-cream base. Pour the mixture into an ice-cream maker. Churn according to the manufacturer's instructions.

Tip: If using frozen peaches, let thaw completely before blending. If using canned, be sure to fully drain any excess syrup before blending.

SAGE, LIME AND VANILLA BEAN ICE CREAM

Makes about 2 pints

When a toddler requests this flavor over chocolate, you know it's gotta be good. Sage, lime and vanilla together create something extraordinary.

2 cups whipping (35%) cream
1½ cups whole milk
½ cup fresh sage (10 to
   12 leaves with stems)
½ cup granulated sugar
2 tbsp fresh lime zest
Seeds from 1 vanilla bean
5 large egg yolks

In a medium saucepan on medium-high heat, combine cream, milk and sage. Simmer gently for 5 minutes. Remove from heat, cover and set aside for 45 minutes, allowing the essence of the sage to fully infuse the milk mixture. Discard sage leaves and stems from milk mixture.

In a medium bowl, combine sugar, lime zest and vanilla seeds (reserve pod for another use). Using your hands, rub mixture together until fully incorporated.

Add egg yolks to sugar mixture and mix well. While mixing, gradually add ¼ cup of the warmed milk mixture at a time, mixing well after each addition.

Transfer mixture to a large pot and heat on medium heat, stirring frequently with a wooden spoon, until the mixture is thick enough to coat the back of a spoon, 10 to 15 minutes. Let cool at room temperature for 30 minutes. Cover and refrigerate for 12 to 24 hours, until you're ready to churn. Pour the mixture into an ice-cream maker. Churn according to the manufacturer's instructions.

Styling Note:
For the background scene, we built up a full-frame image with plenty of ice and fresh limes. A deep metal tray was perfect for holding all the ice in place as it melted.

Settings and Angle:
f/10
ISO 2000
1/125 sec
90 degrees

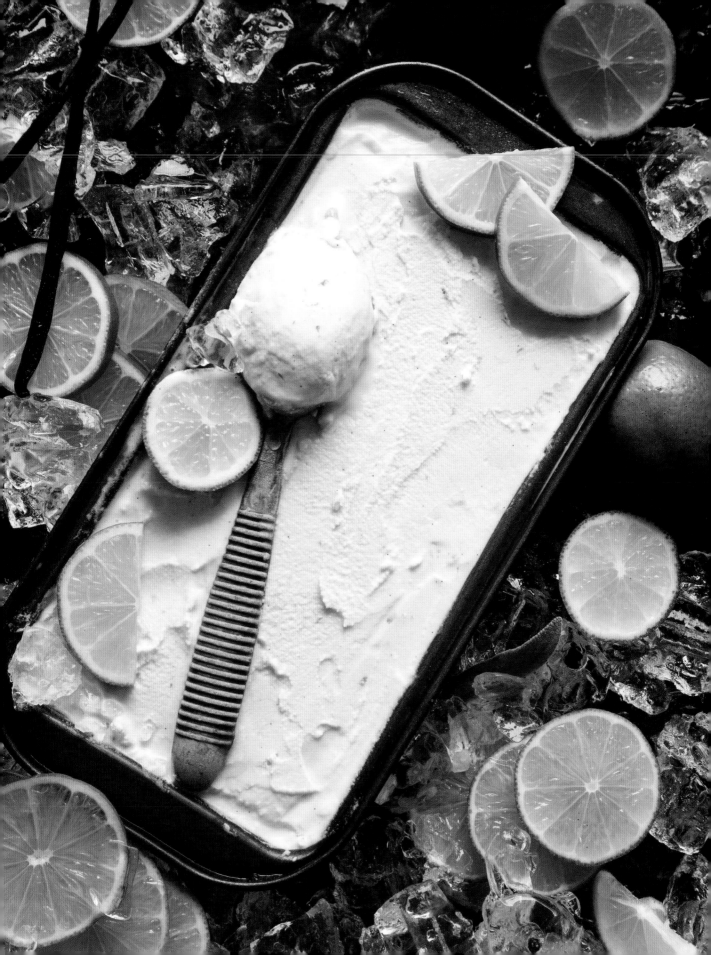

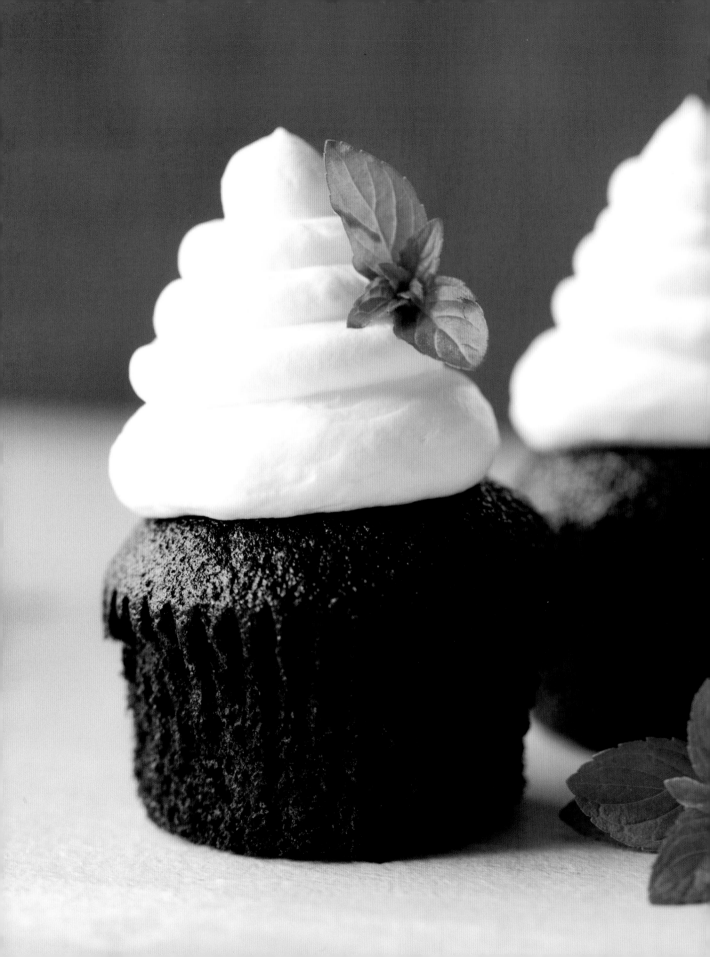

CHOCOLATE MINT CUPCAKES WITH SOUR CREAM FROSTING

Makes 12 cupcakes

Cupcakes will forever have a place on the dessert table, but unfortunately many recipes fail to really stand out and impress. These do.

Cupcakes:

⅓ cup unsalted butter, at room temperature

¾ cup packed brown sugar

2 large eggs

1 tsp pure peppermint extract

1 cup all-purpose flour

¼ cup + 2 tbsp black cocoa powder (see Tip, page 240)

1 tsp baking powder

1 tsp baking soda

1 tsp salt

⅓ cup whole milk

2 tbsp liquid honey

⅓ cup warm water

Frosting:

1 cup whipping (35%) cream

½ cup sour cream

2 tbsp icing sugar

Fresh mint, to garnish

Make cupcakes: Preheat oven to 350°F. Line a 12-cup cupcake pan with paper liners. In a stand mixer fitted with the paddle attachment, cream together butter and sugar. Add eggs one at a time, mixing well after each addition. Add peppermint, and mix to combine. Set aside.

In a medium bowl, sift together flour, black cocoa, baking powder and baking soda. Stir in salt. Set aside. In a small bowl, whisk together milk, honey and warm water. Set aside.

Add the flour mixture to the stand mixer, and mix well. While the mixer is running, gradually add the milk mixture, and mix well (the batter should be thick but pourable). Fill each cupcake liner three-quarters full of batter, and bake in preheated oven for 15 to 20 minutes, until an inserted toothpick comes out clean. Transfer cupcakes to a wire rack and let cool completely.

Make frosting: In a medium bowl, combine whipping cream, sour cream and icing sugar. Using a hand mixer, mix until firm peaks form. Cover and refrigerate until you're ready to frost. Once the cupcakes have completely cooled, top with frosting and garnish with mint.

Styling Note: Because this dessert contains both dark and light colors, we used a backdrop that contrasted each.

Settings and Angle: f/10 ISO 1600 1/80 sec 0 degrees

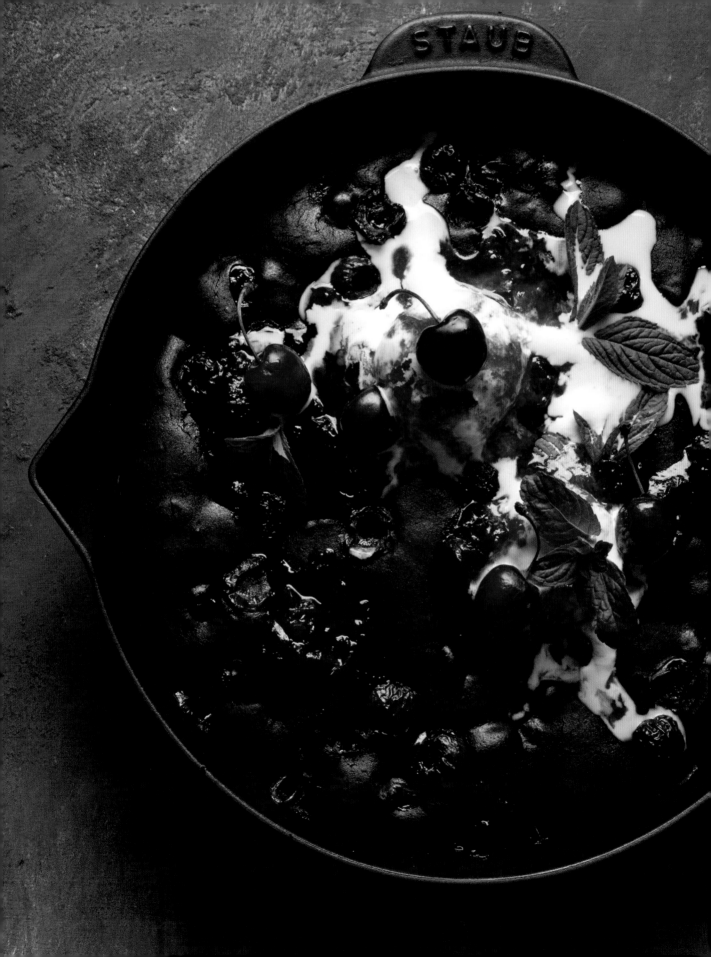

CHOCOLATE CHERRY SKILLET BROWNIES

Serves 8 to 12

This is such a fun dessert to share straight from the skillet. It freezes well, too, which means you can always keep the leftovers (if there are any) for another time. Swap out the fresh cherries for whatever fruit you'd like and make it your own.

Brownies:

1 cup packed brown sugar

3 large eggs

1½ cups chopped dark chocolate

⅓ cup whipping (35%) cream

¼ cup unsalted butter

1 cup all-purpose flour

¼ cup black cocoa powder (see Tip, page 240)

½ tsp salt

1¼ cups cherries, pitted

Ice cream, to serve

Make brownies: Preheat oven to 350°F. Grease a 9-inch skillet with butter and set aside.

In a medium bowl, whisk together brown sugar and eggs. Set aside.

In a small saucepan on medium heat, combine chocolate, cream and butter. Heat, stirring frequently, until melted. Set aside.

In a medium bowl, sift together flour and black cocoa, pushing any clumps through with the back of a spoon. Add the chocolate mixture, egg mixture and salt, and stir well. Fold in 1¼ cups cherries.

Pour batter into the prepared skillet and bake, uncovered, for 35 minutes, or until a toothpick inserted in the center comes out mostly clean. Let cool for 15 minutes before serving.

(recipe continues on next page)

Styling Note:
This shot is all about that irresistible, melty ice cream, which every brownie deserves. Topped with our bright-red cherry sauce, this was devoured immediately!

Settings and Angle:
f/13
ISO 4000
1/100 sec
90 degrees

(continued from previous page)

Cherry sauce:

1 cup cherries, pitted
  and halved
2 tbsp granulated sugar
2 tbsp fresh lemon juice

Make sauce: In a small saucepan on medium heat, stir together 1 cup cherries, sugar and lemon juice until well combined. Bring to a boil, reduce heat and simmer for 15 to 20 minutes, until the cherries are soft and the sauce has thickened slightly. Remove from heat. If desired, blend using an immersion blender until extra smooth.

Serve brownies topped with scoops of ice cream and a good drizzle of cherry sauce.

Tips: Black cocoa powder is a very dark, super-rich alkalized cocoa. It can be found online or at many gourmet retailers.

Be careful when serving the skillet to guests, as it can be extremely hot to the touch.

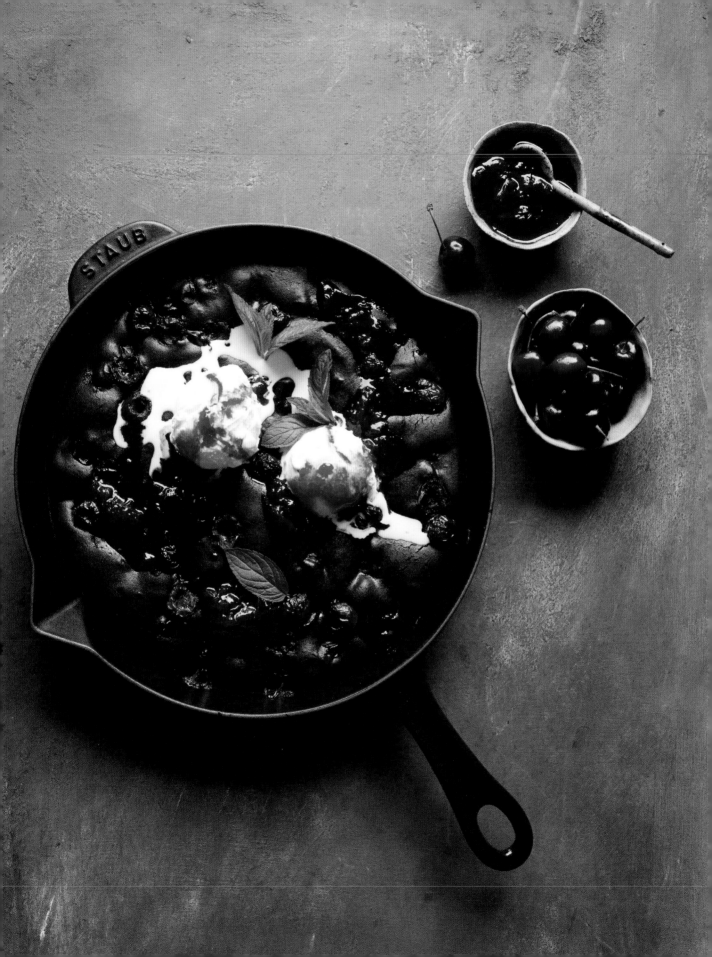

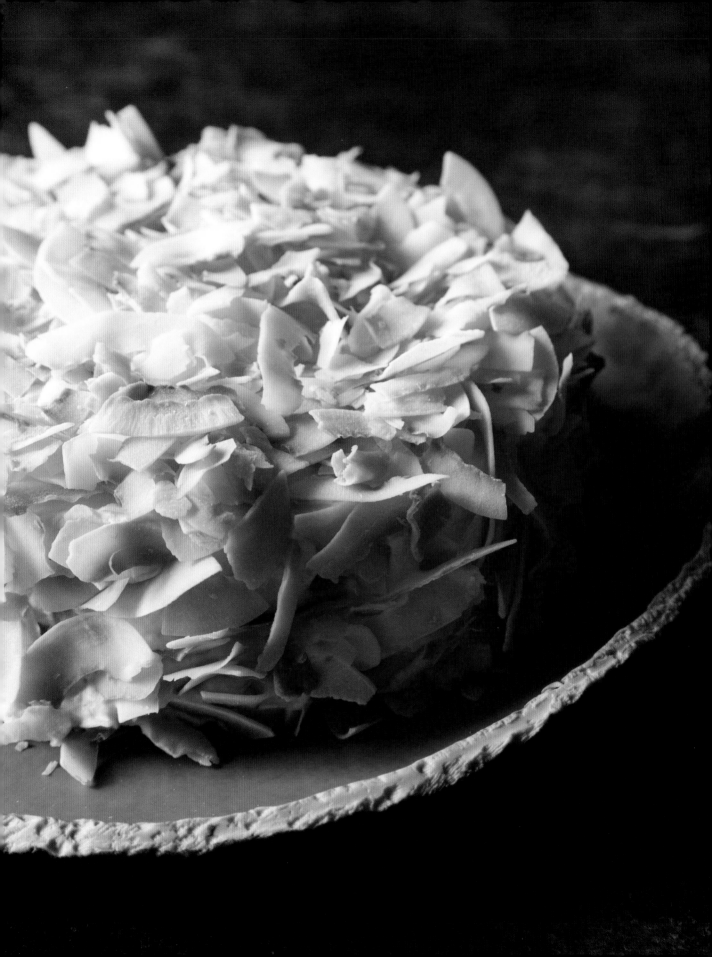

TOASTED COCONUT
MANGO MOUSSE CAKE

Serves 12

*A cake that looks this impressive might have your guests thinking you went
full-on Martha, when really, this baby is a total cinch to pull off. The retro flair
of a mousse cake has timeless appeal, and the unexpected addition of toasted
coconut helps bring this festive dessert to the next level.*

¼ cup butter, at room
   temperature
5 tbsp icing sugar, divided
¼ tsp salt
1 large egg yolk
½ cup + 2 tbsp all-purpose
   flour
1 tsp whole milk or water
2 cups unsweetened large
   coconut flakes
1 package (¼ oz) unflavored
   gelatin powder
2 tbsp water
1 cup whipping (35%) cream
1 cup mango purée

Using a stand mixer fitted with the paddle attachment, cream together
butter, 3 tbsp icing sugar and salt. Add egg yolk and mix until combined. Add flour, and mix well. Add milk, and mix until the dough
comes together. Shape dough into a flat disc, wrap in plastic wrap and
refrigerate for 30 minutes.

Preheat oven to 350°F. Line the bottom of a 6-inch springform pan with
parchment paper.

On a lightly floured work surface, roll out the dough until it's about
¼ inch thick. Cut a 6-inch round. Lay dough inside the springform
base. Bake in preheated oven for 12 to 15 minutes, until golden
brown. Remove from oven and let cool for 30 minutes. Leave oven on.

(recipe continues on next page)

Styling Note:
It's all about the
texture! We used our
100mm lens for a nice
close-up to accentuate the
gorgeous, crispy coconut
coating on the
cake.

Settings
and Angle:
f/10
ISO 1600
1/100 sec
45 degrees

(continued from previous page)

Line a baking sheet with parchment paper. Spread coconut evenly on prepared baking sheet and bake for 5 to 7 minutes, until slightly golden brown. Remove from oven and set aside to cool completely.

In a small bowl, combine gelatin powder and water. Let "bloom" for 5 minutes. Meanwhile, bring a shallow pot of water to a simmer. Place the small bowl over the simmering water and stir until the gelatin has completely liquefied.

Place the cooled cookie base, still in the springform pan, on a parchment-lined baking sheet. Set aside.

Using a stand mixer fitted with the whisk attachment, whip cream until frothy. Add the remaining 2 tbsp icing sugar and continue to whip until soft peaks form. Fold in mango purée and liquefied gelatin.

Pour the cream mixture over the cooled cookie base, smoothing out the top with a spatula. Cover and refrigerate for at least 24 hours.

When ready to serve, warm a knife under hot running water, dry it and slowly run it around the inside perimeter of the pan, carefully releasing the mousse cake. Remove the metal ring around the cake.

Decorate the top and sides of the cake with the toasted coconut, gently pressing with your hands so it adheres to the cake. Cut into wedges and enjoy.

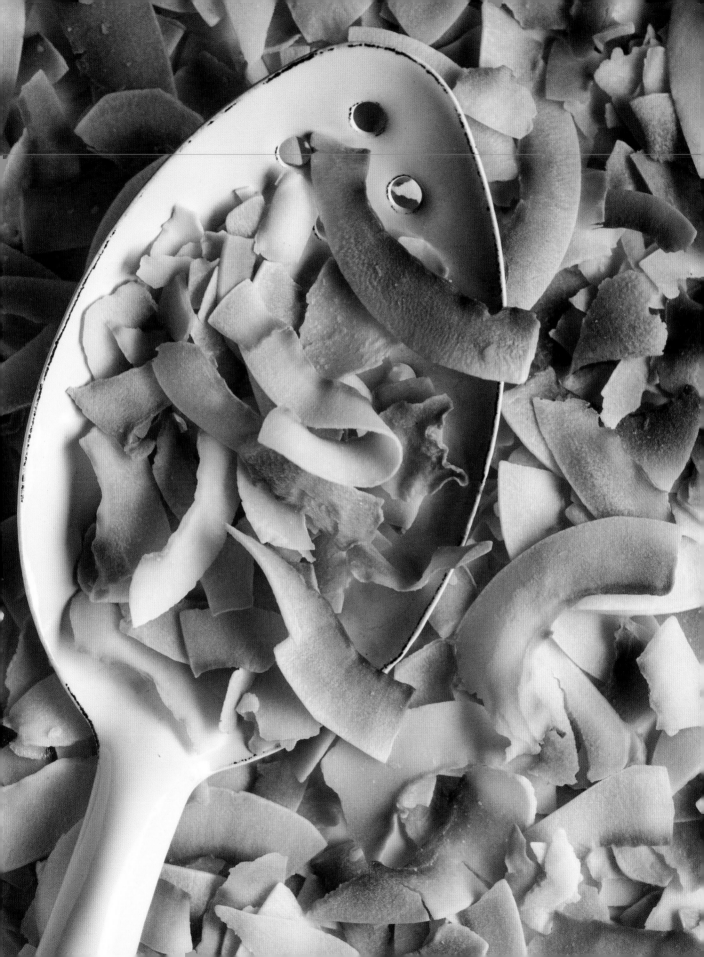

NO-BAKE BOOZY
BLUEBERRY CHEESECAKE

Serves 12

Tequila, meet cheesecake. Need we say more?

1 cup frozen blueberries,
   thawed

¼ cup fresh lime juice

2 tbsp icing sugar

1 package (¼ oz) unflavored
   gelatin powder

2 tbsp water

½ cup + 2 tbsp graham
   cracker crumbs

3 tbsp butter, melted

1 cup mascarpone cheese, at
   room temperature

1 package (9 oz) cream cheese,
   at room temperature

½ cup condensed milk

⅓ cup tequila

Fresh blueberries, to
   garnish (optional)

In a blender, combine thawed blueberries, lime juice and icing sugar, and blend until completely smooth. Set aside.

In a small bowl, combine gelatin and water. Let "bloom" for 5 minutes. Meanwhile, bring a shallow pan of water to a simmer. Place the small bowl over the simmering water and mix until the gelatin has liquefied.

In another bowl, combine graham cracker crumbs and melted butter. Press mixture into the base of a 6-inch springform pan. Refrigerate for 30 minutes.

In a stand mixer fitted with the paddle attachment, cream together mascarpone and cream cheese. Add condensed milk, and mix well. Add liquefied gelatin, tequila and the blueberry purée, and mix well. Spread mixture evenly over top of the graham cracker base. Refrigerate for 18 to 24 hours, until set.

When ready to serve, warm a knife under hot running water, dry it and carefully run it around the inside perimeter of the pan to release the cake. Remove the metal ring around the cake. Garnish with fresh blueberries, if desired.

Styling Note:
The gorgeous purple hue of this cake worked beautifully with a light setup.

Settings and Angle:
f/5.6
ISO 2000
1/100 sec
45 degrees

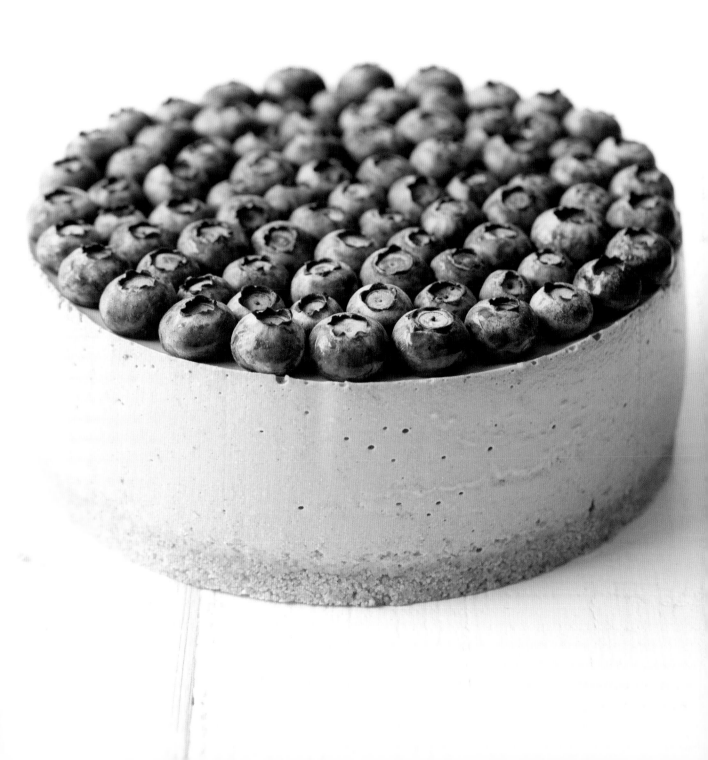

APPLE, CINNAMON AND BEET CRUMBLE

Serves 6

Crumbles are rustic and charming, which is a large part of their appeal. They're approachable, humble even — and the novice baker should have no problem putting one together without too much fuss.

½ cup all-purpose flour

½ cup + ⅓ cup packed brown sugar

1¼ tsp ground cardamom, divided

1¼ tsp ground cinnamon, divided

¼ cup butter, melted

3½ cups peeled, cored and chopped green apples

1¼ cups peeled and chopped beets

2 tbsp fresh lemon zest

¼ cup fresh lemon juice

2 tsp cornstarch

Preheat oven to 375°F. Set aside a 6-inch pie dish.

In a medium bowl, combine flour and ½ cup brown sugar. Add ¼ tsp cardamom, ¼ tsp cinnamon and the melted butter. Using a fork, mix until small clusters of dough form. Set aside.

In a medium bowl, combine apples, beets, the remaining ⅓ cup brown sugar, 1 tsp cardamom, 1 tsp cinnamon and the lemon zest. Set aside.

In a small bowl, whisk together lemon juice and cornstarch. Add to the apple mixture and toss to coat well.

Spread fruit mixture evenly in pie dish. Top with the crumble. Bake in preheated oven for 35 to 45 minutes, until golden brown. Remove from oven and let cool for 5 to 10 minutes before serving.

Styling Note:
Serving the crumble straight from the enamel pan, with a charming blue-and-white checkered napkin alongside the ingredients, lends a casual, at-home feel to the shot.

Settings and Angle:
f/10
ISO 4000
1/100 sec
90 degrees

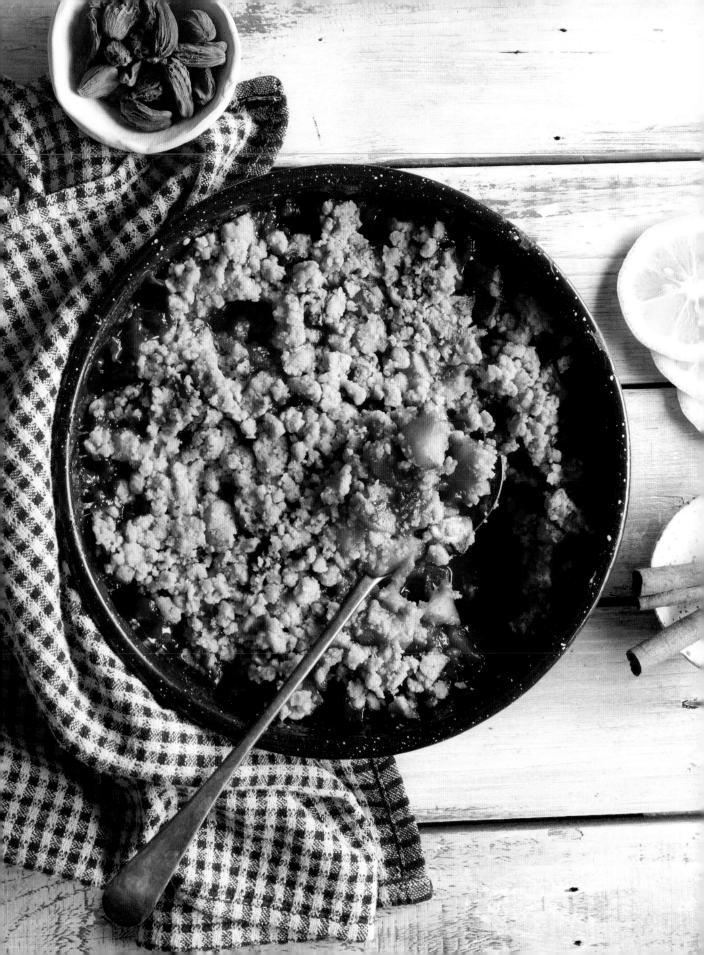

CLASSIC LEMON TART

Serves 12

There's nothing more classic than a lemon tart. We kept things refined, and didn't stray too far from tradition. Top yours with whatever good-looking seasonal fruit you desire.

Dough:

¼ cup butter, at room temperature

3 tbsp icing sugar

1 large egg yolk

½ cup + 2 tbsp all-purpose flour

¼ tsp salt

1 tsp whole milk or water

Lemon Curd:

2 tbsp fresh lemon zest

½ cup fresh lemon juice

½ cup + 2 tbsp granulated sugar

1 large egg

2 large egg yolks

Pinch of salt

6 tbsp butter

Fresh fruit of your choice, to decorate

Make dough: Using a stand mixer fitted with the paddle attachment, cream together butter and sugar. Add egg yolk and mix until combined. Add flour and salt, and mix well. Add milk and mix until the dough comes together. Shape dough into a flat disc, cover in plastic wrap and refrigerate for 30 minutes.

Make curd: In a medium saucepan on medium heat, whisk together lemon juice and 2 tbsp sugar until the sugar is dissolved. Set aside.

In a medium bowl, using your hands, rub together the remaining sugar and lemon zest until completely incorporated. Add egg, egg yolks and salt, and whisk together for 2 to 4 minutes, until mixture is slightly pale. While whisking, add the warm lemon juice mixture (reserve pan) and whisk until completely combined.

(recipe continues on page 252)

Styling Note: Fresh currants always make for wonderful tart toppings, adding a bit of extra drama and flair.

Settings and Angle: f/10 ISO 3200 1/100 sec 90 degrees

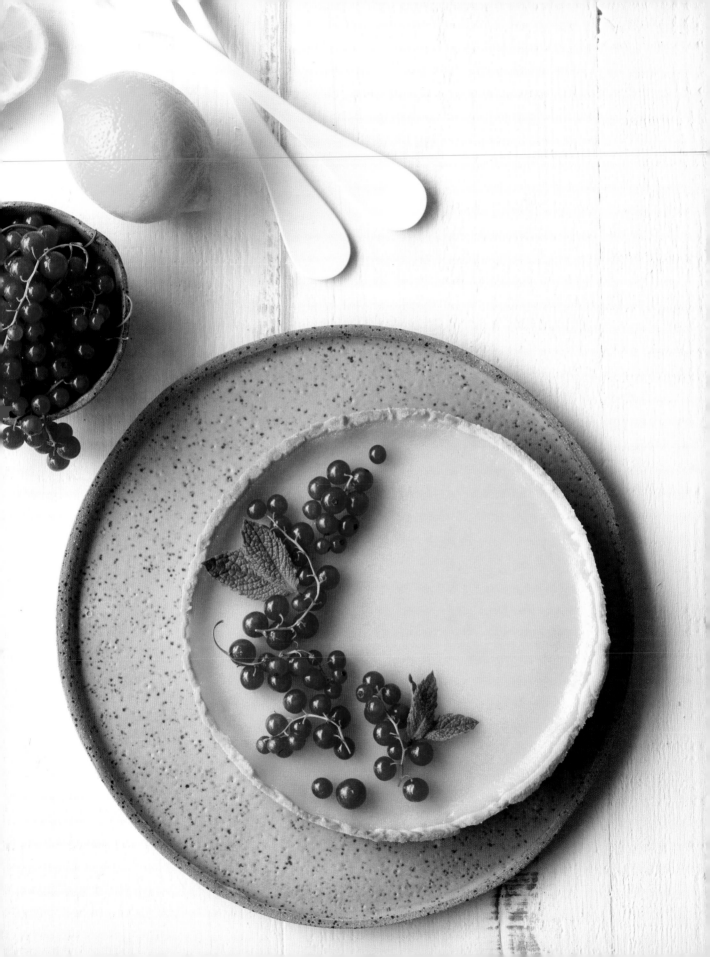

(continued from page 250)

Transfer the mixture to the reserved pan. Warm on medium heat, stirring constantly, until the mixture is thick enough to coat the back of a wooden spoon. Using a fine-mesh sieve, strain mixture into a clean medium bowl (discard solids). Add butter and whisk together until butter is fully melted. Set aside at room temperature.

Blind-bake tart shell: Preheat oven to 375°F. Line a baking sheet with parchment paper. Set aside a 7-inch tart ring.

On a lightly floured work surface, roll out the dough until about ¼ inch thick. Cut a 9-inch round. Place dough inside the tart ring. Cut any excess off the edges, and poke a few fork holes in the dough. Refrigerate for 10 to 15 minutes, until the dough has hardened. Line the empty tart shell with parchment paper, fill with dried beans or pie weights and bake for 10 to 15 minutes, until slightly golden. Remove tart from the oven, remove dried beans or pie weights and let cool completely.

Assemble tart: Preheat oven to 300°F.

Spread the prepared curd evenly over the cooled tart base. Bake in preheated oven for 15 minutes, or until the center is slightly jiggly. Remove from oven and let cool completely on the baking sheet for at least 20 to 30 minutes. For best results, cover and refrigerate for 1 hour (or up to 24 hours) before serving.

Decorate with fruit and enjoy.

PAVLOVAS WITH LIME CURD, BERRIES AND MINT

Serves 6

Some may say that making dessert for no particular occasion might feel slightly lavish or entirely unnecessary, but we beg to differ. While we wouldn't advise you to indulge daily, there are few pleasures more enjoyable in life than a sweet, silky ending to a satisfying meal. Life is short. Eat dessert!

Lime Curd:

¾ cup granulated sugar, divided

Zest and juice of 3 limes (about 2 tbsp zest and ¾ cup juice)

2 large eggs

¼ cup unsalted butter, chilled and cubed

Meringues:

1 tsp pure vanilla extract

1 tsp fresh lemon juice

2 tsp cornstarch

3 large egg whites (about ½ cup), at room temperature

¾ cup granulated sugar

½ pint raspberries, to serve

½ pint blueberries, to serve

Fresh mint leaves, to garnish

Make curd: In a small saucepan on medium-high heat, combine half of the sugar and the lime juice. Cook, stirring frequently, until the sugar dissolves and starts bubbling. Remove from heat and set aside.

In a medium bowl, combine the remaining sugar and lime zest. Using your hands, rub together until well incorporated. Add eggs, and whisk together until smooth and pale green, 2 to 4 minutes. While whisking constantly, gradually add the warmed lime juice to the egg mixture.

Transfer the mixture to a medium saucepan and place on medium heat. Stirring constantly, heat until the mixture is thick enough to coat the back of a wooden spoon. Using a fine-mesh sieve, strain mixture into a clean medium bowl (discard solids). Add butter and whisk together until butter is fully melted. Place bowl in an ice bath (a larger bowl filled with ice and water) until completely cool. Cover and refrigerate for at least 8 hours (and up to 24 hours).

Make meringues: Preheat oven to 300°F. Line a large baking sheet with parchment paper.

In a small bowl, whisk together vanilla, lemon juice and cornstarch until smooth; set aside.

(recipe continues on next page)

(continued from previous page)

In a medium bowl, beat egg whites until foamy. While mixing, gradually add sugar, about 1 tbsp at a time, mixing well after each addition. Once mixture is stiff and glossy, fold in vanilla mixture in two additions.

Using a large spoon, create 6 meringue nests (each about 3 inches wide and 2 inches tall) on the prepared baking sheet, spacing at least 1½ inches apart. Using the back of your spoon, make a small impression on the top of each meringue, swiping the spoon upward to create a decorative peak.

Reduce the oven temperature to 250°F. Bake meringues for 1 hour, or until very pale golden color on the bottom. The outside should be crisp, and the interior should have a hollow sound when tapped. Remove from oven and let cool on a wire rack for 30 to 45 minutes.

Serve meringues topped with the lime curd and berries, or side by side, as desired. Garnish with mint.

Tip: This recipe can be made well in advance and assembled just before serving. Under ideal conditions, the curd can last for up to 14 days in the refrigerator, and the meringues for up to 1 week in an airtight container at room temperature.

Styling Note:
Plating the curd on the bottom and berries on the side makes this dessert look clean and elegant.

Settings and Angle:
f/3.2
ISO 320
1/125 sec
45 degrees

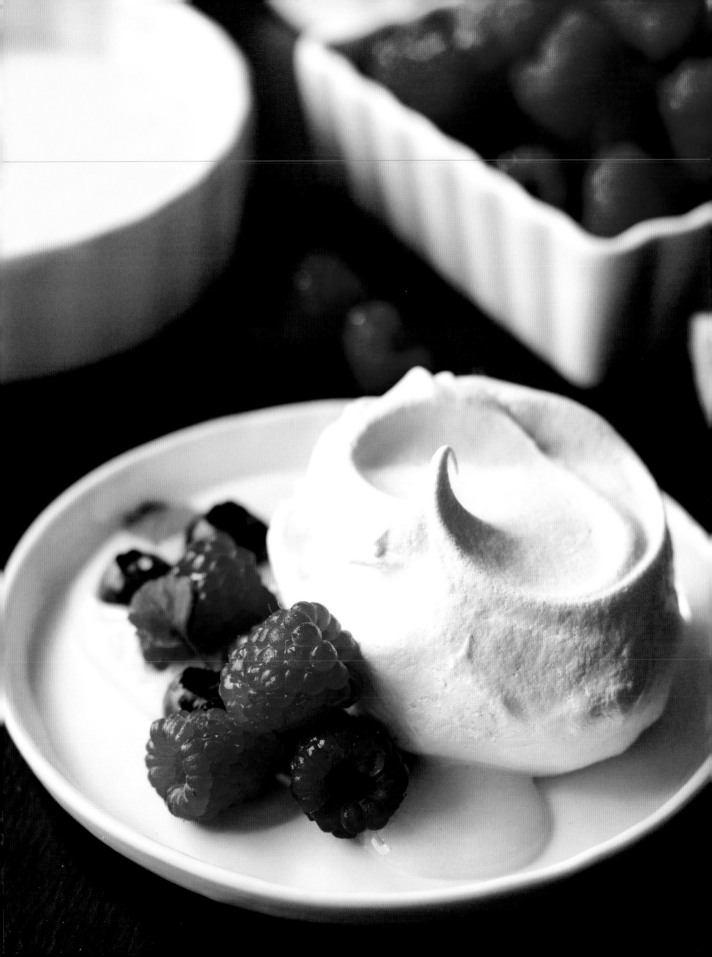

THANK YOU

We had an amazing time putting together this cookbook, hopefully the first of many more to come. We couldn't have done it without our brilliant literary agent, Lori Galvin of Aevitas Creative Management, who was there for us every step of the way.

To our publishers: we can't thank you enough for believing in our concept as strongly as we did and allowing us to bring *Cooking in Color* to life. Thank you to our awesome team, who worked tirelessly to make this project the best it could be: Kirsten Hanson, Noelle Zitzer, Kate Cassaday, Michelle Branson, Tracy Bordian, Alan Jones and everyone else at HarperCollins Canada and Gibbs Smith who had a hand in this creatively cathartic process. We couldn't imagine another home for this book, and we are so happy with how it's turned out. A big thank you to Luis Valdizon for the portraits in this book, and Denise McKenzie-Lee of Enkee Ceramics for the gorgeous handmade pottery.

To all our hungry neighbors, for willingly accepting test batches and half-eaten desserts: we can't thank you enough for helping out—you're all champions. And, of course, to our best buddy, Milo, for being the most loyal clean-up crew we could have ever asked for. We miss you.

Thank you to our beautiful families and friends for the ongoing encourage-ment and enthusiasm, and for being a shoulder to lean on when things felt slightly overwhelming. You helped keep us sane during a difficult yet tremen-dously fulfilling creative year. We appreciate how supportive you've all been throughout this process. It really means the world to us.

Finally, big thanks to *you* for picking up this book, along with all the read-ers who have supported The Food Gays since our journey first began. We're absolutely blessed to be able to do what we love each day.

INDEX